Taking It to the Streets

THEATER: Theory/Text/Performance

Enoch Brater, Series Editor
University of Michigan

Taking It to the Streets

The Social Protest Theater
of Luis Valdez and Amiri Baraka

Harry J. Elam Jr.

ANN ARBOR

THE UNIVERSITY OF MICHIGAN PRESS

To my parents,
Harry J. Elam Sr. and Barbara Clark Elam.
And because unicorns
are still possible.

Copyright © by the University of Michigan 1997
All rights reserved
Published in the United States of America by
The University of Michigan Press
Manufactured in the United States of America
⊗ Printed on acid-free paper

2000   1999   1998   1997   4   3   2   1

A CIP catalog record for this book is available from the British Library

Library of Congress Cataloging-in-Publication Data

Elam, Harry Justin.
    Taking it to the streets : the social protest theater of Luis
Valdez and Amiri Baraka / Harry J. Elam, Jr.
        p.   cm. — (Theater—theory/text/performance)
    Includes bibliographical references (p.   ) and index.
    ISBN 0-472-10793-3 (cloth : alk. paper)
    1. Teatro Camposino (Organization)   2. Workers' theater—
California.   3. Mexican American theater—California.   4. Baraka,
Imamu Amiri, 1934–   —Criticism and interpretation.   I. Title.
II. Series.
PN3307.U6E4   1996
792'.0973—dc21   96-45790
                                                       CIP

Preface

In 1971 I was part of a group of black students from two Boston area private schools—Noble and Greenough School for boys and Beaver Country Day School for girls—that formed a black youth drama organization called "The Family." The objectives of The Family were to promote black consciousness, to increase awareness of racial injustice, and to raise scholarship money for black students at the two schools through our performances. The rhetoric of black nationalism and Black Power informed our theatrical endeavors. As children, we all had witnessed the tumultuous black uprisings of the 1960s, the cries of "Black Power!" the protests and riots exploding in black urban enclaves, including Boston. Implicitly and explicitly, we knew that our existence at these elite prep schools was in no small part a result of such black liberation efforts. Proudly, we wore our Afro hairstyles, greeted one another as brother and sister, and defined ourselves and our organization in relation to those earlier black struggles.

We called ourselves The Family as an explicit invocation of our communality—a communality that we evoked in rehearsals and performances; a collective sensibility that allowed us to turn to one another for needed support, since we represented such small minorities within the two white institutions that were our homes for up to six years. Consciously as well as unconsciously, in our performance work we Family members concerned ourselves not only with community but with cultural identity, with audience participation, and with our relationship to black activist movements. Only years later, when I became an academic involved in researching the theory and practice of black and Chicano social protest theater, did I realize that those same issues, which The Family naively confronted years ago, are consistently critical to the efficacy of social protest performances. Questions of audience involvement, of the performers' social commitment, of the communion between performers and audience, are at the center of the present study. In this book I investigate the conditions that contribute to theater's effective functioning as a tool for social protest and change through a comparative analysis of significant black and Chicano social protest performances during the 1960s and early 1970s. I examine how these past performances impact on our present understanding of social protest performance and cultural resistance.

By "social protest performances" I mean those performances that have an explicit social purpose, that direct their audiences to social action. My definition presupposes that social protest performances emerge solely from marginalized peoples and oppositional struggles. Social protest performances function as counterhegemonic strategies through which underrepresented groups challenge the dominant social order and agitate for change. The representational apparatus of the social protest performance serves to reinforce, reimagine, and rearticulate the objectives of social and political resistance. I use the term *social protest performance*, rather than *radical theater*, to indicate that these performances actively protest against very specific and urgent causes of social need. Social protest performance is an ever-evolving genre appearing wherever oppressed people assert their subjectivity and contest the status quo.

The Family in many ways fell short of this definition: we became increasingly concerned with the intricate and minute details of young adult life and, as a result, less focused on the urgencies that propelled black unrest in the middle and late 1960s. Still, during the years we were in operation we strategically confronted audiences; we experienced the electric bond of effective communion between actors and spectators; we received fervent, participatory ovations; and we even made solid financial contributions to our schools' scholarship funds. Our time with The Family impressed upon my compatriots and me what a powerful political, social, and cultural tool the theater could be.

The interaction between social protest performances and systems of power can prove extremely dynamic. Too often, however, scholarly criticism has either overlooked or denigrated social protest theater because of its ephemerality, its artistic naïveté, and its lack of universality. Yet social protest performances, I believe, can project a vitality unequaled by more mainstream or commercial theatrical endeavors. Social protest theater often engages real life and actual events in profound ways. A desire to provide an alternative scholarly view of social protest performance in part motivates this book. Most certainly, this study is informed by my early experiences with The Family. My memories of those years make me hopeful that this work can provide some service not only to theater students and scholars, but also to present or future practitioners of social protest theater.

Acknowledgments

This book has been many years in the making. Consequently, there are many people to acknowledge. I would like to start with my dear friend, Kim Wiltz, who read the first, very rough version of the book and then sat down with me and helped organize the chapters and refocus the work. Interviews with Amiri Baraka and the late Gilbert Moses greatly aided my research into the Black Revolutionary Theater Movement. In addition, Esmree Bahn, formerly curator of the Moorland-Springarn Archives at Howard University, provided me with access to and assistance with the collected papers of Amiri Baraka housed there. Writer and director Woodie King, playwright Ben Caldwell, and scholar and former student, Judith Williams, all helped me to locate photographs of the Black Revolutionary Theater in the years 1965 to 1971.

I must give thanks to Carlos Morton for whetting my interest in Chicano *teatro* back in 1979 at the University of California, Berkeley. Phil Esparza and the staff of El Teatro Campesino in San Juan Bautista, including Tina Sandoval, were extremely helpful during my research on El Teatro. They provided me with access to films and photographs from El Teatro's past and allowed me to review some of the papers that are held in the El Teatro Archives in San Juan Bautista. Luis Valdez also met with me during his visit to the Stanford campus in 1993 and in person as well as via the phone in 1996. I thank him for his time, his insight, and critique of my work. I want also to acknowledge Julio Gonzales, formerly an actor with El Teatro, for his interview and discussion of the performance practices of El Teatro. My colleague Jorge Huerta, one of the leading scholars of Chicano *teatro*, met with me, originally back in Washington, DC, in the summer of 1991. I thank him for sharing his expertise with me and for expressing real interest in my project.

I thank anthropologist Smadar Lavie, who back in graduate school at the University of California, Berkeley, helped me to explore the connection between ritual and social protest theater. Years later, in 1993, when we were both fellows at the Stanford Humanities Center, she again provided me with sources on anthropology and social change. I thank the Stanford Humanities Center as a whole. My time there allowed me to complete a draft of this manuscript and to think and write on topics of performance and racial identity. My colleague and friend Alice Rayner, of the Stanford Drama Department, assisted me with critical source material and acted as a sounding board for my theoretical concepts. My friend Tracy Rone, Ph.D. candidate in anthropology at UCLA, furthered my knowledge of the anthropology of performance and ritual theory.

Several colleagues have read drafts of this manuscript. I thank Charles R. Lyons, Chair of the Stanford Drama Department, for reading both early and late drafts. His wise counsel and guidance were extremely valuable to me every step of the way. My friend and colleague Horace Porter, Director of African and African American Studies at Stanford University, read an early draft of this manuscript. Although the subject matter was outside his field of expertise, he generously gave of his time and advice to help me along the way. Yvonne Yarbro-Bejarano, Director of Chicano Studies at Stanford University, read a later draft of the book, and I benefited greatly from her knowledge of Chicano theater and culture. I would like to give special thanks to my colleague and friend Janelle Reinelt, Chair of the Drama Department at the University of California, Davis, for her careful reading and constructive criticism, which helped shape the final version of this book.

Throughout the process family and friends have provided me with love and support. My sister, Patricia, read and critiqued an early draft of the first and second chapters. My parents, my brother Keith, sister Jocie, and my aunt Harriet Elam, all encouraged me. My aunt Thelma O'Brien prayed and lit candles for me. My close and dear friend Imani Abalos performed far above and beyond the call of friendship. She read several drafts, proofread chapters, provided me with research information from the University of California, Berkeley, Library, and listened over the phone as I read her sentences, paragraphs, and conclusions. Ron Davies, the Administrator in the Department of Drama at Stanford, has proofread and helped format the various drafts of this manuscript, always with a smile and with commitment to make the work look and read the best that it could.

I must give a very special acknowledgment to Leonade Jones for her love, faith, and support throughout but also for her practical, nononsense reading of the book as we stayed in the Stanford faculty flat in Oxford, England, during the winter of 1994. Her insights were invaluable in shaping the final revision.

Finally, I thank LeAnn Fields, Executive Editor at the University of Michigan Press, for her perseverance and continued belief in this project as well as her knowledgeable guidance in bringing this book to fruition.

Contents

1

An Initiation into the Rituals of Social Protest Theater: The Cultural Politics of El Teatro Campesino and the Black Revolutionary Theater

Repeatedly, in the modern as well as the postmodern United States, oppressed peoples and new political movements have turned to the theater as a means to articulate social causes, to galvanize support, and to direct sympathizers toward campaigns of political resistance. Consequently, the use of theater as a social weapon presents the dramatic scholar, critic, and practitioner with questions of immediate and enduring import. Why use theater—an art form—as a means to effect social change? How does the social protest performance interface with its audience? Does the audience's communion, participation, and emotional empathy inside the theater dissipate or even purge their energy, outrage, and desire to engage in protest activities outside of the theater? Can a theatrical performance affect thought, behavior, and social action? And, if so, how do critics determine the social efficacy of a theatrical performance? What methodology of aesthetic criticism should be applied to theatrical performances that have explicit sociopolitical ends?

My project within the pages of this book is to examine these questions, to analyze specific social protest performances and their interaction with their audiences, and to develop a useful model for social protest performance criticism. As I will explain later in this chapter and throughout this study, the key to the critical analysis of the social protest performance is a recognition and understanding of "the rituals of social protest theater."[1]

I will focus solely on the social protest performances of Luis Valdez's El Teatro Campesino, the farmworkers theater, and Amiri Baraka's (LeRoi Jones's) Black Revolutionary Theater (BRT) during the period 1965 through 1971.[2] The year 1965 marks the beginning of these movements, and in 1971 El Teatro and the BRT both moved away from active, agitational protest theater. I refer to the two manifestations of Baraka's black revolutionary theatrical practice during this era with the label BRT: the Black Arts Repertory Theater School (BARTS), which he founded in Harlem in 1965, and the Spirit House, which he opened in Newark, New Jersey, one year later.[3] I turn to the work of El Teatro and the BRT in the 1960s and early 1970s not simply as paradigmatic of social protest performance but as preeminent examples of social protest theater practice during a momentous and tumultuous historical juncture.

Without doubt the six years from 1965 to 1971 mark one of the most significant periods of American social unrest, in general, and Chicano and black resistance, specifically. During this brief but eventful time the civil rights movement escalated, César Chávez organized the United Farm Workers Union, the Black Power movement evolved, and El Movimiento, the nationalistic movement for Chicano rights, grew to prominence. Corresponding to these sociopolitical events was the emergence of powerful and insistent social protest theater movements. As this study will show, the sociopolitical volatility of these times contributed significantly to the practice of social protest theater.

In March of 1965, one month after the assassination of Malcolm X, Amiri Baraka (then LeRoi Jones) and other black activist artists met in Harlem to form BARTS. With funding from an unlikely source, Harlem Youth Opportunities Unlimited (HARYOU), an antipoverty program established by President Lyndon Johnson's Office of Economic Opportunity, BARTS set about the task of bringing black art to the black masses. With the inception of BARTS, Baraka and the BRT exploded onto the national theatrical and political scene determined to create theater by, for, and about black people. BARTS developed and performed a repertory of short plays written by Baraka and other revolutionary-minded black playwrights. The performance style was direct and con-frontational. The works advocated black nationalist rebellion and the destruction of the dominant, white power structure. The theater became a weapon in the struggle to achieve racialized revolutionary ends.

On 26 September 1965 Luis Valdez went to Delano to participate in a protest march as part of the Grape Pickers strike organized by the newly formed United Farm Workers Organizing Committee (UFWOC). There Valdez, who at the time apprenticed with the San Francisco Mime Troupe, spoke with UFWOC officers Dolores Huerta and César Chávez about the possibility of organizing a farmworkers theater company. Huerta and Chávez embraced Valdez's idea and wel-comed Valdez to Delano. Working with a core group of five members, El Teatro became the cultural voice of the UFWOC within weeks. The troupe developed a broad, presentational performance style that emphasized physical comedy, expressive gestures, bodily movement, and farcical timing. While many critics in the 1970s and 1980s have attributed the genesis of El Teatro's performance style to Valdez's work with the Mime Troupe and his knowledge of commedia dell'arte,[4] Yolanda Broyles-González has more recently established the Mexican popular performance traditions as one of the primary sources for El Teatro's performance work.[5] Through its short, topical, satirical, and improvisational performances, El Teatro contested the oppressive con-ditions of migratory farm labor, raised monetary funds for the strike effort, and challenged the farmworkers to join the new union.

For both El Teatro and the BRT the period from 1965 to 1971 was one of intense social protest performance activity and in this six-year span both groups produced evocative and often dynamic social protest performances. Their performance work over this period established El Teatro and the BRT as two of the more influential social protest theater movements in U.S. theater history. Valdez and Baraka, the charismatic founders and leaders of El Teatro and the BRT, were among the most well-known, powerful, and prominent voices of social protest theater in the 1960s and early 1970s. These men were not only artists but also social activists, cultural theorists, and key players in the social libera-tion movements of Chicanos and blacks, respectively. In speeches, interviews, and written manifestos, both men articulated theoretical paradigms for Chicano and black cultural nationalism as well as for

Chicano and black social protest theater. Inspired by the incendiary theatrics of Baraka, black nationalist protest theaters grew up around the country during the late 1960s. By the early 1970s the efforts of Valdez and El Teatro had sparked the development of Chicano *teatros* throughout the Southwest. El Teatro also stimulated and was in turn stimulated by developments in Latin American theater at that time. Through their respective theatrical practices Valdez and El Teatro and Baraka and the BRT profoundly affected their times, and they continue to influence contemporary Chicano and black theater performance practice and to provide models for social protest theater movements inside and outside the United States.[6]

My emphasis in this study on the "great men,"[7] the "founding fathers," Valdez and Baraka, is purposeful and purposefully problematic. As I focus on the politics and practices of these men, I will examine how distinct concepts of gender informed every aspect of their operations.[8] During this period Valdez's and Baraka's theatrical strategies and social protest ideologies were decidedly male-centric, heterosexist, and patriarchal. In their organizational hierarchies and performance work El Teatro and the BRT reflected the philosophies of male hegemony and female subjugation, which were a significant element of Chicano and black cultural nationalism in the 1960s and 1970s. With this knowledge and within the context of this study of social protest performance, I will consider the role of gender in El Teatro's and the BRT's representations of power, community, cultural identity, and collective consciousness.

While the BRT and El Teatro have each been analyzed, documented, and investigated individually,[9] this text examines them jointly and comparatively. Such comparative, cross-cultural critical inquiries, I believe, are crucial to understanding across difference. The contemporary politics of diversity demand not only that we acknowledge diverse cultural experiences but also that we investigate and interrogate areas of commonality. Only in this way can we move beyond the potentially polarizing divisions of race and ethnicity. Yet, as I begin this comparative project, I must also note that my intention is neither to trivialize the differences nor to overdetermine the similarities between the performance practices of El Teatro and the BRT. Significant differences do exist.[10] El Teatro's plays were performed in a combination of English and Spanish, replicating the ways that Chicanos converse. The BRT's theatrical dialogue reflected the rhetoric of the Black Power revolt and the vernacular of the black inner city. El Teatro used satire, parody, and slapstick humor to educate its audiences and to direct them toward nonviolent resistance. The BRT's performance philosophy, on the other hand, valorized bloody, violent, physical confrontations with the dominant white authority. Perhaps the most profound difference was in the two groups' organizing principles. El Teatro organized originally around the farmworkers strike and focused on the goal of achieving a union contract with the major growers. The BRT, on the other hand, as the "spiritual sister of the Black Power movement," sought to disrupt and overturn the entire U.S. social system.

Still, I believe that defining these groups simply as "different" is too easy and reductive. Instead, I propose a strategy of comparative, differentiated, and differentiating analysis that acknowledges the distinctions while identifying commonalities. Homi Bhabha points out that the concept of "difference" is itself ambivalent and contradictory: "to be different from those that are different makes you the same."[11] El Teatro and the BRT are at once different and the same, separate and connected, particular and yet preeminent examples of social protest performance. Both El Teatro and the BRT emerged in times of social crisis, urged on by determined cries for change. Although they explored and displayed their own particular cultural, aesthetic, and political agendas, El Teatro and the BRT each engaged in performance styles that celebrated the interaction between audience and stage. The social protest performances of the BRT and El Teatro induced and compelled vigorous audience participation. As Geneviève Fabre points out, the power of social protest theater "exists only by virtue of the exchange established between audience and stage."[12]

Examining these two men, Valdez and Baraka, their theaters, and this period exclusively and comparatively enables me to isolate, identify, compare, and contrast social protest performances before distinct constituencies and at specific historical moments. On and through El Teatro's and the BRT's particular and exemplary social protest performances, I will explore the interconnections between the sociohistorical circumstances, the participatory behavior of the audiences, the political sensibilities of the performers, and the social efficacy of the performances. By highlighting the correlation between the performance methodologies, theories, and practices of El Teatro and the BRT in the period 1965 to 1971, I will articulate their cross-cultural commonalities as well as provide insight into the complex genre of social protest performance and its interchange with its audiences.

The Politics of Location

My own interest in the cross-cultural commonalities of social protest performance, and black and Chicano theater in particular, began in graduate school. As a graduate student in the Department of Dramatic Art at the University of California, Berkeley, I was at first primarily involved in research on black social protest theater. Then in 1979, at the outset of my second year in the program, Carlos Morton, Chicano playwright and scholar, asked me to serve as his teaching assistant for a Chicano theater and performance course. Since that initial experience with Chicano *teatro,* I have continued to study Chicano theater specifically and in comparison with black theater. I have found the parallels between black revolutionary practice and Chicano *teatro* in the 1960s and 1970s compelling.[13] My investigation of Chicano social protest theater has informed my understanding of black social protest theater. Correspondingly, my knowledge of black social protest theatrical forms has aided my research into Chicano social protest performance. A continued commitment to cross-cultural analysis drives this book and has propelled me to formulate and maintain its comparative structure. The collision of cultures that comparative criticism encourages can shed light on the practices of both El Teatro and the BRT.

Working with that Chicano *teatro* class in 1979, I gained an early appreciation for, if not yet an intellectual and theoretical understanding of, what contemporary cultural critics such as bell hooks have called the "politics of location."[14] The term *politics of location* refers to the concept that a critic's own location and subjectivity—one's position in relation to the subject of inquiry—is a critical element in his or her interpretation. The politics of location assert that the notion of a disinterested, objective analysis is inherently flawed. Rather, we mediate past and present events through our own present circumstances. Where we position ourselves or are positioned informs how we read a text and, in turn, how we are read as critics.

My identity as an African American located me outside the cultural reference points of the Chicano/a students in that *teatro* class.

And, so, I mediated my study of Chicano culture and my interpretation of the Chicano plays for the course through my own experiences as a theater director and as a person of color in America. On one occasion Carlos Morton arranged for the class to perform scenes that I directed for the Chicano Inmates Association at Vacaville State Prison in Vacaville, California. After the performance several of the Chicano inmates asked me if I were Panamanian or Cuban. They visibly read me as black and therefore not Chicano. Yet they wanted to position me as Latino and to use that location to help them understand why I was working with a Chicano *teatro* class. My subjectivity affected their perceptions of the performance and "colored" how they interpreted my participation in it. I explained that I was black American but that I read Spanish and was studying Chicano theater. Through this response I attempted to reposition myself and to dissipate my status as an outsider.

My current position as an African American theater scholar and practitioner at times confers on me both outsider and insider positionality as I analyze Chicano theater. My knowledge of theater and my research into Chicano theater make me intimately familiar with the materials. Still, my particular cultural background places me outside the specific cultural milieu referenced in the texts. I recognize that, as bell hooks suggests, outsider positionality must be internally and externally interrogated.[15] There is also, I contend, potential benefit from a knowledgeable outside perspective. Informed comparative criticism can provoke new understandings of cultural politics, racial difference, and ethnicity. I firmly believe we must challenge the internal and external social restrictions and cultural expectations often placed upon critics of color to study only their native group. In this comparative study I hope to take advantage of my outsider/insider positionality. From the outset I want to foreground my subjectivity, to acknowledge that my own experiences with issues of racial identity, cultural politics, and social protest performance influence my readings on the pages to follow. My own personal contact with the artistic and social marginalization of African Americans affects my affinity for and sensitivity toward Chicano theater. The politics of location will play a critical role in my analysis of the social protest performances of El Teatro and the BRT.

In fact, I would contend that the politics of location have always figured into critical assessments of El Teatro's and the BRT's social protest performances and the cultural politics of the 1960s and 1970s.

The white critical establishment of that period often leveled disparaging attacks at El Teatro and the BRT in attempts to neutralize the power and energy of their performances.[16] Political conservatism, theatrical paternalism, cultural provincialism, and even racism unconsciously and consciously influenced critical agendas and motivated the dominant culture's attempts to silence the threat to mainstream locations manifested in El Teatro's and the BRT's performances. Removed from the critical mainstream, many Chicano and black critics of the 1960s and 1970s lauded the communion between audience and performers achieved by El Teatro and BRT performances and celebrated the theater as a powerful social and cultural institution.[17] These critics, however, often were as caught up in the revolutionary fervor of the moment and the demands for social and cultural change as the theater practitioners themselves. No critic at that time—Chicano, black, or white—possessed the critical language or the historical distance now available to evaluate adequately and effectively the relationship between the theatrical performance and its social, cultural, and political context.

Interestingly, the aesthetic and historical distance of the 1990s have made it increasingly "academically correct" for leftist-minded cultural critics and scholars to challenge the earlier theatrical practices and ideological orientations of El Teatro and the BRT. Critics have assailed the essentialism of El Teatro's and the BRT's identity politics, the inflexibility of their cultural nationalistic dogma, and the sexism of their theatrical practices.[18] Black and Chicano cultural politics of the 1960s and 1970s have also come under recent attack for their reinforcement of ethnic absolutism and their perpetuation of polarizing racial boundaries of exclusivity.[19] In contrast, postmodern theories of identity have reified the constructed nature and fluidity of identity and have argued that identity is the site of multiple contestations. Through the application of these theories contemporary cultural critics have investigated the past practices of black and Chicano cultural nationalism. They have exposed the 1960s and 1970s claims of homogeneous, absolute Chicano or black identities as naive and overly restrictive. For such essentialist proclamations often did not allow space for diversity and divergent representations of blacks and Chicanos. Recognizing the limitations of earlier conceptions of black and Chicano identity, contemporary black and Chicano theorists have lobbied for coalitional politics that push beyond the earlier platforms of identity to realize contradictions within subject positions and embrace difference.

And yet, while contemporary leftists have decried the strategies of identity practiced in the 1960s and 1970s, the conservative Right and Christian fundamentalist movements have appropriated tactics of identity politics in their appeals to "American values" and their denigration of the so-called cultural elite. In fact, with the putative "Republican Revolution" of the 1990s, developments in contemporary U.S. politics parallel Kobena Mercer's observation that within British politics of the 1980s "the figurative meaning of the left/right dichotomy has been totally reversed."[20] The concept of an "oppressed people" has escaped from its 1960s and 1970s contexts to new usages within contemporary right-wing politics. With the current backlash against Affirmative Action and multiculturalism, conservative activists have redefined white males as an oppressed minority. Clearly, identity politics have not disappeared but have been reformulated. They still play key roles in social and cultural interactions.

The fact is that, while the cultural politics of the 1960s and 1970s were ideologically naive, they were strategically effective. They provided marginalized groups with a needed sense of solidarity and increased subjectivity. For blacks and Chicanos in particular, the period 1965 to 1971 represents a time when intragroup identity, consciousness, and commitment were visibly strong; consequently, despite the inherent deficiencies of 1960s and 1970s identity politics, they still figure repeatedly as either sources for or subjects of contemporary black and Chicano cultural expressions, theoretical paradigms, and even literary theories.[21] In today's dislocated and alienated, postmodern culture, as the New Left "has experienced a crisis of agency that has left it disaggregated and fragmented,"[22] there is an urgent desire by many to revisit and even revitalize the collective sensibilities, cultural unity, and social fervor of those earlier times. And yet within contemporary discourse on culture and identity a tension exists between the need for solidarity and community cohesion to achieve political change and the discomfort with the expected loss of difference and individuality that can result from absorption into a group.

My sense is that a critical reexamination and recontextualization of the ideologies and practices of El Teatro and the BRT during the period

1965 to 1971 can prove extremely beneficial to our understanding of the current manipulations of identity politics and strategies for racial representation and cultural resistance. This project of recontextualization will observe the naïveté of El Teatro and BRT's politics of cultural nationalism but will also consider how these theatrical movements used identity politics and essentialism strategically to agitate for change. My recontextualization will situate the ideologies and dramaturgies of El Teatro and the BRT within the uneven processes of social development.

I believe that an investigation of social protest performances during the period 1965 to 1971 is particularly relevant to current discourse on identity because of the uniqueness of the performative event. Performance, by definition, is inherently ephemeral; each performance is different. Performed identities, the characters or figures onstage, must be constructed with each new performance before an audience and are therefore not fixed. Thus, even with their supposedly absolute racial politics, El Teatro's and the BRT's social protest performances of the 1960s and 1970s strategically constructed identities as they placed performers onstage and used the "transformative power" of the theatrical event to advocate change.

Through their performance work El Teatro and the BRT created idealized and radicalized visions of Chicano and black subjectivity. Implicitly, in their respective agitational projects El Teatro and the BRT exposed the inherent "constructed-ness" of any and all political systems, social communities, historical narratives, and social and cultural identities. They articulated connections between politics, culture, and race that anticipated Stuart Hall's conceptualization of a "politics of representation" as well as the designs and desires for cultural resistance proposed by contemporary cultural critics such as bell hooks, Cornel West, Henry Giroux, and Gloria Anzaldùa.[23]

Our contemporary location not only facilitates my assessment of the relationship between current cultural politics and El Teatro's and the BRT's past practices; it also enables me to examine the social protest performances of El Teatro and the BRT with historical distance and with the employment of new critical methodologies. Recent studies in performance and audience reception theory have pushed audience reception into the foreground as a significant element of criticism and analysis.[24] Developments in American new historicism and British cultural materialism have radically altered critical thinking on the exchange between the historical moment and the dramatic text in performance.[25] In addition, the work of feminist scholars inside and outside of the theater has led to the recognition of gender as "a fundamental condition of experience and category of analysis."[26] Consequently, the efforts of such feminist scholars as bell hooks, Donna Haraway, and Jill Dolan influence my analysis of the social protest performance.[27]

Because of the performances' explicit desire to alter social behavior and revolutionize social systems, I firmly believe that analyzing the social protest performances of El Teatro and the BRT requires an anthropologically informed methodology. The theories of anthropologists Jean and John Comaroff and Victor Turner have supplanted the earlier ritual theories of the Cambridge school of anthropologists and established new models for determining the anthropology of theater and the relationship between the theatrical event and ritual.[28] Their work provides a critical foundation for this study. At the center of my analysis of El Teatro and the BRT is a reimagining of the relationship between ritual and social theater performance. Both El Teatro and the BRT produced theatrical events in which their audiences actively participated. I contend that ritual theory promises the key to understanding why the audience responded in this fashion and to analyzing how this participatory response relates to the possible social efficacy of that social protest performance. When social protest performances operated "ritualistically," they transformed spectators into active participants, and their participatory activity inside the theater was an indicator of or precursor to revolutionary activity outside of the theater.

The Significance of Ritual

From the inception of Western theatrical practice in ancient Greece, if not before, the relationship between ritual and theater has been the subject of research, theory, debate, and conjecture. In the 1960s and 1970s, at the same historical moment that El Teatro and the BRT emerged, avant-garde theater artists such as Peter Brook, Jerzy Grotowski, Judith Malina, Julian Beck, and Richard Schechner all experimented with ritual. Employing a variety of different methodologies, they each sought to capture in their theatrical practice the communal and spiritual effer-

vescence, the gestural and symbolic significance, the collective consciousness endemic to ritual processes. While these experimentalists
purposefully attempted to incorporate ritual into their theatrical work,
El Teatro and the BRT made no conscious effort to inculcate ritual in
their social protest performances. And yet the social protest performances of El Teatro and the BRT often became communal experiences
with the spectators and performers united in a bond of symbolic
protest. Implicitly, El Teatro and the BRT social protest performances
reified the interrelationship between ritual and theater by integrating
the symbolic and the actual, the productive and the celebratory, the
political and the spiritual.

Consequently, uncovering these ritual practices and examining
closely how the "rituals of social protest theater" operate is critical to
determining the oppositional power and aesthetic achievements of El
Teatro's and the BRT's social protest performances. Still, *ritual* is an
overused term whose meanings are often unclear. In order to develop a
paradigmatic understanding of the rituals of social protest theater, I
will appropriate anthropological theories on ritual and apply them to
the social protest performances I discuss. Victor Turner defines *ritual* as
"prescribed formal behavior for occasions not given over to technolog-
ical routine, having reference to beliefs in mystical beings or powers."[29]
The notion of symbolic acts is implicit in this definition. The performance of these symbolic acts links the gathered participants with mystical beings or powers beyond. Expanding on Turner's definition, the
more recent theories of Jean and John Comaroff note that ritual "evokes
the opposition between the enchanted and the secular."[30] Ritual acts as
a form of "symbolic mediation" that negotiates the spaces between the
practical and the spiritual, the sacred and the secular. This "symbolic
mediation" works to inform the spiritual well-being as well as the cultural and social organization of the gathered community.

Yet Jean and John Comaroff maintain that ritual acts not only as
symbolic mediation but also as a "signifying practice" that defines and
authorizes social action.[31] The signifying functions of ritual are both
consecrative and productive, both radical and conservative. In its consecrative and conservative mode ritual can reinforce existing values
and belief systems. At the same time, ritual is capable of imagining new
social orders. Ritual can transform human consciousness and social

behavior and even induce revolutionary action. In this radical and productive capacity ritual constitutes what Jean and John Comaroff refer to as a "vehicle of history-in-the making," which "(re)makes social predicaments" and "(re)casts cultural orders."[32] The impact of the ritual enactment can potentially reach far beyond the immediate historical moment and the current social reality.

As both symbolic mediation and signifying practice, ritual intends to affect the flow of history and the allocation of power in the universe. Through symbolic reformulation, transforming the world of symbol and rite, ritual seeks to control the practical world.[33] Jean and John Comaroff write:

> Ritual is a site and a means of experimental practice, of subversive poetics, of creative tension and transformative action, that under its authorship and authority, individual and collective aspirations weave a thread of imaginative possibilities from which may emerge, wittingly or not, new signs and meanings, conventions and interventions.[34]

Ritual, then, can be subversive and creative. It is a powerful, diverse, multidirectional agent, vital to social processes and to communicating collective, social identities. Turner maintains that ritual "actually creates, or recreates, the categories through which men perceive reality— the axioms underlying the structure of society and the laws of the natural and moral orders."[35] In a similar vein Mary Douglas writes in *Purity and Danger* that "social rites create a reality which would be nothing without them. It is impossible to have social relations without symbolic acts."[36] Ritual is symbolic, collective and meaningful action.

Understanding ritual as a dynamic force, critical to social interaction, enables us to locate ritual practices not simply in "preindustrial" or "primitive" societies, the typical ethnographic sites, but in a variety of other, alternative social spaces. The following chapters document my contention that ritual processes, in the sense that Turner and the Comaroffs define them, were critical elements in the social protest performances of El Teatro and the BRT. The ability of these social protest performances to function "ritualistically" significantly determined their level of interaction with their audience and enhanced their social efficacy. Here I use the phrase *to function ritualistically* to communicate the ability of the social protest performance, the theatrical event as a whole, to replicate the power and spirit of ritual enactments.

Reflecting the dynamism and polysemous nature of ritual, my approach to identifying and analyzing the rituals of social protest theater in this text is intentionally open and flexible. Accordingly, I will argue that the concepts of ritual as both symbolic mediation and as signifying practice are important to interpreting the ritualistic operation of El Teatro's and the BRT's social protest performances. Often their social protest performances acted as symbolic mediations, negotiating the spaces between the current social reality and the struggle for social change. Rather than connecting the participants with the gods or powers beyond, as in tribal ritual ceremonies, the social protest performances of El Teatro and the BRT united the spectators and performers with the greater cause of social action—the Grape Pickers strike (La Huelga) and the UFWOC movement or the Black Power and Black Liberation movements, respectively. When the social performance acted as symbolic mediation, it became more than a theatrical event. The performance functioned as a spiritual celebration, a sacred/secular ceremony.

Margaret Thompson Drewal notes that the Yoruba word for "theatrical performance," *iran*, is the same term that Yoruba apply to most religious rituals.[37] She goes on to note that Yoruba rituals are "socially and spiritually efficacious."[38] As symbolic meditations, the social protest performances of El Teatro and the BRT similarly sought to connect the social and spiritual with the performative. The BRT purposefully appropriated rites and symbols from the black Christian church within its theatrical practices. With El Teatro the invocation of the spiritual was less explicit. Yet El Teatro clearly worked to formulate a spiritual bond between the cause of La Huelga, the farmworkers' strike, and the agrarian roots and early resistance efforts of the Chicano ancestors. The invocation of spirituality served to intensify the meanings of the social protest performance.

As signifying practices, the performances of El Teatro and the BRT reinforced the values and beliefs of their particular movements while directing the audience to take social action. As with ritual, El Teatro and the BRT intended their performances to be transformative and regenerative. Their performances affirmed cultural unity while demonstrating that the spectators' own oppressive social circumstances were ultimately transformable. The ritualistic action of these social protest performances revitalized the oppositional struggles of blacks and Chicanos and confirmed for those in attendance the righteousness of their cause.

The ability of ritual both to affirm and transcend difference is particularly pertinent to this comparative investigation of El Teatro and the BRT. Each ritual enactment is different. The social power and cultural influence of any ritual depend on the specific historical context and constituent audience. At the same time, any individual ritual is representative of the social category of ritual. Jean Comaroff writes that a ritual is "simultaneously unique and yet one instance of a very general class of social movements."[39] Consequently, each ritual is both different and the same, atypical and yet typical.

At times the enactment of ritual produces an infectious enthusiasm among the celebrants, a collective exuberance. According to Erving Goffman, "[ritual] . . . which is accepted at the moment as reality will have some of the characteristics of a celebration."[40] Similarly, the social protest performances of El Teatro and the BRT often became communal celebrations that involved both audience and performers. And yet one area in which theorists and critics have repeatedly sought to differentiate ritual from theater is in the experience of the audience. Critics have argued that, while the audience for a ritual attends out of spiritual need and social obligation, theater audiences normally attend solely out of desire.[41] While ritual celebrants generally function as congregations, theatrical audiences, on the other hand, do not.[42] Consistent with this differentiation of ritual and theater, Turner maintains that rituals represent liminal phenomena but identifies theatrical performances as liminoid phenomena.[43] Liminal phenomena are symbolic enactments, activities, events, and forms that occur at natural breaks within, or "spaces in between," the normal functioning of the social system. They are purposefully integrated into the total social processes of a society. Liminal phenomena, such as rituals, tend to be collective. They stress togetherness and elicit membership and loyalty to the group. Social and cultural necessity reinforce the emergence and existence of liminal phenomena. Consequently, liminal phenomena are concerned with the functioning of the society and with crises within the social order. Turner points out that in liminal phenomena such as "ritual, myth and legal processes—work and play are hardly distinguishable in many cases."[44]

The *oid* in *liminoid* derives from the Greek word *eidos*, meaning "like" or "resembling." Thus, the liminoid resembles but is not identical to the liminal. Liminoid phenomena, as opposed to liminal phenomena, are strictly leisure activities, play, and entertainment. The liminoid is a commodity that one can select and pay to attend. Individuals are free to choose to participate in liminoid phenomena, which occur in "neutral spaces," separated from the mainstream of political and social activities. They develop apart from the central economic and political processes. Unlike liminal phenomena, they tend to be generated by specific individuals and are fragmentary and experimental in character. Turner argues, "One *works* at the liminal, one *plays* at the liminoid. There may be much more pressure to go to church or synagogue, whereas one queues up at the box office to see a play by Beckett, a show of Mort Sahl's, a Super-bowl Game, a symphony concert, or an art exhibit." While Turner classifies church service and attendance as liminal, he identifies theatrical attendance and performances as liminoid.[45]

This book argues, however, that the ritualistic nature and sociopolitical purposes of El Teatro and BRT performances infused the "liminoid realm of theater" with elements of the liminal. The liminal quality of El Teatro's and the BRT's social protest performances served to distinguish these theatrical events from the clearly liminoid functions of mainstream commercial theater. Their explicitly oppositional purposes in conjunction with the tumultuous and tempestuous social mood of the times propelled spectators to attend these performances for reasons that were outside the domain of the liminoid. Perhaps even more significantly, these spectators often actively participated in the theatrical event. As my discussion will show, the cultural and social constitution of the audience, the social environment in which they lived, and the self-conscious construction of the performance itself all contributed to making the social protest performance a participatory experience. Participation alters the constitutive effect of the theatrical performance. Mieke Bal notes that a theatrical performance is most often a "representation of a happening," while a ritual is "a happening itself." Yet, Bal suggests, audience participation can transform this relationship: "Participation in a representational practice can be, under specific circumstances, such as oral, communal performance, a ritual practice."[46]

Within the social and cultural upheaval of the 1960s and early 1970s the spectators for the social performances of El Teatro and the BRT, much like ritual congregations, often joined with the actors in spiritual, subversive, and celebratory protest. The performances of El Teatro and the BRT destabilized the traditional exchange between spectators and the performance. These counterhegemonic social protest performances interrogated and repositioned the power of theatrical representation and manipulated power as a "creative force."[47] Together audience and performers united in the symbolic overthrow of oppression.

The chapters to follow explore the power of social protest performance to articulate social issues, to celebrate cultural identity, and potentially even to direct social action. Each of the next four chapters examines a different aspect of the social protest performance: chapter 2 considers how the surrounding social conditions affect the performance; chapter 3 analyzes the content and form of the social protest play text; chapter 4 investigates the performance space and elements of performance and staging; chapter 5 discusses the social protest performers and explores the role of the audience; and chapter 6 provides a synthesizing conclusion. Throughout these discussions I note the significance that these earlier performances hold for current considerations of cultural resistance and racial representation. My intention is not only to read the past through the present but also to comment on present tensions within cultural politics through an exploration of the past.

Synergy—The Social Environment as an Active Agent: *Black Ice* and *Las Dos Caras del Patroncito*

The turbulent events of the 1960s and 1970s brought issues of race, class, gender, war, and economic deprivation to America's consciousness in profound ways. Significantly, the social, economic, and political realities of the times created an atmosphere conducive to the performance of black and Chicano social protest theater. Synergistically, the social protest performances of El Teatro and the Black Revolutionary Theater informed and were informed by the material conditions of Chicano and black existence. In fact, the surrounding social circumstances actually became critical elements within the social protest performances.

Recognizing the direct relation of El Teatro to the struggles for social change, Luis Valdez declared in 1967: "We shouldn't be judged as a theater. We're really part of a cause."[1] Voicing a similar sentiment, black writer and critic Larry Neal, in 1968, termed the Black Arts Movement "the aesthetic and spiritual sister of the Black Power concept."[2] The avowed social commitment of both of these theatrical groups, their synergistic bond with the contemporary sociopolitical conditions, was critical to the social protest performances of El Teatro and the BRT and their interaction with their audiences. It was on and through the tumultuous surrounding social conditions that the social protest performances of El Teatro and the BRT operated.

In this chapter I will examine closely the relationship between the tempestuous social environment and the social protest performance using two early works of El Teatro and the BRT as models: *Las Dos Caras del Patroncito* by Luis Valdez and El Teatro Campesino and *Black Ice* by black revolutionary playwright Charles Patterson. As John Dollimore and Alan Sinfield note, the reception of any play is "related to the contexts of its production."[3] In *Las Dos Caras* and *Black Ice* the social and cultural contexts not only influenced reception; they were also active agents within the production. *Las Dos Caras* was one of the first "actos" written and performed by El Teatro. The *actos*, as Valdez and El Teatro named their plays, were short, succinct, collectively created pieces used to dramatize the social inequities of the farm labor system and to generate support for the Grape Strike.[4] *Black Ice* was part of the original repertory of the Black Arts Repertory Theater School (BARTS) in 1965.

I have selected these plays not only for their direct and visible connection to the sociopolitical contexts of their production but also because they both work ritualistically to invert the conventional power hierarchy and to legitimate Chicano and black power, respectively. Before turning to the analysis of *Las Dos Caras* and *Black Ice,* however, I want to examine the social context for these works and for the inception of El Teatro and the BRT, to review and foreground the fundamental social conditions that influenced the development of social protest theater in the period 1965–71 and created a supportive environment for it.

Democratic Progression and Social Urgency

The explosion of social antagonisms in the period from 1965 to 1971 would indelibly affect U.S. political, social, and cultural life. At the outset of the 1960s the nation watched intently as civil rights protesters in the South valiantly resisted Jim Crow laws and mob violence, water hoses and attack dogs, racial segregation and discrimination. Out in the Far West migrant workers in the San Joaquín Valley of California, impatient and frustrated with their substandard wages and inadequate housing, followed the lead of the civil rights activists and organized a plan of resistance. César Chávez, head of the United Farmworkers; the United Farm Workers Organizing Committee (UFWOC) strike of 1965; and the subsequent grape boycott would soon garner national attention.

At this same historic moment students of the "baby-boom genera-tion," who had matriculated at colleges and universities in unprece-dented numbers, began to question the relevance of the educational system and to voice their disillusionment with the effectiveness of the government. In 1965 the "free speech movement" originated in Berke-ley, California, and soon spread throughout the country. The escalation of the war in Vietnam, in the mid- to late 1960s, served to exacerbate existing sociopolitical tensions and intensify the atmosphere of unrest both on and off college campuses. By 1969 the continued and increas-ingly visible protests against the war reflected the public's widespread dissatisfaction with the government and with the symbols of cultural and political legitimacy.

These emerging voices of dissatisfaction fought against existing U.S. hierarchies of power but, at the same time, struggled to attain those inalienable rights promised by American "democracy." These resistance efforts still operated within a specific, discursive system. For, as political philosopher Chantal Mouffe states, "People struggle for equality not because of some ontological postulate, but because they have been constructed as subjects in a democratic tradition that puts those values at the center of social life."[5] In the 1960s and early 1970s the social climate in the United States became increasingly volatile, as those who had been silent vociferously cried out for access to the "American dream" of "liberty and justice for all."

The interconnections between these emergent cries for democracy in the 1960s and 1970s reflect a nascent form of what Mouffe and others have recently defined as a "radical chain of democratic equivalences." Building on the work of Antonio Gramsci, Mouffe outlines a theory of "expansive hegemony" in which democratic struggles form links with other democratic struggles, creating a chain of equivalences. She main-tains that "the progressive character of a struggle" depends upon its "link to other struggles. The longer the chain of equivalences set up between the defense of the rights of one group and those of other groups, the deeper will be the democratization process and the more difficult to neutralize certain struggles or make them serve the ends of the Right." Accordingly, Mouffe believes that such radical chains are critical to contemporary progressive politics and the "extension of the democratic revolution into more and more spheres of public life."[6]

The development of coalitions among social protest groups in the

1960s and 1970s provides an early example of Mouffe's contention. They created linkages and a nexus of social activism that contemporary progressives could desire to replicate. The antiwar movement, the civil rights movement, the farmworkers movement, the student protest movements—models of social protest in the 1960s and 1970s—all consciously interacted. Civil rights activists and student dissidents came to Delano, California, some at the invitation of César Chávez and the UFW, to assist with the strike effort. Both Dr. Martin Luther King Jr. and Chávez saw connections between their own struggle for oppressed peoples' rights and the protests against the war in Vietnam. Protest groups, grassroots organizations, militant activists, and champions of reform forged new alliances. During this period a "counterculture" movement emerged, which expressed solidarity across different social struggles and determined to challenge American orthodoxies and systems of power. And yet this chain of equivalences was not without contradictions and examples of uneven articulation of democratic principles. For, as this chapter will show, the social and political subordination of women, gays, and lesbians was—at first—largely ignored by this move toward coalitional politics.[7]

Kobena Mercer perceptively argues that black liberation struggles acted as an influential "metaphor" in the development of social antagonisms and the radical chain of democratic equivalences during this period.[8] For African Americans at this time the desire for economic access and educational opportunity, their willingness to believe the American ideal that "all men are created equal," severely conflicted with the policies of racial segregation. The civil rights and subsequent Black Power movements gave voice to African Americans' opposition to their subordinate positions and their "contradictory interpolation."[9] *Contradictory interpolation,* according to Mouffe, refers to "a situation in which subjects constructed in subordination by a set of discourses are, at the same time, interpolated as equal by other discourses."[10] Such contradictory interpolations affected the production of social antagonisms. Black struggles against subordination empowered other emerging social movements and contradictorily interpolated groups. These groups drew parallels between their own oppositional efforts and the black liberation cause. They appropriated and implemented strategies of civil disobedience first invoked by the civil rights movement. Mercer points out that, in the 1960s and subsequently, "black struggles became universalized in the tactics and strategies of new subjects and agents of democratic antagonism."[11]

César Chávez and the UFW, bolstered by the success of the civil rights movement, used sit-ins, marches, and other tactics of nonviolent resistance in the Delano farmworkers strike. Despite constant abuse and provocation from the growers—"one grower even sprayed pick-eters with pesticides from a crop duster"[12]—the strike remained nonviolent. Not only in Delano but across the Southwest, in rural valleys and urban barrios, Chicanos, like blacks, suffered from discrimination in housing, employment, and education. In cities such as Los Angeles and Houston, Chicanos developed oppositional political organizations and protest movements that benefited significantly from the national visibility attained by black resistance efforts of this period.

And yet historian Rodolfo Acuña notes that, unlike blacks, "Mexican Americans had a difficult time convincing people that they belonged to the civil rights movement. Not until 1970 did the United States courts classify Mexican Americans as an identifiable ethnic minority with a pattern of discrimination."[13] The desire of Chicanos to locate themselves within the economics of the civil rights movement testifies to the "empowering effect of race as metaphor" for "extending the chain of radical equivalences to more and more social groups."[14] The articulation of Chicano social antagonisms and the emergence of a Chicano movement also evidenced the arrival of new, particularly Chicano political subjects and the desire of these Chicano subjects to challenge their subordination on their own terms. Chicanos have a long and separate history of struggle and resistance in the United States. Even before the Battle of Texas in 1836 Chicanos challenged the United States political system for rights to land, resources, and self-determination.[15]

During the 1960s and 1970s the agitational and organizational efforts of Chávez and the UFWOC in Delano, protests by Chicano/a college students for equal access to education and Chicano studies programs, the migration of Chicanos from rural to urban centers, and the subsequent rise in political activism and school boycotts by Chicanos in the urban barrios all demonstrated a growing Chicano subjectivity, an increasing intragroup identification and consciousness.[16] The rise in Chicano identity, awareness, and consciousness supported the contention of sociologists Patricia Gurin, Arthur A. Miller, and Gerald Gurin that group "identification and its transformation into consciousness should be greatest among those strata whose mobility is most blocked and whose channels for redressing grievances are most limited."[17] Chicanos in the 1960s and early 1970s reacted to their lack of social mobility and educational opportunities and challenged discriminatory labor and immigration practices. Certainly, Chicano oppression in the United States was not a new phenomenon. Chicano farm laborers had suffered under a systematic policy of economic discrimination and exploitation for many years. Yet in the 1960s and 1970s—with the increase in the Chicano population, the metaphoric explosion of black Americans against racist subordination, and the breakdown of hierarchical relationships throughout the U.S. social order—pressures for Chicano liberty and equal access surfaced and became antagonistic.

And yet, as Mouffe points out, "you cannot automatically derive antagonisms and struggle from the existence of these objective conditions—they are necessary but not sufficient—unless you necessarily assume people will struggle against subordination."[18] Certainly, the assumption that subordinate subjects will inevitably revolt is naive. My contention is that an understanding of the sociological/psychological condition I term "urgency" is critical in determining *why* social antagonisms occur and in negotiating the gap between the existence of social inequalities and the emergence of radical social protests. Urgency is an invisible but discernable factor in the emergence of radical social struggles. *Urgency* conveys the idea that the frustrations of the disenfranchised have reached crisis proportions; untenable circumstances have pushed oppressed people to the boiling point, and they erupt. No longer willing to endure their subjugation, experiencing the pressures of urgency, the oppressed demand *immediate* reform.

Takeovers of administration buildings on college campuses, riots, spontaneous explosions of outrage on the streets of Detroit and in the grape vineyards of Delano, all manifested the burgeoning mood of urgency in the 1960s and 1970s. Such urgent events provided models that provoked and encouraged other protest activities. In addition, a growing awareness of Latin American and African revolutionary insurgencies and campaigns of guerrilla warfare, like those of Che Guevara in Bolivia and Kwame Nkrumah in Ghana, inspired and helped to intensify the atmosphere of urgency in the United States. Some radical Chicano and black American political movements aligned their own liberation struggles with these and other Third World rebellions.

The feeling of urgency experienced by dissatisfied and radicalized peoples not only compelled them to demand change "now" but also encouraged them to believe that radical change, even revolution, was inevitable. Optimistically, proponents of radical social change, invigorated by the urgency of the times, envisioned the United States on the verge of dramatic and fundamental social and political rebellion. Reflecting back on that period, John O'Neal, one of the founding members of the Free Southern Theater, remarked, "We really believed we were going to change the world in, at most, two or three years."[19] The atmosphere of urgency in the 1960s and 1970s fueled and in turn was fueled by the performativity of the entire social environment. Dramatic social events such as protest demonstrations, draft card burnings, and acts of civil disobedience on the Delano picket lines were notable not only for their subversive political intent but for their performative quality. They were, in fact, public performances before audiences and featuring actual bodies in live performance. In these turbulent times social activists became protagonists in their own real-life dramas. Their acts of protest contained a sense of self-reflexivity, a conscious awareness of their dichotomous positionality as performing/protesting subjects and, simultaneously, objects of the viewing audience's gaze. The concept of the activist-as-performer/performer-as-activist would prove important to the social protest performances of El Teatro and the BRT.

With the concurrent advances in media coverage, protestors became all the more aware of the performative power of social protest events. The 1966 farmworkers' march from Delano to the California state capital of Sacramento, modeled on the 1964 Civil Rights March on Washington, was a self-conscious performative event. The drama of this march and the publicity it received in the print and television media increased visibility, interest, and involvement. Certainly, the demonstrators at the 1968 Democratic National Convention in Chicago recognized that the entire nation and world watched their actions. Yet, as evidenced by the arrests and violence that marked that convention and the highly publicized trial of the "Chicago Seven" that followed, an uneasy tension binds these social performative events and their potential real-life consequences.

The social protest performances of El Teatro and the BRT sought to exploit this tension to their own advantage. El Teatro's and the BRT's

social protest performances reflected and rearticulated the actual experiences of protest and social struggle. The social protest performance of
El Teatro and the BRT held up a "matrical" mirror to the dramatic daily
lives of Chicanos and blacks.[20] The performativity of the entire social
field contributed materially to the interaction between life and art, culture and politics, within the ritualistic social protest performances of El
Teatro and the BRT. Reciprocally, as life became more dramatic, the
social protest performances became more real. Just as acts of civil disobedience functioned as self-conscious performances, social protest
performances operated as acts of protest, visual evidence of social
antagonism with real-life significance and impact.

The performativity and urgency of the social environment affected
not only the development of El Teatro and the BRT but the emergence
of a chain of alternative, experimental theater groups as well. Groups
such as the Living Theater, the Performance Group, and the Open Theater engaged in ensemble, nonlinear processes and actor-based practices designed to displace the director/playwright dyad as the central
force within theatrical creation. Defiantly, these experimental theater
groups pushed the boundaries of American theater and sought to redefine what theater should be. On a variety of levels these theatrical
movements, much like social protest movements of this time, interacted. Cross-fertilizations repeatedly occurred and affected the theaters' practices and even the social protest work of El Teatro and the
BRT.[21] The Radical Theater Festival held in San Francisco in 1968—featuring the San Francisco Mime Troupe, the Bread and Puppet Theater,
as well as El Teatro—was an example of this theatrical interaction. The
puppetry of the Bread and Puppet Theater would influence the development of El Teatro's acto La Conquista de Mexico, which will be discussed in the next chapter. Responding to the explosion of social antagonisms at that time, radical theaters in the 1960s and 1970s voiced their
own frustrations with hierarchical systems inside and outside of the
theater.

New social antagonisms arose in this period infused by the mood
of urgency and as a response to or as a critique of previous antagonisms. The Black Power and Chicano nationalist movements both were
extensions of previous antagonisms. Fueled by the seemingly too deliberate pace of civil rights reform and the assassination of Malcolm X in
1964, the focus and philosophy of black protest shifted away from pre-

vious positions of nonviolence toward a revolutionary paradigm of violent confrontation. On a local and national basis Black Power and black nationalist organizations emerged.[22] At one definitive Student Non-Violent Coordinating Committee (SNCC) demonstration in 1966, Stokely Carmichael, now Kwame Toure, openly challenged his previous mentor, Martin Luther King Jr. He jumped onto the back of a flatbed truck and declared: "The only way we gonna stop them white men from whippin' us is to take over. We been saying freedom for six years and we ain't got nothing. What we gonna start saying now is Black Power!"[23] "Black Power" became a slogan and a movement of national significance. With the emergence of the Black Panther Party in 1966, Americans across the country witnessed on television one of the most dramatic, shocking, and empowering images of the times. Black men clad in black leather, openly carrying firearms, patrolled the streets of Oakland, California, armed and ready for battle. The power of these images was reflected in equally dramatic and violent explosions in the streets of black America. By 1967 racial riots and black unrest had ravaged over twenty cities, including the Watts area of Los Angeles, Newark, Chicago, Harlem, Atlanta, and Detroit. These dramatic social events informed the entire United States that black outrage could neither be ignored nor easily contained.

Correspondingly, the Chicano nationalist movement responded to and galvanized the feelings of frustration emanating from Chicanos in the fields as well as the urban barrios. Chicano communities on the whole, however, never erupted into the riotous conflagrations found in black inner cities. There were isolated violent confrontations with the police, such as the one that resulted in the death of a news reporter, Rubén Salazar, on the day of the Chicano Vietnam Moratorium held in Los Angeles on 29 August 1970.[24] Earlier, on 15 October 1966, in one of the most visible demonstrations of Chicano nationalist insurgency, Reies López Tijerina and 350 members of La Alianza Federal de Mercedes (Federal Alliance of Land Grants) occupied a section of Kit Carson National Forest in New Mexico. They demanded the return of land grants to the "New" Mexicans. Tijerina would stage an armed raid on another national forest, Tierra Amarilla, in the summer of 1967. Tijerina's efforts to establish an independent republic based on land grants became an important symbol within the overall Chicano nationalist movement.

One of the most potent arenas in the 1960s and 1970s for articulating both Chicano and black nationalism was the cultural front. Chicano nationalists declared their spiritual, cultural, and historic connection to Aztlán. *Aztlán* is a Nahuatl word meaning "lands to the north" and indicates the mythohistorical lands of the southwestern United States from which the Aztecs migrated down to Mexico. Chicano nationalism valorized the uniqueness of Chicano culture and differentiated Chicano language and culture from either the black nationalistic or the dominant Anglo culture's orientations. Chicano "cultural" nationalism voiced the subjectivity of previously silenced Chicanos and attempted to articulate a separate and particularly Chicano consciousness.

Because African Americans lacked their own territory and were denied real political access and power, the cultural sphere offered the most logical arena for the Black Power struggle and the representation of a black nationalist ideology. William L. Van Deburg writes: "As the embodiment of the national spirit, black culture was said to be the signal utility of the Black Power movement. . . . For cultural nationalists, black culture *was* Black Power."[25] Black cultural nationalists sought to create a separate black cultural space in which to construct a black identity free from previous cultural definitions and stereotypes.

Within the urgent atmosphere of the 1960s and 1970s disenfranchised black and Chicano peoples gained a new cultural awareness. They appropriated the previously derogatory labels "black" and "Chicano" and transformed them into manifestations of cultural identity and affirmations of cultural resistance. Chants of "Black Power" and "Say it loud, I'm Black and I'm proud," the wearing of Afro hairstyles and dashikis, graphically demonstrated a growing spirit of black identity and black cultural unity. Similarly, shouts of "Aztlán!" "Viva la Raza!" "Viva la Causa!" and "Viva La Huelga!" echoed throughout the West and Southwest and revealed a burgeoning Chicano cultural collectivity. No longer willing to be ignored or invisible, the black and Chicano communities of the 1960s and early 1970s cried out against their marginality, proudly asserted their ethnic difference, and demanded social action.

Noticeable in black and Chicano strategies of cultural consciousness and nationalism was a naive articulation of what Stuart Hall, in his important essay of 1985, "New Ethnicities," terms a "politics of representation." According to Hall:

How things are represented and the "machineries" and regimes of representation in a culture do play a *constitutive*, and not merely a reflexive, after-the-event, role. This gives questions of culture and ideology, and the scenarios of representation—subjectivity, identity, politics—a formative, not merely expressive, place in the constitution of social and political life.[26]

Black and Chicano cultural nationalists were very much concerned with the machineries and regimes of representation. By foregrounding culture in their liberation struggles, they acknowledged and attempted to maximize the formative capabilities of cultural representation in "the constitution of social and political life." The valorization of culture as a space for political struggle enabled black and Chicano cultural nationalists—including Baraka and the BRT and Valdez and El Teatro—to construct strategic political positions that challenged the political status quo and previous representations of blacks and Chicanos.

Thus, as we will see throughout this study of El Teatro and the BRT, cultural nationalism in the 1960s and early 1970s was a complex, contradictory, and dichotomous project. At times the politics of cultural nationalism were prescient, predicting contemporary constructivist strategies of racial representation and ethnic politics. And yet, rooted in the urgencies of their specific historic moment and focused on the desire to achieve black and Chicano cultural and political consciousness and self-determination, black and Chicano cultural nationalism often reinforced notions of essentialized, homogeneous black and Chicano identities.

Evident within the 1960s and 1970s politics of Black Power and cultural nationalism, El Movimiento Chicano and Chicano cultural nationalism, was an emphasis on collective action and communal modes of empowerment. At this time black urban areas throughout the country experienced a surge in community organizing and an expansion of community organizations. As August Meier and Elliot Rudwick note, "a spirit of self-help and racial solidarity" united "ghetto residents for concerted action culturally, economically, and politically."[27] Similarly, Chicanos on the rural farmlands and in the urban barrios came to understand that access to social rights and political power depended on their identification with and active advocacy of notions of a unified Chicano "community." The concept of a "Chicano community" symbolically united the geographically and socially distinct rural farmworkers' struggle with the urban movements for Chicano rights and access under one united cultural-political front. Sociologist Paul Gilroy argues that the formation of communities is often critical to the foundation of oppositional strategies of social movements and efforts of collective resistance.[28] The construction of these symbolic Chicano and black communities of interest also represents, on a micro level, a manifestation of a radical chain of democratic equivalences. The politics of community united diverse antagonistic issues such as housing discrimination, fair labor practices, and bilingual education as democratic equivalences.

The valorization of community and the advocacy of collective action became critical components in the identity politics and social performance practices of El Teatro and the BRT. Valdez and Baraka envisioned their theaters as significant institutions within their marginalized communities, institutions that explicitly promoted the development of communal power, cultural awareness, and self-determination. Significantly, in their post-Delano residences—first in Del Rey, California, in 1967 and then in Fresno in 1969—El Teatro did not merely establish theatrical homes but also created community cultural centers. In addition to housing dramatic presentations, these cultural centers also sponsored a full range of Chicano cultural and artistic activities. When Baraka moved from Harlem to Newark, New Jersey, in 1966, he too established a cultural center, Spirit House. At Spirit House he initiated a diversified range of programming, including the African Free School for Youth. He named the new cultural center Spirit House because he hoped to move peoples' spirits and to function as integrally in the life of the community as a grocery store.[29]

Yet communities and communal modes of empowerment do not only operate as foundations for "collective radical action."[30] As Gilroy notes, "Community is as much about difference as it is about similarity and identity."[31] Communities establish, define, and separate themselves from others in terms of difference. With the development of Chicano and black communities of interest came the establishment of boundaries of exclusivity. The strategic promotion of communities of interest and resistance ran the risk of reinscribing external racist notions of ethnic absolutism. As an unfortunate consequence of the exclusive promotion of one's community's interests, Chicano and black groups at times found themselves in competition over limited resources.[32] For both El Teatro and the BRT the promotion of "the communal mode of empowerment" potentially restricted the expression of divergent ideas in order to reinforce the aesthetic principles of cultural nationalism.[33]

In addition, Norma Alarcón points out that, while the "communal mode of power" often appears to be the "only" model of empowerment that the oppressed have, it remains a "paternalistic model" that "limits the participation of women."[34] In times of urgency and upheaval Chicano and black cultural nationalism emphasized overcoming the domination of white culture and neglected their own subjugation of women. Yolanda Broyles-González points out that

> putting women's issues second, or discounting them altogether, was common among leftist groups of the 1960s in the United States and around the world. The liberation of people "in general" was considered the chief priority. Ironically, those engaged in struggles for human equality were slow to recognize that class struggles and ethnic struggles would not necessarily better the lot of women.[35]

The politics of black and Chicano cultural nationalism responded to what they construed as the needs of "their people." Yet, as Broyles-González notes, their definition of "their people" was decidedly male-centric and, consequently, did not always include, nor reflect, the particular oppressive conditions of women. The dearth of women's issues within the Black Power movement and El Movimiento Chicano, among others, demonstrates the uneven processes of social development. Contradictions and hierarchical relationships exist not only within dominant structures but within subordinate systems and movements agitating for change as well. Because of what Gramsci describes as the complex interplay of social and material relations, a political interest group may move toward or even achieve equality of access and opportunity on one front while it simultaneously ignores or even reinforces other issues of injustice and oppression.[36]

In part as a response to and even as a critique of leftist movements of the period that failed to recognize their inherent sexism or the rights of women as a legitimate political objective, a women's movement emerged in the late 1960s and early 1970s. The women's movement and subsequent feminist movements created legal and political campaigns, alternative institutions, and cultural organizations directed at empowering women and giving voice to their subjectivity. Reacting to the heterosexism present in the social practices and ideologies of the Left as well as the Right, the gay rights movement, and specifically the Gay Liberation Front, also came into being during this period, their members united around issues of identity and oppression. The gay rights and the women's movement each experienced their own sense of urgency, demanding immediate rights for gays and women, and also formed coalitions with other "oppressed peoples" and social movements. Consequently, both groups attempted to extend further the links in "the radical chain of democratic equivalences."[37]

Following the Black Power and Chicano movements, both the gay rights and women's movements serve as foundations for critiques—such as that by Yolanda Broyles-González—of the inherent gender biases, homophobia, and essentialism of both these earlier sociopolitical struggles. From our present, privileged location in the 1990s, we can observe how the development of gay and feminist theories enrich our understanding of the structural and ideological limitations of black and Chicano cultural nationalism in the United States during the period from 1965 to 1971. The cultural politics at that time simply did not actively address or emphasize the interactions of race, class, gender, and sexuality. Valdez notes that bringing women performers into El Teatro presented particular cultural problems because of the farmworkers' perceptions of the craft of acting and their conceptions of women's roles within the community.[38] An attempt to have a married woman read the part of La Virgen de Guadalupe in an early *acto* met with severe criticism and was quickly abandoned. The farmworker audiences strongly maintained that no woman who was not a virgin herself could be allowed to perform as La Virgen. Even the men within the troupe, according to Valdez, faced resistance and needed to overcome the derogatory label "puta," or "punk," which was how many farmworkers conceived of actors.[39] These confrontations over gender and performance testify to the inadequacies of labeling El Teatro's practices as sexist or heterosexist without recognizing the cultural and sociohistorical contexts of the group's operation.

Although the political platforms of black and Chicano nationalism in the 1960s and 1970s did not emphasize issues of gender, class, or sexuality, this does not mean that participants within these movements, particularly women, did not engage these issues. In her article "Black Nationalism: The Sixties and the Nineties" Angela Davis explains that a nascent concern over the intersections of systems of oppression was present within the politics of black nationalism in the 1960s:

> We may not have been able to talk about gendered racism, "sexuality" may have still meant sexiness, homophobia, as a word may not yet have existed, but our practice, I can say in retrospect, was located on a continuum that groped and zigzagged its way toward this moment of deliberation on the pitfalls of nationalism and essentialism.[40]

Davis's personal observations reveal that cultural politics in the 1960s lacked the language presently available to express the intricacies and interconnections of racial, class, and sexual oppression. The articulation of counterhegemonic struggles that purposefully work across and through these issues has required time and distance to evolve. Equally significant, Davis's words again point out that black nationalism at that time was not a monolithic concept but, rather, a "very complex and contradictory project."[41]

The later women's and gay rights movements were not without their own contradictions and inequalities. Subsequent critiques of the early women's and gay rights movements by women and gay critics of color have pointed out that racism was very much present in these movements. Such critiques reinforce our understanding of the uneven processes of social development. Continued critical interrogations and rereadings of supposedly progressive social developments can affect the revelation of new social inequities, the emergence of new political subjects, and the development of new social antagonisms.

The conception of both the gay rights and women's movements did help to extend the "democratic revolution into more and more spheres of social life." The fact that they originated when they did and in response to the politics of that time testifies to the overwhelming sense of urgency and political volatility that were then present. El Teatro and the BRT also emerged and operated in this tumultuous atmosphere. The period 1965–71 was a precarious and contradictory time, filled with both peril and potential. Cries for the destruction of the social order commingled with demands for self-determination and a call for the creation of new political and cultural systems. Attitudes toward hairstyles, dress, drugs, sex, music, and politics drastically changed as the counterculture attempted to reconfigure U.S. society. Battered by the confluence of social unrest, cultural and economic upheaval, and political instability, the U.S. social environment experienced new and unprecedented uncertainties.

Ritualization, Performativity, and Social Dramas

The desire to redress the urgent American social crises of the 1960s and early 1970s produced not only substantive policies and material action but also ritualistic measures: "symbolic mediations" and "signifying practices" designed to restore or redefine the social order. The performative nature of the social environment encouraged similar modes of redress. The United States in the 1960s and 1970s was ripe for, and in many ways in need of, ritual. Here, again, I am invoking the definitions of ritual established in the first chapter. Rituals are particular and privileged social practices whose purposes are both generative and regenerative. They can act as performative models for new social systems as well as work to reaffirm existing values and beliefs. Transferring ritual theory to the social field of the 1960s and 1970s may appear a bold move, but I believe that, clearly, during this period symbolic acts were critical to the maintenance and perpetuation of social relations. In this time of urgency activities of an implicitly and explicitly ritualistic nature emerged in a variety of arenas.[42] The dominant culture as well as those groups whose projects of protest and liberation stood in direct opposition to it often engaged in ritual practices in order to solidify social values or to reaffirm activist commitments.

My contention is that this emergence of ritual activity was particularly acute in the underprivileged and underrepresented Chicano and black communities. The propensity for and preponderance of ritual practices among blacks and Chicanos were due in part to the particularly insistent crises of social need that have surfaced from these underrepresented populations. It also reflected their respective spiritual and cultural orientations and experiences. Historically, for blacks as well as Chicanos performance, spirituality, and resistance have been interconnected. Early in African American history music functioned not only as a means of performance but also as a way to carry coded messages of rebellion. Drums warned of insurrection and, as a result, were confiscated by white slave owners. Negro spirituals such as "Swing Low Sweet Chariot" detailed escape plans along the Underground Railroad. Sermons, baptisms, call-and-response singing, and other rites enacted within the black Christian church were highly performative and participatory. Blacks molded Christianity to their own functional and spiritual needs. The black church operated as an important, and at times the only, space for African American cultural, political, and social interaction. As a result, religion and spirituality—from before the time of Harriet Tubman up to and through the era of Martin Luther King Jr. and Malcolm X—played critical roles in black political and resistance struggles. Outside of the church as well as inside, black cultural practices enjoined the spiritual and political spheres. The ode "We Shall Overcome," sung along civil rights picket lines in the 1960s, purposefully infused the political moment with a spiritual power and linked the marchers with the higher cause of freedom beyond. Furthermore, as Angela Davis notes, it was not only the black Christian tradition but also black Muslim practices that connected black spirituality with black political agency. According to Davis, the Nation of Islam has remained a "movement that accords nationalism the status of a religion."[43]

The spiritual component was equally important in the Chicano movement and the UFWOC strike in the 1960s and 1970s. As Broyles-González points out:

> During the early strikes . . . the back of César Chávez's old station wagon often functioned as a portable shrine replete with holy images, flowers and picket signs. Striking workers kept vigil there twenty-four hours a day; union meetings and daily mass were celebrated at the station wagon shrine parked next to the vineyards.[44]

Strikers carried religious symbols along with strike materials and picket signs. César Chávez was perceived as a spiritual leader as well as a political one. These intersections of politics and spirituality were consistent with the fact that, fundamentally, Chicano Catholicism was and is a syncretic faith borne out of Indian ritual practices and resistance as well as Christian ideology. La Virgen de Guadalupe is one of the most visible examples of this syncretism: she is at once a manifestation of the Virgin Mary and the Aztec deity Tonantzin.[45] La Virgen continues to figure prominently in Chicano religious, political, and performative practices. She remains not only the patron saint of Mexico but also a symbol of Chicano resistance and, more recently, a contested figure in Chicana feminist cultural critiques.

The cultural heritage of Chicanos features continuous intersections of the mythical and the miraculous, the performative and the religious, the spiritual and the political. When the Spanish invaders came to Mexico in 1510, they found among the indigenous populations a rich heritage of ritual spectacles and religious performances. They adapted the native forms and instituted a Christian liturgical drama that attempted to inculcate the doctrines of Christianity in the lives of Native Americans. Pageant plays and religious spectacles survive in Mexican and Chicano culture. Performed on religious holidays and festivals, these pageants purposefully incorporate spiritual and performative elements. Yet implicit within these texts are also political statements about the relation between the colonized native populations and the Spanish colonizers. Broyles-González notes that "these pageants enact the spiritual dimension of domination and subordination."[46]

The conflation of the political, spiritual, and performative within Chicano and black cultural practices informed the creation of El Teatro's and the BRT's ritualistic social protest performances[47] and also affected the receptivity of their audiences to these and other ritual enactments. During the 1960s and early 1970s many blacks and Chicanos experienced not only the transformational upheaval of the times but also a growing cultural consciousness and a willingness to combat their sociopolitical subjugation through cultural acts. The ritualistic social protest performances of El Teatro and the BRT were significant manifestations of such agitational cultural acts. When most effective, the celebrations of political optimism and cultural commitment achieved at these performances were equally moments of spiritual affirmation.

Moreover, I believe that the functioning of social protest performances in urgent, performative times correlates directly with the operation of ritual within what Turner terms the "crisis phase of social dramas." Turner notes that rituals were commonly enacted in preindustrial civilizations as a means of redressing the crisis stage of "social dramas."[48] Correspondingly, within this crisis phase social protest performances were performed as a mode of effecting social change. Turner delineates the process of social drama as follows:

> A social drama first manifests itself as the breach of a norm, the infraction of a rule, law, morality or custom or etiquette in some public arena. This breach may be deliberately, even calculatedly, contrived by a person or party disposed to demonstrate or challenge entrenched authority—for example, the Boston Tea Party— or it may emerge from a scene of heated feelings. Once visible, it can hardly be revoked. Whatever the case, a mounting crisis follows, a momentous juncture or turning point in the relations between components of a social field—at which seeming peace becomes overt conflict and covert antagonisms become visible. . . . In order to limit the contagious spread of the *breach* certain adjustive and redressive mechanisms, informal and formal are brought into operation. . . . The mechanisms may range from personal advice and informal arbitration to formal juridical and legal machinery, and to resolve certain kinds of crisis, to the performance of public ritual.[49]

Certainly, the dramatic and tumultuous events of the 1960s, the social upheavals occurring in the Delano grape vineyards and black urban America, could be classified as social dramas. Extending Turner's theory, the UFWOC strike and the picket lines in Delano form the initial stage of a social drama. "La Huelga" represents a deliberate "breach of the norm" and a challenge to the authority of the ranchers. A crisis phase was clearly evident in Delano as "overt conflict and covert antagonisms" came to demarcate and define the relationship of the striking farmworkers with the dominant social order.

Turner points out that, "in large scale complex societies, redress may be through rebellion, or even revolution, if the societal value-consensus has broken down, and new unprecedented roles, relationships, and classes have emerged."[50] Similarly, Chicanos and blacks emerged as new political subjects in "new and unprecedented roles" and attempted to resolve their particular social dramas by revolting against the hegemony of the dominant culture. These marginalized ethnic groups now asserted their own values in opposition to the dominant cultural norms and sought to build consensus and solidarity solely among themselves.

Applying Turner's social drama model to the social conditions of blacks and Chicanos requires certain adjustments. Still, understanding the urgent conflagrations of the 1960s and early 1970s as social dramas provides insight into the synergistic bond between the ritualistic social protest performance and the concurrent sociopolitical conditions surrounding the production. Within the urgent atmosphere of the times El Teatro and the BRT envisioned their social protest performances as measures of redress, mediating the urgent crises in Chicano and black communities and directing social action. Similar to ritual redress, the social protest performance worked to transform the world outside of the performance, the social drama. Functioning ritualistically, the social protest performances of El Teatro and the BRT worked as symbolic mediations and signifying practices connecting their audiences to a higher power—the social cause beyond.

Black Ice and Las Dos Caras del Patroncito

The original outdoor performances of Black Ice and Las Dos Caras specifically reflected and benefited from the surrounding atmosphere of urgency and upheaval. The content of and the contexts for the performances of these plays involved "mini" social dramas in which the audience participated. The first performance of Las Dos Caras occurred in 1965 on the actual picket lines in Delano amid an atmosphere of tension and anxiety. Because of the social circumstances—the presence of the ranchers' armed guards—the actual performance was itself an act of resistance. Within this social drama of "confrontation on the picket line," the social protest performance of Las Dos Caras operated like a ritual. The performance worked to redress the present social drama by symbolically disempowering the ranchers and revealing the potential power achieved through collective farmworker participation in the strike. The performance of Las Dos Caras was at once within and outside the other strike activities on the picket line. Through the power of performance El Teatro contested conventional power relationships and the subordination of farmworkers within the agribusiness hierarchy.

Prior to each street performance of Black Ice, BARTS would create a

phony racial confrontation in order to draw spectators to the performance. Baraka explained: "We sent Shammy [a BARTS troupe mem-
ber] with a pistol chasing one of the characters in Black Ice. The bloods
seeing a brother with a gun chasing somebody who looked like a white
man made a crowd instantly and the show began."[51] Unaware of the
fictitious nature of this racial incident, spectators immediately assembled. BARTS's pistol chase prologue skewed the lines between the illusion of the stage representation and concurrent racial realities. In 1965
Harlem, the image of a black man with a gun chasing a white man was
a powerful signifier. BARTS designed its fictitious racial confrontation
to capture the emotional involvement of an actual racial incident. Provoked by the staged chase and the racialized atmosphere of urgency,
concerned black spectators congregated with anticipation as a "community of interest" to watch the insurrection unfold. Their decision to
follow this black/white conflict made them participants in the action.

The action of the chase capitalized on and intensified the urgency
of the moment. BARTS had created an imaginary social drama. The fic-
tionalized social drama then evolved into a symbolic social protest performance that proposed the redressive solution of revolutionary insurgency. Performed in the crisis phase of this social drama, Black Ice, like
Las Dos Caras, functioned as ritual; and context is critical to ritual. As
Catherine Bell notes, "the social or cultural context of ritual does not
exist separately from the act."[52] The constructed chase helped to foreground the relationship between the performed events and the existent
dynamics of the black struggle against white oppression.

Within its particularly intensified social environment Black Ice
operated as a signifying practice, directing black spectators toward collective and violent revolutionary action. At the outset of Black Ice a sect
of black nationalists forced a white congressman—a synecdoche for the
white capitalist system—to sit, bound and powerless, in a chair. In a
vain attempt to assert his authority, the white congressman informed
his black nationalist captors: "You'd be surprised at the power a Congressman has. We run this country."[53] Yet Yargo, the leader of the black
kidnappers, reprimanded him, "You're not in a bargaining position,
Congressman" (BI, 562). The black nationalists were now in control,
and the hegemony of Congress, of the "white power structure," was
symbolically undermined by the stage representation. Yargo and the
black nationalists, with their guns and rhetoric of revolution, embodied

a new conceptualization of power. The action deconstructed any notion that the hegemony of the dominant culture was either ontological or essential. BARTS, in creating this social protest performance, achieved what Eric MacDonald considers a "poststructuralist" understanding of power as a "creative force" that can be controlled and transformed through cultural production.[54]

Las Dos Caras also functioned as a signifying practice, generating farmworker optimism, reaffirming self-worth, and emphasizing that oppressive circumstances could be overcome. This play, like Black Ice, reimagined power as a creative force. Las Dos Caras deconstructed and demystified the hegemony of the white grape ranch owner, or "Patron," as he was known to Chicano farmworkers. El Teatro adjoined the diminutive form -cito to Patron, the boss character's name, to diminish symbolically his stature and his power. The powerful rancher boss in life became the "Patroncito," or "little boss," onstage, a far less threatening figure. Weary of the demands of power, the Patroncito in Las Dos Caras longed for what he perceived as the simple life of the farmworker and asked the Farmworker character if they could exchange places. After he received the agreement of the Farmworker, the Patroncito removed the symbols of his power—his pig mask, his large cigar, and his whip—and handed them to the Farmworker. Through this disrobing process, the Patroncito became as "human" as the Farmworker. The Patron was literally undressed, or deconstructed, as all-powerful Other. Removing the external signifiers of power disempowered the Patroncito and transformed the dialectic of dominance and resistance. The Farmworker exclaimed, "Patron, you look like me!"[55] El Teatro suggested through the comically charged image of the Patroncito disrobing that his power was not essential nor internal within the body but, instead, constructed.[56]

In an article on the use of form in Las Dos Caras, "The Cruciform Farce in Latin America," Andrea G. Labinger articulates a similar thesis. She maintains that "the external trappings are the only determinants of social status. Role reversal, or the transfer of these trappings from one character to another can topple the entire social order."[57] I would argue that the exchange between the Patroncito and the Farmworker inverted but did not topple the social order. The hierarchy of Patron and farmworker remained in place. Still, the onstage exchange symbolized the type of status and power deflation that the UFWOC intended to effect in actuality. The UFWOC strike sought to remove some of the external trappings of power possessed by the ranch owners. The objectives of the strike—the signing of a contract with the UFWOC, the formation of a union hiring hall—would, in effect, redistribute certain vestiges of power to the previously powerless farmworkers.

Prior to the UFWOC strike the California agribusiness industry had systematically exploited migrant workers and maintained a structure of ethnic and economic stratification. Single men lived in dilapidated bunkhouses; large families were forced to live in extremely cramped substandard living quarters with an inadequate supply of food. Each workday morning flatbed trucks arrived and shuttled the farmworkers to the fields. Virtually indentured servants, the farmworkers received salaries far below the minimum wage. In 1960 the average income of Chicano farmworkers in the Southwest was $1,256 for 183 days' work.[58] They did not benefit from overtime guarantees or workers' compensation. The nature of the work and the low pay required long, difficult hours of labor. Since many of the Chicano farmworkers lacked the proficiency in English to secure employment for themselves, they often fell prey to the Chicano farm labor contractor, who would find employment for migrant workers in exchange for a percentage of their salary. The labor contractor was derogatively named El Coyote by the farmworkers because he preyed on the vulnerable migrant worker in need of employment. He was all the more despicable because he, like the farmworkers, was a Chicano. Thus, he exploited his own people. El Coyote was an important figure in the *acto Quinta Temporada* (which will be discussed in chap. 4). Abused by the labor contractor as well as the ranch owner, without the opportunity for legal redress or alternative employment, the farmworkers suffered, enslaved by what Vernon M. Briggs Jr. calls "America's most exploitative industry."[59]

The oppressive conditions of migratory labor figured prominently in *Las Dos Caras*. Immediately after exchanging places, the Patroncito discovered that the life of a farmworker had demands and indignities he had never previously imagined or experienced. He found himself subjugated to the Farmworker-turned-Patron. In keeping with the broad, physical performance style of El Teatro, the Farmworker's abuse of the Patron involved parody and slapstick humor. The Farmworker kicked the Patroncito, and, when the Patroncito asked why, the Farm-worker responded: "Because I felt like it boy! You hear me, boy? I like your name, boy! I think I'll call you boy, boy!" (LD, 17). The continuation of the abusive grower–migratory laborer relationship suggested that the oppression of the farmworker was an inherent component of the farm labor system, regardless of who was at the helm.

Las Dos Caras asserted that only the systemic changes advocated by UFWOC could end the exploitation of farmworkers. The abused Patroncito demanded immediate assistance, but, since he was dressed as a farmworker, his own henchman, Charlie, did not recognize him: "Charlie, you idiot, it's me! Your boss!" (LD, 18). Exasperated and defeated, the Patroncito ran from the stage calling for César Chávez and the support of the union. As a direct consequence of his beating by the Farmworker, the Patroncito came to understand the necessity of collective struggle as a strategy to achieve a reimagining of the agribusiness system. He desperately desired the communal power that each individual farmworker attained by joining the union and supporting the policies of Chávez.

The comic exploitation of the Patroncito by the Farmworker symbolically avenged the daily abuse that farmworkers suffered in the California agribusiness system. It expressed the desire of many farmworkers to redefine their position within California agribusiness and to strike back at their oppressors. In Chicano Satire Guillermo Hernández observes:

> To an audience of farmworkers, who know the dehumanized conditions confronted daily in the fields, the debasement of the figure represented by the Patroncito was an important turning point in the assertion of their dignity.[60]

This acto affirmed the new awareness of self-worth and cultural pride among "los de abajo" (the underdogs)[61] who had for too long been subjected to a system of cultural, psychological, and economic degradation. Las Dos Caras exposed the vulnerability of the ranch owner and encouraged farmworkers to arise as new political subjects in their own real struggle against subordination.

Interestingly, the onstage drama of the black nationalists acting in defiance of black subordination in Black Ice paralleled the real-life

power struggles that BARTS encountered in 1965. BARTS came under
fire from local and national government officials for misusing government funds (its Harlem Youth Opportunities Unlimited [HARYOU]
grant) to promote antiwhite propaganda. Republican state representative Paul Fino was adamant in denouncing BARTS and demanding the
revocation of their funding. Fino declared that the funds "had been
used to produce plays that advocated Negro revolution and the murder of white persons and portrayed whites as degenerate homosexu-
als."[62] Eventually, Office of Economic Opportunity (OEO) chief Sargent
Shriver labeled the Black Arts funding an "outright mistake in financ-
ing."[63] Baraka, on the other hand, felt that, as taxpayers, he and the
members of BARTS were entitled to their congressional subsidy. In its
own social drama of funding, BARTS attempted to resist and even
negate the expectations and authority of the Congress and the traditional white power structure.

Fiercely committed to creating theater by, for, and about blacks,
BARTS productions often prohibited white audiences and critics from
attending. In fact, while in New York to tour the programs he adminis-
tered, Sargent Shriver was denied admission to BARTS. This manifestation of intragroup exclusivity mirrored other assertions of black
nationalistic separatism at that time. Through this purposeful action of
exclusion BARTS symbolically exorcised the authority of the dominant
culture and practiced what Stephen Greenblatt terms "radical subver-
siveness"—that is, "not merely the attempt to seize existing authority
but as a challenge to the principles upon which authority is based."[64]
Correspondingly, in *Black Ice* the black nationalists contested fervently
the morals and beliefs of the U.S. capitalist system. While they held the
Congressman captive the black nationalists attacked the values of the
white power regime that he represented. The black nationalist, Martha,
pistol-whipped and upbraided the Congressman:

> You, the prince of thieves call me insane! You who cheated the
> world and robbed and murdered in the name of God—hell! You,
> who butchered half the world. Call me insane! You degenerate bas-
> tard! (*BI,* 564)

With these vituperative, accusatory remarks, Martha voiced the anti-
Western, anti-imperialist platform of black nationalism: white Western

rule has oppressed, subjugated, and murdered people of color for centuries and therefore must be destroyed. The illegitimacy and historic abuses of white power justified immediate and violent black resistance.

As the kidnappers awaited the anticipated exchange of the white Congressman for the black nationalist, political prisoner, John Chambers, they soon realized the futility of their plan. The black nationalist Green explained to the Congressman:

> I know they won't exchange Chambers for you. My brother will die this day. My brother will die this day! We can't save him. But the project isn't a failure. We have you, butcher! Your death should step up the pace of the revolution. (*BI*, 560)

Green's words proved prophetic. The exchange plan failed. Several collaborators died in a shoot-out with the police. As a consequence, the defiant Martha then murdered the white Congressman in the name of freedom. This execution of the white Congressman symbolized the anticipated escalation of the black revolutionary offensive to be achieved outside of the theater.

By recognizing that the murder of a white congressman by black militants would intensify the already tense racial climate, Green asserted the significance of urgency. For urgency was an invisible but tangible agent in *Black Ice*. It played a critical role in how both "black" and "white" power were constructed and conceived. Implicitly and explicitly, the play informed its audience that the time to act for black liberation was now. Martha's execution of the Congressman signified to the black spectators that they, too, must "step up the pace of the revolution." Urgency fostered a climate in which BARTS could represent the kidnapping and execution of a congressman as a possibility. And, more important, urgency created an atmosphere in which this murder could be perceived as a viable black revolutionary tactic.

The action of *Las Dos Caras*, like that of *Black Ice*, worked to intensify the existing atmosphere of urgency. The Farmworker in the *acto* was radicalized as he came to understand that change could be achieved through the application of insistent and immediate pressure. The downtrodden Patroncito-turned-Farmworker reacted to the urgency of his own social drama, which both symbolized and was buttressed by the actual atmosphere of urgency that suffused farmworker life in Delano in 1965. And yet the physical action represented in *Las Dos Caras* was markedly different from that depicted in *Black Ice*. While the Farmworker-turned-Patron in *Las Dos Caras* comically abused the Patroncito-turned-Farmworker, the black nationalists in *Black Ice* tortured and eventually killed the white Congressman. The difference in the nature of the violence in these two plays reflected a distinct difference in the dramaturgical philosophies of El Teatro and the BRT. El Teatro, embracing the nonviolent strategies of César Chávez and the UFWOC and emanating from the Mexican performance tradition, employed slapstick and satire as its primary means of theatrical communication. Incorporating the violent, fiery rhetoric of the Black Power movement, the plays of the BRT erupted in violence and decreed that violent revolution was the inevitable solution to white oppression. *Las Dos Caras* focused on reforming the particular situation of the strike in Delano, while *Black Ice* encouraged the disruption of the overall U.S. governmental system.

Despite these differences, both plays shared a similar, synergistic relationship to the social environment. They were affected by, but in turn sought to effect change in that environment. These social protest performances of El Teatro and the BRT attempted to articulate critical social, political, and economic desires of their respective Chicano and black constituencies and to locate these immediate and urgent concerns within the overall missions and objectives of the two social protest movements. Like ritual enactments, *Las Dos Caras* and *Black Ice* attempted both to reflect and to transform the social reality.

Reconsidering the Effects of Urgency

The power of social protest performance in these urgent times to articulate social and cultural principles and to dramatize specific current events made it a unique and often effective social and cultural weapon. John Weisman, in *Guerrilla Theater,* relates an incident in which César Chávez purposefully utilized the power of the social protest performance to aid the efforts of the UFWOC:

> Chávez used the Teatro when regular organizers met with failure. In one small town near Selma, California, the Teatro succeeded in convincing field hands of the need to organize after UFW professionals had tried for weeks and failed.[65]

As Weisman claims, the social protest performance was, at times, a more effective means of promoting resistance than other, more conventional approaches. As a result, the social protest performances of El Teatro and the BRT became important participants in the Chicano and black social and cultural liberation movements of the 1960s and 1970s. These performances not only influenced the social environment but were products of that environment as well. The volatile social environment was critical to the emergence of El Teatro and the BRT and a powerful agent within their dramaturgy.

Los Vendidos by Luis Valdez and El Teatro Campesino, 1968.
(Photograph by George Ballis, courtesy El Teatro Campesino Archives.)

Luis Valdez as the Patroncito and Augustin Lira as the Farmworker. *Las Dos Caras del Patroncito* by Luis Valdez and El Teatro Campesino, 1968.
(Photograph by George Ballis, courtesy El Teatro Campesino Archives.)

Augustin Lira as the Farmworker, Douglas Rippey as the Grower,
Luis Valdez as Winter. *Quinta Temporada* by Luis Valdez and El Teatro
Campesino, 1968. (Photograph by George Ballis, courtesy El Teatro Campesino
Archives.)

La Conquista de Mexico by Luis Valdez and El Teatro Campesino, 1970.
(Photograph by George Ballis, courtesy El Teatro Campesino Archives.)

Augustin Lira as the Farmworker and Daniel Valdez as the Patroncito.
Quinta Temporada by Luis Valdez and El Teatro Campesino, 1967.
(Photograph by George Ballis, courtesy El Teatro Campesino Archives.)

Luis Valdez as
La Raza, Douglas
Rippey as The Unions.
Quinta Temporada by
Luis Valdez and El
Teatro Campesino,
1968. (Photograph by
George Ballis, courtesy El
Teatro Campesino
Archives.)

J. Errol Jaye as the Minister, Carl Bossiere as the Burglar. *The Prayer Meeting or The First Militant Minister* by Ben Caldwell, July, 1968. Woodie King Jr., director. (Photograph by Charles Pinckney, courtesy of "A Black Quartet" produced by Woodie King Jr.)

A Black Mass by LeRoi Jones/Amiri Baraka. Afro-American Studio Theatre Center, September, 1972. (Photograph by Bill Doll, courtesy of the Billy Rose Theatre Collection, The New York Public Library for the Performing Arts, Astor, Lenox and Tilden Foundations.)

Slave Ship by LeRoi Jones/Amiri Baraka. Gilbert Moses, Director. Theater-in-the-Church, January, 1970. (Courtesy of the Billy Rose Theatre Collection, The New York Public Library for the Performing Arts, Astor, Lenox and Tilden Foundations.)

Auction block scene from *Slave Ship* by Amiri Baraka. Free Southern Theater production. Gilbert Moses, Director, New Orleans, 1970. (Photograph by Larry Songy, courtesy of the Free Southern Theater Collection, Amistad Research Center, Tulane University, New Orleans Lousiana.)

3

Generating Social Change and Cultural Affirmation: Content and Form in the Plays of El Teatro and the BRT

In the previous chapter I discussed the impact of the 1960s and 1970s social context upon the social protest performances of El Teatro and the BRT. Urgency suffused and infused the social environment of that time and helped to create an atmosphere conducive to the performance of social protest theater. This chapter will examine closely and exclusively the dramatic text and how it figures in the overall social protest performance. Through a comparative discussion of four plays—*A Black Mass*, by Amiri Baraka; *The Prayer Meeting or the First Militant Minister*, by Ben Caldwell; *La Conquista de Mexico* and *Los Vendidos*, both by Valdez and El Teatro—I will analyze how content and form contribute to the BRT's and El Teatro's projects of social protest by communicating cultural affirmation and political rebellion.

Symbolic elements within social protest dramas often "functioned ritualistically" to reaffirm cultural consciousness and collective action, and the form of these dramas could then work to reinforce content and to generate audience participation in the theatrical event. Here the phrase "functioned ritualistically" has a somewhat different connotation than that established in the first chapter. What I want to propose by my use of the phrase in this context is that given units within the content of the play text acted much like symbols act within the structure of ritual. Turner considers the symbol the most basic unit of ritual that still contains the principles of ritual. He believes that ritual symbols can condense meaning and unify disparate signification.[1] Once again expanding Turner, Jean and John Comaroff maintain that ritual symbols can also reproduce and re-present meanings: "The symbol, in short, contains the basic chemical processes that impart social life to complex orders of signification—and significance to the complex life of social orders."[2] Accordingly, functioning ritualistically, symbolic elements within social protest performances conveyed, combined, and condensed meanings. The concatenation of symbols within the play text aided the social protest performance's ability to function as a symbolic mediation and a signifying practice.

Jean and John Comaroff note that much of Turner's and other anthropologists' work on ritual has been concerned only with content and not with form. They point out that theorists "have shown far greater sensitivity to its [ritual's] symbolic content than to its formal properties, to *what* it says rather than *how* it says it. . . . Precisely *how* they [rituals] are mobilized to work their magic goes unexplored."[3] Without such anthropological support theorizing the ritualistic effects of the social protest play text's form could be difficult. Recent Marxist literary criticism, however, can provide useful insight into the interrelationship of content and form. Marxistentics have argued that content and form inform and are informed by each other. According to Terry Eagleton, the relationship of content and form is dialectical.[4] Content, Eagleton maintains, acts to determine form, while the choice of form is ideologically circumscribed and reflects back on content. Similarly, Fredric Jameson argues that form is a transformative product of the inner logic of content.[5] The emphasis of these critics on the synergy between content and form is important to understanding how form operates within ritualistic social protest dramas. Turning again to ritual, Jean and John Comaroff note that "it is now coming to be recognized that rites deploy such things as poetic tropes, juxtaposition, and redundancy to implode and (re)order experience."[6] In other words, the form or structure of ritual has been shown to reinforce and even influence content. Consistent with both Marxist literary theory as well as Jean and John Comaroff's analysis of ritual form, I will argue that the form of El Teatro's and the

BRT's social protest texts worked along with their content to structure the interaction of cultural affirmation and political protest.

There is another element of ritual theory that I believe is particularly relevant to this examination of form, namely the concept of "antistructure." As antistructure, Turner maintains that rituals operate outside of normative structural constraints and disrupt the normal social order. Antistructural rituals are liminal, creative, and subversive. They can generate experimental possibilities and can propose new models for social interaction. Turner argues that, similar to antistructural rituals, revolutions within a social system can constitute antistructural subversions.[7] The paradigm I want to posit here is that both El Teatro and the BRT strategically used antistructural tropes to interrupt the narrative form and flow of their play texts. These antistructural intrusions worked in a manner similar to that which Turner outlines for antistructural rituals. They were symbolic, irreverent, self-conscious moments designed to arouse audience interest and involvement. These tropes were inherently deconstructive: they disrupted the actions and meanings of the play texts and added new interpretive significance. At the same time, they attempted to provoke social action on the part of the spectators and to create disruptions in the structural hierarchies maintained by the dominant culture outside of the theater.

El Teatro's and the BRT's use of antistructural tropes encouraged the audience to join with the performers, to cross the conventional separation between spectators and the stage. By inviting the audience to participate, the overall structure of social protest plays—as Kimberly Benston suggests—moved away from mimesis, "the representation of an action," and closer to what he terms "methexis," a "communal helping out."

> Spiritually and technically, this movement is from mimesis, or representation of an action to methexis or "communal helping out" of the action by all assembled. It is a shift from drama—the spectacle observed—to ritual, the event which dissolves traditional divisions between actor and spectator, between self and other.[8]

Benston theorizes that, structurally, social protest performances formulated a more proactive, spiritual relationship with their audience than traditional performances did. The move away from mimesis to methexis represented a shift from the conventional dramatic structure and processes of representation to a more ritualistic theater that called for spectators and performers to interact as equal participants. Such communal participation, I believe, was critical to the efficacy of social protest theater.

Communal involvement in the ritual ceremony was in large part a response to the collective interpretation of the ritual symbols. Jean and John Comaroff, as well as Turner, contend that the meanings of all ritual symbols depend on the sociohistorical context of their enactment. Symbols attain power and meaning as a consequence of their usage in a specific historical moment. Thus, the impact of ritual symbols can change visibly over time. According to the Comaroffs, "These [ritual] signs and techniques often come to be potent precisely because of the historical circumstances in which they acquire their meanings."[9] Correspondingly, the form and content of social protest dramatic texts must be understood to be what feminist critic Donna Haraway terms "situated."[10] Their meaning and impact are situational, dependent upon the particular social, political, and cultural context.

The situated contents and forms of El Teatro's and the BRT's social protest plays privileged the subjugated, particularized, and suppressed perspectives of black and Chicano communities. Haraway writes: "Situated knowledges are about communities, not about isolated individuals. The only way to find a larger vision is to be somewhere in particular."[11] By understanding that the form and content of El Teatro's and the BRT's plays were situated within and determined by their specific social contexts, we can establish how form and content articulated the particular voices of underrepresented Chicanos and blacks in the 1960s and early 1970s, revitalized their cultural consciousness, and agitated in that unique historical moment for social action.

Myth and History

In May 1966, at Proctor's Theater in Newark, New Jersey, Amiri Baraka's theater troupe, the Spirit House Movers, first performed *A Black Mass*. Baraka wrote and directed the play, which was based on the Black Muslim creation myth. According to the myth, black scientist Jacoub, or Yakub, was angry at his treatment by Allah. Through a process of color grafting he produced a bleached-out, white devil race from the original black people. When Allah viewed the destructive power of Jacoub's creation, he banished Jacoub and the white devil race to the caves of Europe, where the white race was destined to rule the world for some six thousand years. After that time world power would be restored to the original black people. Black Muslim doctrine maintained the period of white rule would soon expire.

Baraka imagines this play as a ritual, a "black mass." The ritual processes of *Black Mass* are to inculcate black spectators in this Black Muslim mythology and to renew black self-esteem, cultural pride, and social struggle. The symbolic action explicitly conflates spiritual, political, and performative elements. Larry Neal calls the play "Jones's [Baraka's] most important play mainly because it is informed by a mythology that is wholly the creation of the Afro-American sensibility."[12] Baraka presents a mythology that valorizes black people as the original people and the source of all creation. The performative action of *Black Mass* relates the subjugation of blacks, by the dominant power structure, to the mythological transgressions of the black scientist Jacoub and his creation of a genetically deficient, white "devil" race. Baraka's use of myth correlates with Robert Weimann's observation that "there is a point at which myth encompasses both religion and knowledge, illusion and a sense of reality."[13] *Black Mass* reifies the Black Muslim creation myth as religious and historic truth.

La Conquista also reveals the impact of past histories on present circumstances. Originally staged as a puppet show in 1968 at the El Centro Campesino Cultural Center in Del Rey, California, *La Conquista* retells the story of the Spanish conquest of Mexico, the initial contact between Hernán Cortés and the indigenous Indian population. The title suggests that the fall of Mexico was the result of external forces. The play reveals, however, that the siege of Mexico would not have been possible without the collusion of certain Indian tribes and chiefs, including Moctezuma. This *acto* exposes the sacred mission of Cortés and the Spanish missionaries as a fraud. *La Conquista* denigrates Cortés and the Spanish conquistadors—traditionally glorified in Western history as religious missionaries and valiant explorers—as imperialist mercenaries. According to *La Conquista,* cultural chauvinism and economic greed fueled Cortés's mission and his destruction of ancient Indian civilizations. Valdez appropriates the power of historical representation to deconstruct the traditional image of Cortés and to relate the subjugation of Chicano peoples in the 1960s to the suppression and destruction of Mexican-Indian beliefs, values, and practices by the Spanish conquerors.

An allegorical figure, Piedra del Sol, the Aztec stone calendar, narrates *La Conquista*. As the symbolic embodiment of Indian ancestral ingenuity as well as colonial acquisitional expansionism, Piedra del Sol conveys to the Chicano audience the importance of controlling one's own history. The creation of the Aztec stone calendar—a large, elaborate, and complicated structure—was a testament to the high level of early astronomical achievement by the Aztec people. Independent of Western knowledge and discovery, the Aztecs developed an extremely accurate system of time measurement based on their observations of the sun. This system, uniquely theirs, offered a particularly Aztec understanding of the days, seasons, and length of each year. Ironically, Western history credits Cortés with discovering the stone calendar and bringing it to Western attention in 1519. In the counterhistory of *La Conquista*, however, instead of Cortés reporting the "discovery" of the stone calendar, Piedra del Sol, as narrator, recounts the "truth" of Cortés's discovery and conquest of Mexico. Piedra del Sol reimagines and reproduces the meanings of the Aztec stone calendar. Symbolically, the play returns the power to record time and significant historical occurrences, usurped by Cortés and the Spanish conquerors, to Piedra del Sol.

Time is also a significant element of *Black Mass*. In this and other black revolutionary works, however, Baraka posits time as a destructive white, Western invention that restricts and represses black humanity. In the critical work, *In Our Terribleness*, he calls "time" simply, "A LIE."[14] According to Baraka, the white, Western fabrication, time, structures human existence within an unnatural cycle. Conversely, traditional African societies, Baraka maintains, existed without any obsession with time. Thus, black people, Baraka argues, need to transcend time and return to their African origins. He writes, "The key is to lift above the cycle."[15] At the outset of *Black Mass* black magicians Nasafi and Tanzil ceremoniously prepare a libation designed to destroy the power of time. Their devout processes parallel the priest's consecration of the bread and wine before the offering of communion in the Catholic Mass. Correspondingly, the mixture that the black magicians create is also meant as an offering. Nasafi proclaims that all who taste the magical potion that they concoct "will dance mad rhythms of the eternal universe until time is a weak thing."[16] Nasafi's anticipated victory over time symbolized a sociocultural change that Baraka fervently believed black people actually needed to effect.

One of the most significant symbolic elements in *Black Mass* is Baraka's representation of blackness. The color black in Western culture has traditionally represented darkness, evil, wickedness, and sin. White, in contrast, has denoted honor, virtue, innocence, and purity. In *Black Mass* Baraka constructs a cosmology that inverts this binarism. Blackness now symbolizes beauty and humanity. Black magic, formerly associated with diabolism, sorcery, and Satan worship, becomes a positive and most powerful life force—for black magic has produced "the beauties of creation" (*BM*, 22). The play opens in "Jet blackness" with "Soft peaceful music (Sun Ra). Music of eternal concentration and wisdom" (21). This "black endless space" is not threatening but perceived by the black magicians as "beautiful reality." Blackness, as a symbol, is reimagined and re-presents new meanings of cultural affirmation. Purposefully, Baraka's valorization of blackness in *Black Mass* directly correlated with the burgeoning black cultural consciousness and identity movements of the 1960s and 1970s.

In juxtaposition to the dominant culture's representations of whiteness as goodness and purity, both *Black Mass* and *La Conquista* represent whiteness as negative and destructive. The black magicians Tanzil and Nasafi, in *Black Mass,* caution their compatriot Jacoub against the deleterious effects of whiteness on the black world order. The lesson goes unheeded. While the other black magicians prepare a potion to combat time, Jacoub creates a White Beast that loves time and that will soon turn on its creator. The gross, evil White Beast symbolizes the depravity, the callous self-interest, the corruption, that Baraka and other black cultural nationalists believed were endemic components of the dominant white culture's imperialist project. The White Beast can only repeat, "White! White!" and "Me! Me!" Correspondingly, Piedra del Sol, in *La Conquista,* describes the Spanish conquerors not as humans but as inhuman and bestial: "The chief of the white men was a bearded coyote named Hernan Cortez. . . . With him was another white devil named Pedro de Alvarado."[17] *La Conquista* clearly delineates between the good "Indians" and the evil white characters. Disregarding the spiritual ideals of their mission, the white Spaniards lust for gold; they abuse, exploit, and kill the indigenous peoples. Both *Black Mass* and *La Conquista* contrasted the virtuous and original black and native peoples with evil whiteness in order to reassert black and Chicano cultural identity and to promote positive self-images.

Yet, from our contemporary critical vantage point, the argument can be made that defining Chicano and black as humanistic and white as antihumanistic does not destroy but, instead, reinforces racial absolutism. By asserting Chicano and black difference and inverting the typical binary system of representation, both *La Conquista* and *Black Mass* potentially reinscribe the cultural imperialist paradigms they intended to subvert.[18] As Minh-Ha Trinh points out, difference can be "that which undermines the very idea of identity."[19] In enslaving blacks and conquering native Americans, white colonialists justified their actions through a doctrine of difference and racial absolutism. They maintained that an essential difference existed between them and the inferior others. By separating the white devils from the "authentic humans"—black people—Baraka continues this essentialist process. Promoting difference, in the words of Trinh, allows for an "apartheid ideology" and "separate but unequal development."[20] Extending Trinh's point, one could argue that, by juxtaposing images of evil whites with virtuous people of color, *La Conquista* and *Black Mass* restricted the process of democratization by maintaining social hierarchies and reinforcing a system of polarizing binarisms.

Women are similarly restricted in their positions in both texts. While the powerful black male magicians in *Black Mass* consider the great questions of culture, religion, and creation, the powerless black women can only respond with their emotions and their sensuality. When the women violate the sanctity of the black magicians' laboratory, Nasafi rebukes them, "What are you women doing running into this sanctuary?" The women writhe and twist in "their thin garments," while the men, "dressed in long exquisite robes," rationally consider the cosmos. Even as the play advocates a radical altering of the subject position of black people, it reinforces the subordinate role of women and exhibits an uneven distribution of power among men and women.

La Conquista emphasizes the significance that the native woman La Malinche plays in the destruction of Mexico. La Malinche in *La Conquista* betrays her people and becomes the guide for and concubine of the Spanish invaders. Piedra del Sol derogatively calls her "the first Mexican-American." Within the politics of Chicano cultural nationalism she represents "La Vendida," the ultimate sell-out. Using cynicism and derision, the action of the play reveals her licentious behavior with Cortés and his "white devil" comrades. La Malinche's sexual betrayal has not only historical but also contemporary consequences for Chicanas and for Chicano perceptions of female sexuality. Yvonne Yarbro-Bejarano, in her article "The Female Subject in Chicano Theater: Sexuality, Race, and Class," argues that, as a result of the myth of La Malinche, "female sexuality becomes the site of degradation and evil."[21] Yarbro-Bejarano further points out that "the myth of La Malinche is crucial to understanding the link between cultural nationalism and the exclusion of the female subject."[22] The myth of La Malinche enabled cultural nationalists to posit the independent and "sexual" woman as undesirable traitor, while championing the activism of men and placing them in the subject position. Chicanas who challenged cultural nationalistic representations of women risked being branded "malinchistas," or traitors. Thus, the expected role for Chicanas onstage and in reality remained the passive support of their men.

While I realize that such contemporary critiques provide insight into the political limitations of *La Conquista* and *Black Mass*, I also believe that a recognition of the situated nature of the symbols within these plays can expand our understanding of the complexities and continued significance of El Teatro's and the BRT's cultural politics. The symbolic potency of blackness in *Black Mass* or whiteness in *La Conquista* is situated and situational, dependent upon the theatrical and sociopolitical context. Within their respective social protest performances El Teatro and the BRT constructed these symbols strategically to serve their overall projects of advocating cultural consciousness and directing social change. As Baraka in his 1984 autobiography admits, the practices of the Black Revolutionary Theater in the 1960s and 1970s involved the "artification of certain aspects of history to make a recipe for 'blackness.'"[23] Such symbolic strategies potentially represent an early manifestation of what Gayatri Spivak terms "the strategic use of essentialism,"[24] a possible method for negotiating the contradiction between postmodern theory's opposition to the notions of a "whole person" or a "constituted subject" and the desire of marginalized groups and new political subjects to articulate for themselves an "authentic" identity.[25] The strategic use of essentialism entails the situational adoption of an essentialist identity or ideology because of its particular political advantage at that specific historical moment.[26] Accordingly, the creation of *Black Mass* and *La Conquista* consciously and subconsciously involved the employment of various strategic processes.

Spivak cautions, however, that the strategic use of essentialism depends on one's consciousness of the possible restrictiveness and perils of essentializing: "So once you begin to selectively use . . . essentialism as [a] position promised within an awareness of the limits of (self) positioning—individual—collective—then you can see [it] to be strategically effective."[27] Spivak's warning suggests that political subjects must maintain an intellectual distance and constant awareness of their subject positions. Valdez, Baraka, and the practitioners of El Teatro and the BRT were not particularly concerned with the sociopolitical dangers of essentialism but, rather, with the power attained, in urgent times, by championing cultural difference and romanticizing the past. Situated within the urgencies of the 1960s and 1970s, El Teatro and the BRT privileged strategies of expedience in order to achieve their sociopolitical ends. In contrast to Spivak's statement, then, their strategic employment of essentialism did not depend on a consciousness of its limits but, rather, a recognition of its tangible and immediate benefits.

The "situated" forms of both *Black Mass* and *La Conquista* reinforced the topical significance of their contents. Both plays were adapted from popular cultural genres. Their forms comforted and confronted their audiences, employing both structural and antistructural elements. *Black Mass* unfolds much like a Gothic horror story, similar to *Frankenstein.* Following the horror story structure, a mad scientist, Jacoub, disregards the warnings of his colleagues, Tanzil and Nasafi, and creates a new human organism. The experiment, however, goes awry. The scientist has created a monster. Baraka's stage directions call for stage lighting and cinematic special effects that heighten the horrifying emergence of Jacoub's evil creation, the White Beast:

> Another intense explosion, the room is silent and dark, and then a sudden hot white glare. . . . Now the glare, glowing wild bright, seems to split. The sound is like glass being scraped on a black-

board. A crouched figure is seen covered in red flowing skins like capes. . . . The figure is absolutely cold white with red lizard-devil mask which covers the whole head and ends up as a lizard spine cape. (BM, 29–30)

Once created, the White Beast immediately leaps upon the gathered black women and black magicians and turns them into White Beasts as well. Then, adhering to the typical plot structure of a mad scientist horror film, the White Beast turns on its own creator, Jacoub.

Baraka also intends for Black Mass to transcend the boundaries of the horror film form. He asks that the White Beasts exit through the audience and indiscriminately attack and confront audience members as they retreat. This antistructural device allows for the improvisation of the performers. The White Beasts' confrontation of audience not only interrupts the flow of the play; it also disrupts the spectators kinesthetic distance from the production and transforms the relationship between the audience and the performers. Understood within the context of racial upheaval, the play's structure encourages the spectators to relate this invasion of their personal space by the White Beasts to the impositions, threats, and abuses that black people must endure under the oppressive white power structure.

Baraka follows this moment with another antistructural interpolation designed to elicit audience reaction. As the White Beasts exit through the audience at the end of Black Mass, the voice of an offstage narrator—a figure visibly, or rather invisibly, outside the action of the play—is heard. The narrator interrupts the dramatic action and directly addresses the spectators. He exhorts them and alerts them to their own significance within the developing, dramatic social crisis:

And so Brothers and Sisters, these beasts are still loose in the world. Still they spit their hideous cries. There are beasts in our world, Brothers and Sisters. There are beasts in our world. Let us find them and slay them. Let us lock them in their caves. Let us declare the Holy War. Or we cannot deserve to live. Izm-el-Azam. Izm-el-Azam. Izm-el-Azam. Izm-el-Azam. (BM, 39)

This call to action adds new significance to the play. The audience is not merely to recognize the danger of the White Beasts but to act to remove that danger. The message is urgent: only a "Holy War" can restore the original black world order. Consequently, the exorcism of the White Beasts is not only a secular but also a sacred endeavor. The Islamic chant "Izm-el-Azam" reinforces the religious import of this battle against white hegemony. Ritualistically, this final invocation endows the black liberation struggle with spiritual sanction and entreats the spectators to participate.

Borrowing from the theories of Antonin Artaud's "Theater of Cruelty," Baraka envisioned an antistructural, confrontational black theater that would impel the audience to act. In his 1965 manifesto of the Black Arts Movement, "The Revolutionary Theater," Baraka adamantly declared:

> Revolutionary theater should force change. It should be change. . . . Revolutionary theater must Expose! . . . Revolutionary theater must accuse and attack anything that can be accused and attacked.[28]

Baraka imagined a proactive theater that directly challenged the spectators and demanded that they take action. In *Black Mass* he attempted to put theory into practice.

La Conquista also confronts its audience but in a distinctly different fashion. The form of *La Conquista* relies on the Mexican popular culture traditions of storytelling and oral performance. Oral historians in preliterate Indian societies transmitted culture and history through their voices, bodies, and memories to the gathered community. As Broyles-González points out, oral culture is always "situational," dependent upon "the performer's momentary positioning relative to the community and its extended history."[29] Situated within the Mexican oral performance tradition as well as the 1960s and 1970s struggle for Chicano liberation, *La Conquista* functions as a "historical narrative," presenting its audiences with a revised history of the conquest of Mexico.

Hayden White, in *The Content of the Form,* associates the process of historical narrative with storytelling and the creation of mythical views of reality:

> Far from being a neutral medium for the representation of historical events and processes, historical narrative is the very stuff of a

mythical view of reality, a conceptual or pseudoconceptual "content" which, when used to represent real events, endows them with an illusionary coherence and charges them with the kind of meanings more characteristic of oneiric than of waking thought.[30]

White and other contemporary scholars have worked to deconstruct the power and authority traditionally associated with historical narrative and historical discourse. They contend that history should no longer be understood as a fixed point of objective truth but, rather, as a construct open to subjective interpretations. Predating this postmodern scholarship, *La Conquista* engages in the construction of history. Piedra del Sol's historical narrative/oral history seeks to affirm the mythical/historical foundations for the Chicano liberation movement. Clearly, the historical narrative/oral performance form of *La Conquista* is not a "neutral medium." It explicitly informs its audiences of past mistakes that require organized, collective, corrective action.

In the final scene of *La Conquista* the Indian Chief Cuahtemoc (Falling Eagle) directly addresses the audience and acts out an antistructural trope. He interrupts the flow of the action and usurps the power of Piedra del Sol to narrate events. Cuahtemoc explains how the early Mexicans participated in their own destruction, because they mistook the white imperialist conquerors for gods. Then Cuahtemoc rhetorically provokes the audience and assures them that a similar lack of unity could never impair Chicano resistance efforts again. "Ojala que todavia no sea asi! Verdad, sol? [I hope, that it will not always be so! Right, sun? (*LC,* 65)]." In this way he encourages audience participation, while he predicts and attempts to structure the future.

The antistructural use of Cuahtemoc is also significant because of the historical importance of this Indian chief. Called the "last Aztec and first Mexican,"[31] Cuahtemoc fiercely resisted the siege of Cortés at Tlatelolco in 1521. Despite the collusion of other Indian tribes and leaders with Cortés, Cuahtemoc defended Tlatelolco. Eventually, the strength of Cortés and his forces overwhelmed the army of Cuahtemoc. He was taken prisoner by Cortés on 13 August 1521 and soon executed. A statue to this Indian chief stands with raised spear at the intersection of Insurgentes Avenue and Paseo de la Reforma in Mexico City. Harold Coy writes, "Cuahtemoc, the last Aztec king, with his scorched feet, resisting his tortures, is the symbol of our [Mexican] nationality—not Cortés, thirsting for treasure."[32]

At the conclusion of *La Conquista*, after Cuahtemoc speaks, Piedra de Sol, the narrator, returns to the stage. He punctuates Cuahtemoc's words by instructing the Chicano spectators to unite: "Simon! Organicense raza!" Piedra del Sol and Cuahtemoc, as symbolic embodiments of ancestral spirits, incite the audience and invite them to join in a communion of resistance. Their deliberate call to action unites the spiritual with the political and joins past ancestral history with present crisis.

Both plays, situated within the context of the black and Chicano social struggle and identity politics, explicitly connect historical events and past transgressions to the social reality of the times. Valdez and Baraka wanted their audiences to understand the historical chain of oppression and to realize that the only avenue to freedom was through united and organized resistance.

Satire and Parody

While *La Conquista* and *Black Mass* consider the historical and mythical roots of social conditions in the 1960s and early 1970s, the contents of *Los Vendidos* and *The Prayer Meeting* exaggerate and contest that reality through biting social satire. In both *Los Vendidos* and *The Prayer Meeting* the satire evolves from a farcical premise. *Los Vendidos* takes place at a "Used Mexican" lot. Parodying a used car salesman, Honest Sancho sells used Mexicans. *The Prayer Meeting* satirizes an evening prayer session with an accommodating black minister who literally has "a talk with God." A black burglar, previously intent on burglarizing the minister's house, answers the praying minister as "the voice of God." Henry Louis Gates Jr. notes in *The Signifying Monkey*, "Effective parody depends on an intimate knowledge of the subject."[33] The political effectiveness of these social protest parodies also hinges on the spectator's familiarity with the subjects. Both plays parody popular culture icons and subvert stereotypes. The plays act as cultural correctives and social commentaries as the parodied subject is held up to ridicule, revised, and critiqued.

Los Vendidos and *The Prayer Meeting* purposefully ridicule characters who have assimilated into or have accommodated white American culture. In the urgency of the 1960s and early 1970s, assimilation to black and Chicano cultural nationalists, connoted betrayal of one's own ethnic identity, or "selling out." Assimilation, they believed, devalued the cultural traditions of the ethnic minority while privileging the values of the dominant culture. Consequently, Chicano and black identity politics of the 1960s and early 1970s valorized ethnic solidarity and continually confronted and opposed assimilation. They assaulted accommodationist positions and redefined existent representations of Chicano and black identity and power.

The title *Los Vendidos* literally means "the sell-outs," and both Honest Sancho and his customer, Miss Jiménez, are shown to be exactly that, traitors to their Chicano identity. Honest Sancho accommodates the white power structure by selling and devaluing other Mexicans. Miss Jiménez is a continuation of the La Malinche character of *La Conquista*. Just as La Malinche prostitutes her services to Cortés, Miss Jiménez sells herself to then California governor Edmund Brown Sr. As an employee in Governor Brown's office, Miss Jiménez, like La Malinche, betrays her own people by acting as an emissary for the white oppressor. Brazenly, she visits Honest Sancho's looking for a "Mexican type" for the administration, "a brown face to be in the crowd at one of the Governor's speeches." Divorced from her cultural heritage, Miss Jiménez pronounces her name with an anglicized *J* sound and corrects Sancho when he addresses her using the Spanish pronunciation: "My name is *Jim*-enez. Don't you speak English? What's wrong with you?"[34] Miss Jiménez is also the only Chicana in the *acto*. Implicitly, then, because of the lack of other representations of women, the *acto* suggests a connection between her gender and her assimilationist ideals. This *acto* ridicules Miss Jiménez' position and admonishes other Chicanos who would believe success in the United States lies solely in the emulation of Anglo culture.

The Minister in *The Prayer Meeting*, like Miss Jiménez in *Los Vendidos*, has betrayed his people. He has preached a doctrine of accommodation and docility, and his position within the black community results from his complicity with the white power structure. When the Minister enters his home, he kneels and prays to God. He asks for assistance in quelling the violent mood of his black congregation. His parishioners want to rise in protest over the recent killing of a young black man, Brother Jackson, by a white police officer. The Minister rationalizes his passive response to Brother Jackson's death in his prayer to the Lord:

> I tried, Lord. I tried to keep them from the path of violence. I tried to show them where it was really Brother Jackson's fault for provokin' that off'cer. There's a time for protest and a time for silence. They say the off'cer hit him a few times. Brother Jackson could've taken a beating. It wouldn't be the first time he'd taken a beating.[35]

For many blacks in 1969, sensitized to and frustrated by the abuse of blacks by white police officers, the Minister's rationalization sounded simply absurd. The Minister's attitude in prayer demonstrated his duplicitous accommodation of the dominant culture.[36]

In this drama Caldwell consciously reimagines the problematic figure of the black minister. In black folk culture the black preacher is often represented as a comic opportunist looking to line his pockets by passing the collection plate among his parishioners and searching for a free fried chicken dinner after Sunday services. Since slavery the minister has also served as a prominent social, political, and spiritual leader within the black community. In the 1960s the predominant example of the minister as political and spiritual leader was the nonviolent Martin Luther King Jr. *The Prayer Meeting* makes reference to the various roles played by the black minister as it associates this figure with negative self-interest.

Other BRT plays, including *Slave Ship* by Baraka (which will be discussed in the next chapter), also questioned the role of black Christian ministers in the black liberation movement. According to the BRT, the black Christian church was a reactionary and accommodating tool of white oppression retarding the revolutionary effort. The BRT as well as the Black Power movement encouraged blacks to perceive the Christian church as tangential to their social, spiritual, and political survival. Ironically, even as the BRT's playwrights denigrated black Christianity in plays such as *The Prayer Meeting*, they still appropriated ritual elements from the black Christian tradition to provoke a ritual sensibility in their audiences. *The Prayer Meeting* invokes the sacred while deconstructing its associations with Christianity and realigning it within the context of black nationalism.

Immediately upon entering the Minister's house, the Burglar recognizes the home owner's position as self-serving opportunist and his connection to the dominant white capitalistic system: "I shoulda known this was a preacher's pad. A nigger livin' like this, either a preacher, a politician, or a hustler. Really ain't no difference though. All of 'em got some kind of game to get your money!" (*PM*, 29). Then, observing the Minister's return home, the Burglar quickly hides behind a chair. After he hears the Minister praying to God asking for direction, the Burglar castigates the Minister, acting as the voice of God:

> You so sure that if they go up 'gainst the white man they gon' lose and whitey won't need *you* no more. Or if they go up 'gainst whitey and win, then they won't need you. Either way yo' game is messed up. So you want things to stay as they are. You tell them to do nothin' but wait. Wait and turn the other cheek. As long as you keep them off the white folks you alright with the white folks. MY PEOPLE got to stop catching hell so you can live like this! (32)

The Burglar/God uses a language peculiar to the black inner city in order to communicate a revolutionary message to the Minister and the black spectators. This language is potent and forceful, capable of commanding new faith, new actions, and new policies. As Geneviève Fabre explains:

> The virulence of his [the Burglar's] speech literally steals language in order to tear the pastor away from his apathy. The prayer no longer harks back to formulas; it becomes an act, and the utterance is made event. The inflated language of the robber/God is not only a parody of the discourse of authority; it also corresponds to the event it predicts: the unheard-of word proclaims that the time of submission has passed. God is calling the pastor to take up arms, not to turn the other cheek.[37]

The Burglar's inflammatory discourse with the Minister is an antistructural intrusion that disrupts the traditional Christian ritual of prayer and replaces it with a new ritual. The Burglar offers the Minister and his black parishioners a new radicalized gospel of liberation through violent protest. Through the intervention of the Burglar the parodied ritual of evening prayer becomes a ritual of revolution. Discussing the dynamic potential of ritual, Victor Turner observes, "As 'a model of' ritual can anticipate, even generate change, as a 'model for,' it may inscribe order in the minds, hearts and will of participants."[38] The new ritual of revolution in *The Prayer Meeting* is intended to affect not only the Minister's social reality but the spectator's social behavior as well. Functioning ritualistically, this moment of *The Prayer Meeting* presents both the Minister and the social protest audience with models for a new social order. This symbolic action condenses the meanings of the black revolutionary struggle into the rhetoric of the Burglar/God. The brief meeting of the Burglar/God and the Minister transforms black, accommodationist religion into a theology of activism.

As a direct consequence of his talk with God, the Minister undergoes a radical conversion. Seeing "the light" of this new God reconstructs the Minister as a militant activist. Similar conversions were an important component of agitprop drama. In the Workers Theater of the 1920s the capitalist proletarian character quickly learned of the inherent contradictions in the current social system and converted to communism. In *The Prayer Meeting*, however, the symbolic transformation is not simply a political one, as in agitprop, but also a spiritual and cultural one. *The Prayer Meeting*, like *Black Mass*, unites the spiritual with the sociopolitical, creating the "first militant minister" as well as a new black religion that endorses and impels black revolutionary struggle. After his conversion the stage directions call for the Minister to open his Bible, the symbol of the old accommodating religion, and to pull from its center a gun, a symbol of the new revolution. This is a powerfully ritualistic moment. It effectively combines and conveys spiritual, cultural, and political meanings. Its signification is also situational, dependent upon its historical moment. Given the currency of slogans such as "The bullet or the ballot" and "By any means necessary" in the black vernacular of the late 1960s and the popular representation of the black Christian minister as nonviolent integrationist, the image of the newly radicalized Minister extracting a gun from the pages of the Bible would have held a particular potency.

Instructed by the Burglar/God to "lead a protest march to end all protest marches," the Minister, holding the gun and the Bible, delivers an impassioned oration in preparation for the next day's march:

Brothers and sisters, I had a talk with God last night. He told me to tell you that the time has come to put an end to this murder, suffering, oppression, exploitation to which the whiteman subjects us. The time has come to put an end to the fear which, for so long, suppressed our actions. The time has come. (*PM*, 36)

Speaking directly to the audience, the Minister's words incite the audience to act. His words challenge the audience to recognize that the time for rebellion in their own lives has arrived and to understand the correlation between the Burglar's invocations, the Minister's final sermon, and their own social circumstances.

Interestingly, the Minister's revolutionary address effectively employs the rhythms and rhetorical strategies of the traditional black Christian preacher. Barbara and Carlton Molette, in *Black Theater: Premise and Presentation,* discuss the Afro-Christian church and the black sermonic tradition as the basis for a ritualistic and spiritually invigorated collective drama.[39] The Molettes argue that, through the use of repetition, rhythmic emphasis, and pitch variance, the black preacher heightens the congregation's emotional intensity and produces spontaneous shouts and dances, communal ecstasy, and total spiritual involvement.[40] The final sermon of the Minister in *The Prayer Meeting* uses the black sermonic form to exhort communal ecstasy and collective action. The Minister's rhetorical repetition of the phrase "The time has come" conveys to the spectators the immediacy and urgency of the liberation struggle. Caldwell's adaptation of this black Christian tradition to a speech of black nationalist fervor also reflects John and Jean Comaroff's contention that the meanings of ritual symbolism depend on the specific context of its use.[41] By situating this revolutionary address within a new religious context, playwright Caldwell unites the spiritual, cultural, and the political within the doctrine of black nationalism. The new radical message of the militant black Minister signals the transformation of the black liberation struggle into the "Holy War" that Baraka called for in *Black Mass.*

The Prayer Meeting argues that black people will be blessed in this "Holy War" because God is on their side. The Burglar/God constantly refers to black people as "My People." Finally, the Minister asks the Burglar/God if black people are in fact God's "chosen people":

MINISTER: Lord you keep saying "my people." Are black people
             our "chosen people?"
BURGLAR: You goddam right! and you and everybody else better
             act like it!

(PM, 33)

Black people, proclaims the Burglar/God, share a unique relationship
with God and will overcome because they are His chosen people. Per-
ceiving blacks as God's chosen challenges traditional interpretations of
the Old Testament. It also inverts Talmudic readings that denigrate
blacks as the "damned children of Ham." The signs, images, and
actions of *The Prayer Meeting* transform the implications and meanings
of the phrase "chosen people" to reflect the context, referents, and situation of its use. As a result, *The Prayer Meeting*, like *Black Mass,* affirms
black self-worth.

Los Vendidos reinforces the self-image of Chicanos by subverting
stereotypes. Honest Sancho parodies Honest John, an Anglo used car
salesman, whose ads saturated the southern Californian television
market in the 1950s. The models in Sancho's Used Mexican lot are all
stereotypes that define and delimit Mexican representation in the
United States. White America's perpetuation of these stereotypical
Mexican images has inhibited Chicanos' self-image and retarded the
development of Chicano cultural identity and self-determination. Honest Sancho shows Miss Jiménez the various Mexican models available
to her. These include: the Farmworker model, "The Volkswagen of the
Mexicans"; Johnny Pachuco, the urban "low-riding" model; El Revolucionario, the "standard Revolucionario and/or Early California Bandit
type"; and Eric Garcia, the Mexican American model representing "the
apex of American engineering." The presentation of these "Used Mexicans" satirizes the stereotypes and denounces the dominant culture's
acceptance and perpetuation of confining images of Mexicans.

Sancho's display of these negative Mexican models not only
indicts the dominant culture but also suggests the complicity of Chicanos in their social and economic subjugation. Sancho's models are
victimized by their own internalized oppression. The Farmworker
model, Sancho explains, will also work as a "scab," or strikebreaker.
Johnny Pachuco suffers from a "deep inferiority complex" that causes
him to steal from his own people and to ingest drugs into his body.

While the symbolic action of this *acto* encourages Chicano spectators to laugh at the farcical situations and the satirical exaggerations, it also functions correctively, asking the spectators to recognize their own culpability and their need to be self-critical. Carlos Ynostraza explains:

> El Teatro makes us laugh at ourselves. But at the same time, it forces us all to be aware of where we stand with the white power structure that's so prevalent today. And they show us how far we're going to have to go to claim our self-respect and racial pride.[42]

Corresponding to the power inherent in ritual symbols, the symbolic and satirical presentations of the Used Mexican models unite disparate meanings—meanings designed to contest dominant cultural representations as well as those intended to induce Chicano self-criticism.

Later in *Los Vendidos,* seemingly without provocation, the most accommodating of Used Mexican models becomes a Chicano activist. As soon as Miss Jiménez purchases Eric Garcia, the Mexican-American acculturated model, he transforms from Mexican-American reactionary into Chicano revolutionary. The radicalized Eric, along with the other models, turn on Miss Jiménez, spouting the rhetoric of rebellion: "Viva la Raza! Viva la Causa! Viva la Huelga! . . . Chicano Power!" (*LV,* 48). The putative transformation of Eric is a particularly potent symbolic moment. It underscores the potential for revolutionary action in even the most seemingly nonpoliticized Chicanos. Furthermore, it reveals the inherent dangers when the dominant culture adopts and promotes simplistic, reductive representations of underrepresented peoples. Beneath Eric's surface lies a dormant rage, a frustrated and complex psyche that the dominant culture has underestimated and ignored. The unleashing of Eric's previously unexposed militancy destroys the dominant culture's expectations of and authority over Chicano images.

Los Vendidos appropriates the power to represent Chicanos and posits this power in the control of those most confined and controlled by these representations, the used Mexican stereotypes themselves. After chasing Miss Jiménez from the stage, Eric and the other previously repressed stereotypes control their own fates. As he carries Sancho—frozen in a statuelike pose—offstage Eric remarks to the audi-

ence, "He's the best model we got" (*LV*, 49). This unexpected denoue-
ment reveals that Sancho is the only real model and that it is he who is
controlled by the others. Eric never really was a conformist Mexican
American. His transformation into Huelgista was a ruse used to dupe
Miss Jiménez. The four models now split the profits of their intrigue.
Previously constructed as separate and psychologically damaged Mexican models, the men are now symbolically unified and strengthened
by a shared vision. They have defeated authority, overcome stereotypical representations and expectations, and gained the ability to self-
define. Symbolically, they have broken free from the deleterious effects
of internalized oppression. They have taken what Richard Scharine
notes is a critical step for any "emerging minority," "the reclamation of
its cultural forms and imagery."[43]

Eric's direct address to the audience is again an antistructural
intrusion within the play's form. At this moment he is a liminal figure,
neither totally inside nor outside of the action. His remarks compel the
spectators to reassess the meanings of the *acto*. For now the spectators
realize that they, too, have been deceived. Eric invites the audience into
his confidence. They now become "co-conspirators," vicarious participants celebrating the spoils of the Mexican models' victory. Previously
in the play, when the used Mexican salesman, Honest Sancho, presents
his models to Miss Jiménez, he presents them to the audience as well.
Consequently, the audience plays the role of used car buyer engaged in
a battle of wits with the salesman. They too attempt to decipher the
truth of the merchandise from the hyperbole of the sales pitch.
Throughout the *acto* the form invites audience participation and structurally approaches Benston's theoretical conception of methexis, "the
communal 'helping out' of the action by all assembled."

Similarly, the communal helping out is effectively initiated in *The
Prayer Meeting* through a dramatic structure that enables the spectators
to watch the farcical premise, the Burglar as voice of God, with an
awareness beyond the Minister's purview. While the Minister accepts
the voice of God as reality, the spectators know the truth and, as a
result, become the Burglar's "coconspirators." They participate in and
laugh at the Burglar's ruse. As Benston explains, the move toward
methexis creates more "flexibility of dramatic form," which allows the
spectators and performers to interact more freely and directly and
results in a more "participatory theater."[44] The forms of both *The Prayer*

Meeting and *Los Vendidos* are interactive, encouraging conspiratorial communion and celebration.

Still, for some critics the spectacle of four Chicano men rejoicing over their deception did not seem particularly revolutionary. Betty Ann Diamond critically inquired:

> And what is the point of the supposedly "revolutionary" action they have taken? The way it stands, the action is a way of ripping off the man. There is emotional satisfaction at seeing Miss Jiménez chased off the stage defeated, but this is vengeance, not revolution.[45]

Jorge Huerta reports that some Chicanos were embarrassed by the images of deceit and theft represented in the play.[46] As a result of such criticism, El Teatro revised this *acto* and changed the ending for a 1973 version of the play that was videotaped for television station KNBC in Los Angeles.

> The revised version of the *acto* relied on the transformation of the many "Mexican-American models" that were placed throughout the nation to bring about changes necessary to improve the Chicano's condition, thus indicating that their transformation would spur society's.[47]

The new version emphasized the message of antiassimilation and Chicano cultural affirmation. The action of the four Used Mexican models celebrating the spoils of their victory was removed.

A similar criticism of inappropriate "criminal" activity could be leveled at *The Prayer Meeting*. For at the conclusion of *The Prayer Meeting* the Burglar carries through on his original mission and robs the Minister.

MINISTER: This is a heavy burden you place upon my shoulders, Lord.
BURGLAR: I feel I'm takin' some of your burdens away.

(PM, 34)

The Burglar leaves with the Minister's property, and his crime remains unpunished. Yet I contend that neither the trickery of the "Used Mexicans" in *Los Vendidos* nor the burglary in *The Prayer Meeting* diminish the respective play's social efficacy. When understood as situated within their particular social and cultural contexts, both actions represent irreverent, symbolic victories over systems of power and authority.

The identity politics, the revolutionary ideologies of both the Black and Chicano Power movements, were predicated on antistructural irreverence. In order to foment structural change these movements rejected and demeaned the institutions, values, and traditions of the dominant culture. Correspondingly, in both *Los Vendidos* and *The Prayer Meeting* traditional symbols of authority and power are treated irreverently and subverted. Not only do these plays challenge figures of authority, but, through the deception of the Mexican models and the Burglar's theft, the plays also undermine the social order itself, by challenging society's fundamental values of right and wrong. The definitions of right and wrong, like the definitions of normative behavior and the "American Dream," all have been constructed by the dominant culture. White—often racist—hegemony has determined what is or is not "criminal." Repeatedly in the 1960s and 1970s, the white power structure attempted to diminish, devalue, and even defeat the political insurrections of marginalized groups by relabeling these revolutionary outbursts as criminal activities. One of the key strategies of the FBI's counterintelligence program (CONTELPRO) in its war against revolutionary organizations such as the Black Panthers and the Chicano Brown Berets was to contain and to retain their members on criminal charges. Even the nonviolent César Chávez was jailed for his protest activities in 1970. Situated within this historical context, the actions of the Burglar and the Used Mexican models can be construed as a creative, counterhegemonic, antistructural reallocations of power that contest the fundamental legitimacy of the dominant culture.

The situated forms and contents of *Los Vendidos* and *The Prayer Meeting* practice structural irreverence while celebrating the popular cultural tradition of the trickster hero. The trickster figure, prominent in both black and Chicano folklore, solely relies on wit and guile to undermine and often embarrass figures of strength, power, wealth, and dominance. In *The Signifying Monkey* Gates traces the African American trickster figure back to Africa and the Yoruba god Esu-Elegbara and on through the subversive figures in black vernacular tales—Briar Rabbit, Stagolee, and the Signifying Monkey.[48] Correspondingly, Broyles-González connects the tradition of the "comic underdog-trickster" in contemporary Chicano culture back to early Indian and Mexican oral performances:

> Popular fascination with the underdog trickster figure traverses Mexican popular performance genres. This generic character appears in numerous guises yet always bears an inordinate critical thrust couched in humor. It is the Pedro de Ordimalas figure, the Quevedo figure, or the Pepito figure prominent in joke telling tradition. It is the anthropomorphic rabbit, the poor *ranchero*, or the Indian peasant.[49]

Broyles-González sees the Mexican comedian Mario Moreno, or "Cantiflas," as the embodiment of this comic underdog-trickster figure. In both black and Chicano traditions the trickster, whether Cantiflas or the Signifying Monkey, outsmarts more powerful or dominant adversaries. The subversion, ridicule, and outwitting of authority by the trickster signifies a victory for the underclass, the oppressed. Accordingly, Geneviève Fabre writes, "Stated in terms of a popular tradition that sees the trickster as a hero, the revolutionary message [of *The Prayer Meeting*] loses neither its relevance nor its impact."[50] Through the subterfuge and irreverence of the tricksters, *Los Vendidos* and *The Prayer Meeting* reject authority and reaffirm the cultural validity of marginalized peoples.

Still, one potential danger with the employment of the trickster as a symbol of antistructural irreverence is that the trickster acts as an individual. As a result, his or her actions are principally for his or her own benefit and not for the good of the community. His or her self-focused acts of deception could compromise the social protest performance's goals of generating collective action and solidifying community. In *The Prayer Meeting* the juxtaposition of the Minister's final inspirational speech with the Burglar's criminal activity mediates against the dissolution of community. The changes that Valdez and El Teatro instituted into the script before the 1973 televised version of *Los Vendidos* can be perceived as an acknowledgment of this problem with the trickster as social protest hero. In the revision the self-serving action of the four Chicano tricksters was replaced by collective assertion of the need for Chicano cultural and social consciousness.

Content and Form and Audience Participation

During a unique time of urgency, the content and forms of the plays discussed in this chapter united culture and politics through the assertion of cultural identity and political resistance. Implicit and explicit within these situated forms and content was a critique and a subversion of Western cultural authority. The situated content and forms of these plays were intended to raise audiences' sociopolitical awareness and to induce their involvement in the social protest event. Symbolic elements within the play texts intensified the spectators' relationship to the texts and propelled audiences to participate in the "communal helping out."

Because of the concurrent social upheaval, "situated" spectators were better able to understand the correlation between the play's content and their own real lives. Turner notes that ritual symbols are dynamic and contain the capacity to "instigate social action. . . . People are induced to want to do what they must do. In this sense ritual action is akin to a sublimation process, and one would not be stretching the language unduly to say that its symbolic behavior actually 'creates' society for pragmatic purposes."[51] Similarly, symbols within the social protest play text impelled the audience to want to "help out." The "symbolic behavior" that the performers and audience members enacted together as coparticipants constructed new models for society and for social change. For the "ideal" social protest audience members, as I will detail in the subsequent chapters, participation within the social protest performance potentially affected social thought and served as a precursor to social action.

4

Rehearsing the Revolution Onstage: The Social Performance Text and the Performance Space

The last chapter established how the form and content of the social protest play text functioned ritualistically to reaffirm cultural pride, inform social consciousness, and induce audience participation. In this chapter I will extend this argument by examining the "performance text" and performance space. It is the performance text, the visual and oral components that constitute a performance, which is read by the audience. This chapter will show that symbolic elements within the social protest performance text, for both El Teatro and the BRT, expanded, visualized, and concretized concepts expressed in the dramatic content. Chants, music, gestures, physical action, and comic business all served to convey and compel both cultural affirmation and social action. Jean and John Comaroff write that "ritual in fashioning signs can make new meanings, new ways of knowing the world and its meanings."[1] Correspondingly, by employing the "transformative power of theatrical performance," the performances of El Teatro and the BRT created new meanings for and new ways of knowing established social processes.

By the "transformative power of theatrical performance" I mean that the theatrical performance can transform a seemingly simple act into a powerful moment of theatrical as well as social and cultural significance. This concept relates to the transformational power that Margaret Thompson Drewal and Jean Comaroff, among others, associate with certain ritual practices.[2] Rituals are often enacted as social interventions with the express purpose of transforming the social reality. Similarly, El Teatro and the BRT used the transformative power of theatrical performance to persuade their audiences that their own real-life "social dramas" were ultimately transformable. The represented action transformed and transcended the current and immediate social conditions. The performances often conflated past, present, and future while predicting and visualizing the actualization of El Teatro's and the BRT's revolutionary goals. The conflation of time symbolically reaffirmed the urgency and significance of the present performative moment. By predicting revolutionary victory, the performances renewed the audience's commitment to struggle. The success of the social protest cause was shown to be distinct, specific, and attainable.

This chapter will examine the social protest performance text and performance space using two particular social protest plays in performance: *Slave Ship,* written by Amiri Baraka and directed by Gilbert Moses at the Chelsea Theater Center in Brooklyn in November 1969; and the *acto Quinta Temporada,* originally conceived and performed by El Teatro Campesino in 1966, at a Grape Strike meeting held at Filipino Hall, in Delano, California. Jorge Huerta calls *Quinta Temporada* "a classic of its genre."[3] Clayton Riley writes that *Slave Ship* is "a mood: established by ritual concept."[4] I have chosen to discuss *Quinta Temporada* and *Slave Ship* because in their respective 1960s productions, these plays evidenced effective strategies of ritualistic social protest theater.

These plays, however, used markedly different styles. *Slave Ship* exploded with brutal, inflammatory images and incited black revolutionary violence. *Quinta Temporada,* on the other hand, employed farce and slapstick to predict the collective benefits that accrued from nonviolent support of the UFWOC and La Huelga. And yet I believe that a comparative analysis of these disparate plays in performance can provide insight into how social protest performances can potentially affect audience reception. Signs, symbols, images, and actions in the performance texts of both *Slave Ship* and *Quinta Temporada* presented their particular constituencies with new models for social change. The performance spaces for and performative action of *Slave Ship* and *Quinta Temporada* each induced audience participation as well as communion between audience and performers. At the same time, they impressed upon their spectators that these performances were not meant merely as entertainment but held actual social consequences.

The Theatrical Space

El Teatro's traveling performances required a performance space that was flexible and easily transportable to each new performance site. Aesthetically, the *actos* demanded a space that was representational rather than realistic, adaptable to the staging of each individual play. With these artistic and practical requirements, the back of a flatbed truck became the stage floor. The scenery, at first, consisted solely of a red and black banner bearing the name of El Teatro Campesino and a large National Farm Worker Association (NFWA) strike banner, a red field with a black Aztec eagle inside a white circle. Valdez explained the significance of the strike banner's colors: "The red is the blood of sacrifice, the black is the sorrow and the white is the hope."[5]

This simple, functional, boldly iconographic stage became a powerful theatrical symbol for El Teatro's audience of fieldworkers. In El Teatro's performances the flatbed truck operated as a dual symbol: an ever-present reminder of those other flatbeds that served as the primary means of transportation for the migrant farmworkers to and from the fields; and an open space that connoted and promoted rebellion. Just like the social circumstances that surrounded it, El Teatro's open performance space was liminal and dynamic—capable of signifying the past and present struggle as well as the farmworkers' optimistic future. The NFWA strike banner in the background established for the audience an immediate connection between the *actos* performed and the union strike rhetoric. For many the banner symbolized hope for the imminent achievement of migrant workers' rights and established a sense of unity, binding all those who encompassed its significance.

When El Teatro took its productions out into the fields, the campesinos had to leave or interrupt their work in order to watch the performances. At times the participation of these audiences subjected them to danger. Throughout the duration of the strike the growers as well as the police sought systematically to intimidate Chávez and his fledgling union. They used guard dogs, sulphur insecticide spray, arrests, and physical beatings to prevent picketing farmworkers from spreading their campaign for farmworkers' rights and encouraging more workers to join their rank and file. These attempts to disrupt the union spilled over into the performances of El Teatro and the atmosphere that surrounded those performances. Armed field supervisors and police maintained a constant vigil as the farmworkers crossed over to the El Teatro stage. The actual threat of violence created by these armed forces heightened the realism and urgency of the proceedings.[6] At times El Teatro's performances fulfilled the ideal of Nigerian playwright Wole Söyinka that "true guerrilla theater occurred when it was as dangerous for the audience to be present as it was for the actors to perform." At such performances attending as well as acting in the performance represented a risk. Necessarily, the performance of the *actos* under such circumstances constituted far more than entertainment.

In an interview in *Drama Review* Valdez told the details of one performance, in June 1966, at the edge of the DiGiorgio ranch in Arvin, California. At first the workers were extremely reluctant to leave the fields and move any closer to El Teatro's truck.

> We were on the truckbed calling them over, but they wouldn't come, so we started singing and then we began our first acto—Felipe [Cantu] came out. We started to get some stragglers, and as it got darker more and more people came out. By the time we were into our show, all of the camp were out there—a couple hundred people. They cheered, they laughed, they applauded.[7]

The act of "crossing over" radically changed the spatial relationship between spectators and performers. It literally brought the farmworkers closer to the El Teatro performance. Altering the spatial and physical distance of the audience to the production helped to change the spectators' psychological distance from and their interaction with the production. More significantly, the act of crossing over was truly an act of social defiance on the part of these farmworkers.

For El Teatro the reality of the fields became a theatrical device, a critical element in its performance. By performing in the fields, the very site of oppression, El Teatro intensified the relation between the signified and the signifier, between the sign vehicle and the spectator interpreter, heightening the import and immediacy of the performance. Performing at the site of oppression impelled the campesino spectators to become more active participants. Throughout the performance these spectators remained acutely aware of their surroundings and of the potential violence of the current labor crisis. As discussed in chapter 2, La Huelga constituted what anthropologist Victor Turner termed a "social drama." Viewed within the context of this social drama, El Teatro's outdoor mobile performances functioned as a "play within a play" and the farmworker audience as players in a larger drama of greater consequence. The fields themselves held specific iconic identity. El Teatro's performances converted real space into iconic space, symbolically transforming the reality of the farmworker. Then the performance itself rearticulated and reimagined the fields not only as a site of the farmworkers' exploitation but also as a site of resistance and even the actualization of the strike cause.

Unlike El Teatro, Gilbert Moses could not stage *Slave Ship* at a literal "site of oppression." Still, he attempted to transform the performance space into a slave ship—a critical, historical site of black degradation and collective social memory. Set designer Eugene Lee, resident designer for the Trinity Square Repertory Theater in Providence, Rhode Island, designed a set, in consultation with Moses, that captured "the feeling of a slave ship that if cut in half the audience could see into. In fact, it actually rocked back and forth."[8] As a historical site of unconscionable racial violence, the slave ship potently communicated to its spectators an African American heritage of struggle and survival.

In the Moses production of the Baraka text the slave ship symbol contained not only historical connotations but contemporary meanings as well. Moses and Baraka wanted the audience for *Slave Ship* to understand that contemporary "America in a lot of senses is just a replay or a continuation of that same slave ship, that it's not changed."[9] As the action of the Moses production shifted in geographical locale and historical period, the dominant, iconographic symbol of the slave ship remained. Kimberly Benston observed:

Baraka [Moses] transforms the entire theater into the slave ship whose black passengers' historical journey is from first enslavement to contemporary revolution, and whose mythical journey is from African civilization through enslavement to spiritual resendency.[10]

By maintaining the slave ship as the setting for all of the play's action, Moses connected African American experiences of the past and present. Through this visual representation Moses wanted the spectators to understand that African American existence in America remained slavelike, devoid of a sense of belonging or ownership.

Moses staged the play environmentally; the whole theater became a performance space, "where action might erupt at any point. Action could happen in back of you or right beside you."[11] Moses created the sensation, for the audience, that they were actually aboard a slave ship. The spectators endured their own personal "middle passage." Moses, like the El Teatro performances, converted iconic space into real space affecting the audience's spatial, physical, and psychological distance from the production. The audience witnessed slaves in the ship's hold being pitched and tossed about. They heard the slaves scream, cough, and vomit. One slave woman was raped, another killed herself, a third gave birth, all as the audience watched. Moses eliminated any distance the audience had from one another or from the performers. Walter Kerr remarked, "Black bodies seem to come straight through the floor of the slave ship."[12] The production disrupted the spectators' normal expectations of theatrical proxemics and aesthetic distance. To effect further the experience of a slave ship, the audience sat extremely close together, on hard, uncomfortable, wooden benches. Don Isaacs observed that the positioning of the slave ship set and the audience's benches "forced the audience to hunch over to see what was happening during the first half of the play."[13] The treatment that the spectators endured represented the real overcrowding and discomfort that slaves suffered within the hold of a slave ship. As a result, attendance at *Slave Ship* held actual physical consequences for the audience.

By reproducing the site of oppression and its accompanying sensations, Moses forced the spectators to be more active participants in the theatrical event. At one point in the performance slaves were auctioned off to members of the audience, and the audience again was compelled to participate. Jerry Tallmer of the *New York Post* reported that, on the night he attended the production, "A beautiful little black boy of about 10 was 'sold' to drama critic Edith Oliver of the *New Yorker*."[14] By trespassing the normal barriers that separate audience and performers, Moses created an atmosphere of disorientation and even hysteria.[15] Moses believed that the discomfort and dislocation of the spectators would make them more susceptible to the play's messages of militancy and revolution.

To influence further the audience's response, Moses and his performers, in their rehearsals, experimented with what he termed "emotional space."[16] Emotional space connoted the distance between the notes of a song or two lines of dialogue or two bars of music. These moments of silence were often taut, filled with anticipation for the spectators. Effective orchestration of emotional space, manipulating the silences and pauses, could create feelings of anxiousness and tension in the audience members. The idea of emotional space came from Moses's training with Paul Sills and had much in common with the practices of the experimentalists Peter Brook and Richard Schechner. The employment of emotional space was also common in black Christian church rites. Within black church practices the manipulation of emotional space by the preacher in the sermon, or by the choir in song, often produced momentary feelings of spiritual ecstasy and exaltation. Moses appropriated this technique for the purpose of fomenting audience participation and a communion of revolutionary spirit. In Moses's experimentations with emotional space, music played an integral role as Moses, who wrote significant portions of the music for the *Slave Ship* production, brought in five musicians to work with the actors in rehearsal. The rehearsals resulted in the creation of a rhythm that in performance, according to Moses, "produced a communal euphoria and a cognizance of a cultural commonality."[17]

One could argue that through music, improvisation, and humor, El Teatro also manipulated emotional space. El Teatro's use of emotional space, however, did not produce militant outrage or incitation to riot. El Teatro's manipulation induced the spirit of a folk festival rather than tension and hysteria. Performances began and ended with music and encouraged an atmosphere of a "carnivalesque" celebration. Adapting the theories of Mikhail Bakhtin, Baz Kershaw writes of the carnivalesque:

> Carnival undermines the distinction between observer and participant; it takes place outside of existing cultural and social institutions, occupying real space-time in streets and open spaces . . . it is accessible and it is excessive, enjoying spectacle and grotesque exaggerations of the norm. Above all, carnival inverts the every-

day, workaday rules, regulations and laws challenging the hierarchies of normality in a counterhegemonic, satirical and sartorial parody of power.[18]

This understanding of the carnivalesque is particularly appropriate to El Teatro's performances. As in the carnivalesque, the performances of El Teatro in the fields, the actual workplace, interrupted and challenged the norms and regulations of the workday. El Teatro's performances would begin and end with folk songs in which the spectators were invited to participate. The use of music, physical humor, and techniques of audience interaction created an atmosphere of festivity and celebration that, as Kershaw writes of the carnivalesque, broke down the separation between performers and spectators. Still, one assumption within the discourse on the carnivalesque is that after the disruption of the social order, the hierarchical structure is restored, and the status quo returns. This reinstitution of the old order should not, however, be perceived as totalizing. The celebration of the carnival in its very composition entails excess, seepage, the permeation, of existing boundaries.[19] El Teatro's manipulation of the emotional space, the troupe's agitation through music and performative action for social change, purposefully encouraged and helped to produce such slippage.

By manipulating the emotional space in carnivalesque celebration, El Teatro returned to the "carpa," or tent theater, an early Mexican oral performance tradition. Yolanda Broyles-González maintains that the *carpa* was the most important source for the work of El Teatro.[20] Similar to the traditions of the *carpa*, El Teatro employed music, folklore, humor, stock characters, and open, generalized performances. Broyles-González notes the difficulty for contemporary scholars in defining exactly what constituted a *carpa* performance: "It is impossible to define the Mexican *carpa* as one thing for it encompassed a field of diverse cultural performance practice popular amongst the poorest segment of the Mexican populace."[21] Broyles-González affirms that, despite its various permutations, historically the *carpa* "served as a counterhegemonic tool of the disenfranchised and oppressed."[22]

In the early 1900s traveling burlesque theatrical troupes performed a form of *carpa* exclusively for working-class audiences in Mexico. The content of these performances often served as a political review. Nicolás Kanellos reports that "The carpas functioned quite often as popular tribunals, repositories of folk wisdom, humor and music, and were incubators of Mexican comic types and stereo-types."[23] These *carpa* performances were crudely and quickly staged. The atmosphere was always both festive and subversive. Real space became transformed into performance, or iconic, space. The audience accepted the crude simplistic backdrop of the canvas *carpa* as a theatricalized location.

As El Teatro performed on the back of transformed flatbed trucks, they invited the spectators to enter their performance space and to join in *carpa*-like subversive celebrations. Yet, while these *carpa* performances transcended the reality of their location in order to entertain their audience, El Teatro performances, because of their explicitly social purposes, never wanted their audiences to escape totally into the illusion of the theater. Instead, the performances in the fields constantly reminded the spectators of the link between the performative action and the farmworkers' actual, urgent, social struggle.

El Teatro's performing at the site of oppression as well as Moses's reproduction of the oppressive slave ship environment purposefully kept their respective spectators aware of the extremely real forces of oppression that surrounded them. These performance spaces were in themselves dichotomous, both confrontational and comforting. Moses's re-creation of a slave ship for the Chelsea Theater Center's production of *Slave Ship* and the outdoor performance environment for El Teatro's *actos* compelled a tactile interaction, a visceral response, from their audiences. As a result, audiences became, potentially, more receptive to and engaged in the ritualistic action of the plays.

The Performance Text: Signs and Symbols in Performance

The images and signs in the performance text of *Quinta Temporada* purposefully drew upon the daily experiences of the campesinos in the San Joaquín Valley. At the outset of *Quinta Temporada* a performer, wearing khaki shirt and pants and bearing a placard that read "Farmworker," steps onto the stage and addresses the audience: "My name is José . . . and I'm looking for a job. Do you have a job? I can do anything, any kind of field work."[24] Even before his first words the sign as well as his khaki uniform define and identify the Farmworker. The complex yet simple Farmworker was a character central to the early *actos*. He symbolized the heritage of Mexican experience, the continually oppressive conditions of agricultural oppression, as well as the eventuality of revolutionary change through support of the UFW. The Farmworker became a powerful symbol, not simply within the plays of El Teatro but also within the context of the UFWOC strike and the Chicano movement as a whole. Bruce-Novoa explains:

> All that was needed was unity, and at the center of a unified Chicano community stood the farmworker. The appeal of this well-designed and dynamically staged propaganda, was confirmed in the success that Teatro Campesino enjoyed, not only with Chicanos, but among liberal elements of the non-Chicano communities. Through that success the image of the farmworker was confirmed as an icon on par with the mestizo head and the United Farm Worker Flag.[25]

In *Quinta Temporada* El Teatro condensed and re-presented the exploitative labor experiences of all Chicano farmworkers through the representative image of the Farmworker character. He represented an allegorical Chicano "Everyman."

As *Quinta Temporada* continues, another performer, dressed in khaki pants but covered with money, walks out onto the stage and announces, "I am Summer." At this moment Valdez and El Teatro expected farmworker audiences to laugh with recognition. According to Maria Shevtsova, "The laughter provoked [by a performance] is laughter acknowledging the significance of signs commonly understood."[26] Valdez explains his reasons for choosing this representation of summer:

> This is the way the farmworkers look at summer. As a kid I can remember my family going north towards the prune and apricot orchards. My image was of leaves and fruit clustered on the tree and all this turning into flows of dollar bills.[27]

Within the specific context of the migratory labor experience a man dressed in khaki clothing and covered with dollar bills became an effective symbol of summer. Valdez's anthropomorphic representation of summer compressed the migratory farmworkers' sensory and intellectual responses to this important farming season into a visual image. Intrinsically, Valdez understood the power of the *actos'* performance symbols to reproduce and re-present social meanings. Valdez stated that the images presented in the *actos* "are directed at the farmworker; they're supposed to represent the reality that he sees. It's not a naturalistic representation; most of the time it's a symbolic, emblematic presentation of what the farmworker feels."[28] Valdez used the symbolic, "tropic play of images" to communicate meanings that reached beyond the surface-level understanding inherent in naturalistic representations.

A comic "lazzi" of exploitation all too familiar to the farmworkers immediately follows the symbolic revelation of Summer. After the Farmworker picks the money off the clothing of Summer and sticks it into his back pocket, the evil and exploitative labor contractor, Don Coyote, removes the money and hands it back to the Patron, leaving the Farmworker with nothing. The Farmworker onstage is, at first, oblivious to this deception. The farmworkers in the audience, on the other hand, witness the money exchange. El Teatro intended for the farmworker spectators to perceive this comic monetary interplay as emblematic of their own economic abuse under the migratory labor system. Labor contractors—derogatively termed "coyotes" by the farmworkers—prayed on the migratory workers' powerless position by securing them employment in exchange for a percentage of their wages. In *Quinta Temporada* the labor contractor is subversively named "*Don* Coyote." The name parodies the name of the heroic and mythical figure Don Quixote. More significantly, as Huerta notes, "The title, *Don,* which is usually reserved for distinguished older men, is here used to ridicule the character and reveal his true stature."[29]

The subsequent action further emphasized to the spectators the untenable economic circumstances of the Farmworker. The symbolic *lazzi* of "money picking" is repeated when a performer representing Autumn, dressed like Summer, but not as abundantly covered with money, comes onto the stage. Then, following the departure of Autumn, the character Winter leaps onto the stage bringing with him cold facts: no work and bills that must be paid. While the Patron and the labor contractor successfully pay off Winter, the Farmworker, lacking financial means, must suffer Winter's assault. Winter drags the Farmworker across the stage and drops snow from a pouch onto the Farmworker. Once again this physical action reproduced disparate meanings and induced a dichotomous response from the original campesino audiences. It entertained as well as disturbed. While its slapstick humor caused the farmworker/spectators to laugh, they laughed with the realization that the Farmworker's exploitation onstage represented the reality of their own oppression under the seasonal system of farm labor.

The action of *Quinta Temporada* not only reveals the economic exploitation of the farmworker but explicitly infers that the only viable and valid response to this economic oppression for the "Everyman" Farmworker onstage, as well as those farmworkers in the audience, is to strike and to support the UFWOC. Abused and beaten by the contractor and Patron, the Farmworker seeks some means of redress. Spring, a woman wearing a lightweight spring dress, skips onto the stage. She instills in the Farmworker the resolve to resist further exploitation by going out on strike. With the assistance of Spring the Farmworker is reborn as a "huelgista." Huerta observes that "Spring, symbol of resurrection, rebirth, and renewed vegetation, offers hope to the farmworker both figuratively and literally, just as it did for the agrarian ancestors of these humble folk."[30] The image of the anthropomorphic Spring coming to the aid of the struggling Farmworker visually demonstrates that the power of the seasons can be harnessed and turned to the farmworkers' advantage. Significantly, a woman portrays Spring. This casting and its visual iconography reinforces conventional gender roles and representations of women as nurturing support systems.

With the Farmworker on strike, Summer and Autumn pass by unattended. Characters portraying the churches and La Raza help to bolster the Farmworker in his protest. Through the representation of these anthropomorphic figures El Teatro symbolically links the spiritual, cultural, and political in the realm of the performative. Their interconnection confers spiritual sanction on the farmworkers' radicalization. The union of these forces justifies and reaffirms the strike. The presence of Spring, church, and La Raza convey to the audience that the Farmworker is not alone in his current struggle. He has collective power and agency.

This *acto* transforms the subordinate relationship of the seasonal farmworker to the land. Rather than solely representing the land as a commodity and a complicit partner in the subjugation of the Farmworker, the land becomes a tool within the Farmworker's resistance effort. When he goes out on strike, the Farmworker develops a new cooperative interaction with the land, which purposefully recalls the ancient Aztecs' religious, cosmic, and practical connections to the earth and soil. Geneviève Fabre refers to this assertion of the agrarian Aztec past as the "masks" of this *acto*.[31] Unlike most of the original El Teatro *actos*, including *Las Dos Caras del Patroncito*, *Quinta Temporada* did not involve the use of actual masks. In other *actos* El Teatro used masks as well as placards hung around each character's neck to support the symbolism and meaning of the performative action.[32] While *Quinta Temporada* did not use actual masks, Fabre maintains:

> The masks of this *acto* [*Quinta Temporada*] are an investigation into the rich cultural past of former Meso-American agrarian societies where cultivation of the land and intellectual pursuit were conceived as complementary. The past is opposed to the bleak present in which land has become an instrument of oppression and the campesino has lost his sense of place in the cosmic order. The number five as indicated in the title refers to a complex symbolic system related to Mayan cosmology.[33]

As Fabre notes, the concept of a "quinta temporada," a fifth season, consciously invokes the symbolic significance of the number 5. The ancient Aztecs considered themselves the people of the "Fifth Sun." The Fifth Sun was the epoch of the Aztec civilization in Aztlán. Under the concept of a Fifth Sun the Aztecs developed a complex cosmology.[34] During the 1960s and 1970s the historical, spiritual, and cultural connotations of the Fifth Sun became important to Chicano cultural nationalistic practices. Armando B. Rendon writes in the *Chicano Manifesto:* "The Chicano is unique in America. He[35] is a descendant of the Fifth Sun, bound to the land of Aztlán by his blood, sweat and flesh."[36] In the fall of 1967, in Berkeley, California, a group of committed Chicano writers and artists created a publishing house devoted solely to the promotion of Chicano arts and culture and named it *Quinto Sol*, the Fifth Sun. Correspondingly, *Quinta Temporada*, through its symbolic use of the number 5, its anthropomorphic representations, its recollection of the ancient Indians' communion with the land and the forces of nature, forges a spiritual bond between the Aztec past and the Chicano farmworkers' present.

In the performance of *Slave Ship* playwright Baraka and director Gilbert Moses also sought to connect the cultural past with their immediate social struggle. They created images and action that infused the present historical moment with symbols of African cultural heritage. Through sparse dialogue, music, sound, and movement, *Slave Ship* chronicles African American history from Africa through the middle passage to the civil rights and black power struggles of the 1960s and 1970s. The symbolism in Moses's production of *Slave Ship* emphasized the survival of African culture, spirituality, and communalism in African American experience.[37] Yoruba dialect was spoken during the first twenty minutes of the play, while the beating of African drums remained constant throughout. As the action moved from the roots of black civilization in Africa through slavery to the 1960s, the characters continued to chant and speak phrases in Yoruba and pray to African deities. This visual portrayal of African cultural retention informed the spectators that, despite the pressures from white America to conform, African traditions continued to survive in African American culture and experience.

Because the plot and character delineation of *Slave Ship* were so sparse, the other elements of the production increased in significance. The performance of *Slave Ship* emphasized gestures and symbols over the spoken word. Spectacle, music, sounds, and smells all combined to bring audience and performers together in an atmosphere of intense feeling. Created by jazz musician Archie Shepp and director Gil Moses, the music covered the historical spectrum of black music, from African drums to jazz to rhythm and blues. This music suffused the entire production, intensifying the emotional impact of onstage moments. Critic John Lahr in the *Village Voice* called the production "genuine musical theater."[38] Kimberly Benston asserted that the music in *Slave Ship* "is thus the strength, memory, power, triumph affirmation—the entire historical and mythical process of Afro-American being."[39] As suggested by both Lahr's and Benston's comments, the music acted as much more than background. The conjunction of historical and contemporary African and African American musical styles symbolized and reaffirmed the African presence in the African American cultural continuum.

As in *Quinta Temporada*, the action of *Slave Ship* was not real but, rather, symbolic re-presenting, re-producing meanings for its audience. Paul Carter Harrison noted, in his response to the performance of *Slave Ship*, that the director "Moses was able to heighten our sensitivity to the context of oppression without duplicating the experience in a static representation of reality, as in a natural life photograph; instead he relied upon our response to inform the spirit of outrage."[40] Rather than realism, Moses employed powerful stage symbols. Turner writes that ritual symbols act as "instigators and products of temporal sociocultural processes."[41] Correspondingly, the oppressive socioeconomic conditions of black American life inform and were informed by the symbolism of *Slave Ship*. The play's action compressed the horrors of the middle passage and the degradations of centuries under white racist hegemony into succinct stage moments. *Slave Ship*'s representational account of black history flowed from slavery to civil rights, omitting any record of emancipation. This deliberate omission emphasized that oppressive conditions for blacks have been continuous.

Baraka and Moses also used action and images within *Slave Ship* to challenge and transform conventional social and cultural meanings. Like *The Prayer Meeting*, *Slave Ship* contested the legitimacy of and the black spectators' faith in traditional black religion. Baraka visually associated the civil rights ministry, the legacy of Dr. Martin Luther King Jr., with betrayal and complicity, by having the Uncle Tom house slave of the early slavery scenes and the assimilationist black preacher in later scenes portrayed by the same performer. When the preacher first appeared, the stage directions read: "Now lights flash on, and preacher in modern business suit stands with hat in his hand. He is the same Tom as before."[42] Audiences close to and familiar with the achievements of the immensely popular Dr. King could potentially have found such an association troubling. Still, the signs and symbols connected with the black preacher in *Slave Ship* transformed the meanings embodied in the image of the black preacher–as–civil rights crusader. The depiction of the black preacher in *Slave Ship* worked to, as Jean and John Comaroff suggest, "make new meanings, new ways of knowing,"[43] out of established images.

The transformation of the Uncle Tom slave into the black preacher

called into question the preacher's credibility within the black liberation struggle. As a result, the representation of the preacher in *Slave
Ship* reads not as a symbol of black pride and authority but, rather, as a
caricature in the minstrel tradition, a stereotype of accommodation.
According to the stage directions, "He [the preacher] tries to be, in fact,
assumes he is, dignified, trying to hold his shoulders straight, but only
succeeds in giving his body an odd slant like a diseased coal chute" (*SS*,
142). With the guidance of these stage directions as well as the language
that Baraka creates for this character, the performer who played the
preacher presented him as a demeaning and deferential "Steppin
Fetchit"–like character. The play remakes the nonviolent preacher as an
accommodating obstacle to the black liberation cause.

With newly awakened political consciousness and militancy, the
other black characters onstage rise en masse and murder the black
preacher. The execution of the preacher visually dramatized the need
of the gathered black spectators to eliminate from their own consciousness any tendency to accommodate oppression. Significantly, the black
masses execute the preacher in the same stage area previously used as
a slave auction block. Their violent actions transform the space and
exorcise the negative vestiges of slavery. The transformations of space
and of the complacent black masses into militant activists symbolized
for the audience that oppressive circumstances could be overcome,
"transformed," through collective revolutionary action.

The killing of the black preacher is followed by the symbolic execution of an offstage "White Voice." This offstage White Voice, an
invisible but extremely tangible symbol of the powerful psychological
and sociological effects of white oppression, hovers above the play,
inhibiting black interaction. Implicitly and explicitly, the representation of the White Voice critiques and comments on the power of representation. Although not physically present, the White Voice is powerfully represented. At one point the White Voice announces to the
onstage black masses: "I'm God. You can't kill white Jesus God. I got
long blond blow hair. I don't even wear a wig. You love the way I look.
You want to look like me!" (*SS*, 145). These words underline racist representations and assumptions that have conditioned the treatment of
blacks by whites and have also constrained blacks' self-image. By controlling the representational apparatus, the dominant culture has per-
petuated its values and superiority. As a result, some blacks have inter-

nalized their inferiority and accepted and coveted everything white, including, according to *Slave Ship*, the concept of a white, blue-eyed, blond-haired "Jesus" god. The play charges the oppressive United States, capitalist system with the perpetuation of a spiritually bankrupt Christian ethos that promotes and legitimizes racism.

The black masses literally destroy and disempower the White Voice, symbolically deconstructing its representational authority. Subdued by the oncoming black onslaught, the White Voice changes from confident disdain to fearful pleading and finally to screams of horror. Simultaneously, other black cast members remove an effigy of Uncle Sam with a cross around his neck—a grotesque representation of the connection between the Christian ethic and U.S. capitalism—from the upstage wall and smash it. By controlling the representational apparatus of *Slave Ship*, Baraka empowers the black masses and black cultural representations. Through the execution of the White Voice the visible and invisible hegemony of the dominant culture and cultural representations is symbolically expunged.

Slave Ship explicitly invites the black spectators to become participants in this symbolic overthrow of the White Voice. Chanting "When we gonna rise. Rise, rise, rise cut the ties, Black man rise" (*SS*, 143), they cross out into the audience, shaking hands with the black audience members, challenging and encouraging black audience members to stand, to join with them in the chant and in their attack on the White Voice. This antistructural interpolation is at once inside and outside the action of the play. It is both creative and destructive as it allows for the improvisational flexibility of the performers and destroys the conventional boundaries between stage and spectators. Through this antistructural trope *Slave Ship* moves toward Benston's notion of methexis, the ritualistic and communal helping out. The participatory and symbolic action—the chanting and shaking of hands—encouraged audience members to commune, to help out.

Occasionally, white audience members as well as black desired to stand and participate. Critic Stan Machlin observed, "The powerful play hypnotizes like a religious ritual; a mass in secular times. This was so extreme that many whites attempted to stand up and join the singing chanting blacks—both audience and actors, even though it was their own destruction."[44] Machlin's allusion to *religious ritual* is particularly telling. The performance functioned as a symbolic mediation linking

the gathered participants with the greater cause beyond, the black liberation effort. Like a religious ritual, it purposefully connected the spiritual and political and generated communal participation. Present in
the symbolic, stage victory over white oppression was a feeling of spiritual exaltation. Machlin's observation that white as well as black spectators attempted to stand attests to the infectious power of the ritualistic performance event. The music, the action, the rhythm and
symbolism, of the production could potentially induce participation
and inculcate audience allegiance regardless of race. The cumulative
effect of *Slave Ship* resembled the communal celebration that Erving
Goffman associated with ritual ceremonies, as the audience and performers united in celebratory protest.[45] Machlin's perception of a common cross-racial response to this event suggests the possible effectiveness of ritualistic social performances as strategies within postmodern
political movements that reach across boundaries of ethnicity in
attempts to effect social change. Still, there were problems in efficacy
and reception whenever the BRT or El Teatro performed a social
protest play, such as *Slave Ship* or *Quinta Temporada,* before a mixed or
nonconstituent audience. In the next chapter, I will discuss in more
detail the effects of audience composition on the social protest performance and the value to El Teatro and the BRT of addressing ethnically
specific and segregated audiences.

The symbolic action of *Slave Ship* not only functioned as a symbolic
mediation but also as a signifying practice. It defined and authorized
violent social protest as the only recourse for black liberation. Stefan
Brecht wrote of the incendiary effect of *Slave Ship:*

> The final revolt is a genocidal call to arms to young Afro-American
> audiences—a call for killing of the white man. There is a symbolic
> overthrow of Uncle Sam. The play joins the present with clenched
> fists, hymns, new flags. . . . The play incites to violence.[46]

By presenting new symbols of violent revolutionary change and inviting the audience to participate in the symbolic defeat of oppression,
Slave Ship acted, like ritual, to "affect the flow of power in the universe"
and to influence audience actions outside of the theater. The performance encouraged audience participation and revolt while predicting

in simplistic, visual terms the actualization of the black nationalist movement.

Using a distinctly different approach to violence, *Quinta Temporada* imagines a successful conclusion to the Grape Pickers strike and challenges its audience to participate on the picket lines outside of the theater. With the Farmworker on strike, the Patron has no one to pick his "money" crop. As a result, the Patron's finances are depleted, and he cannot escape the inevitable onslaught of Winter. Winter drags the Patron across the stage, pummeling him with snow. Winter's previous abuse of the impoverished Farmworker is subverted as the Farmworker is replaced by the Patron, who now must suffer the brunt of Winter's attack. This transformed *lazzi* of Winter visualizes the effects that the strike will have on the ranch owners. The symbolic persecution of the Patron empowers the campesinos onstage and in the audience by revealing that the power of the seasons, even Winter, can be harnessed and turned to the farmworkers' advantage through collective support of the strike.

The defeated Patron concedes to the striking Farmworker's demands for a union contract and hiring hall. Using a giant pencil, a symbol of the collective strength of the union, the Patron signs a union contract. The victorious Farmworker/Huelgista exclaims, "Ganamos! [We won]." The character portraying Winter then kicks the labor contractor off the stage. The physical act of kicking the labor contractor offstage symbolizes the erasure of such parasitic procurers, which the UFWOC hoped to effect in the immediate future. The signing of the union contract and the adoption of the union hiring hall were to render the labor contractor's services unnecessary and to nullify his ability to exploit unwitting migratory workers. Significantly, the onstage victory predicts the eventual real-life triumph of the UFWOC cause. The action of the play transforms and transcends the current reality, creating an unrealized but desired future and rallying the spectators to increase their efforts to achieve that future.

As in *Slave Ship*, the form of *Quinta Temporada* incorporates the principles of methexis. The ending for *Quinta Temporada* offers an antistructural direct address that invites the audience to participate. In the final scene the former Winter announces to the audience his symbolic transformation. He no longer represents Winter but, instead, the Fifth

Season, "the season of social justice": "Si alguien pregunta que paso ese contratista chueco, diganle que se lo llevo la quinta chin—LA QUINTA TEMPRADA! [If anyone asks what happened to that crooked labor contractor, tell him he was taken away by . . . the Fifth Season (*QT*, 34)]." This direct address further dispels the theatrical illusion. The words of the Fifth Season reaffirm and validate, for the spectators, the righteousness of the strike effort. As in *Los Vendidos*, his words also make the spectators accomplices in determining the fate of the labor contractor.

Symbolically, this ending establishes for the farmworkers a future-oriented season of their own—one to fight for, to depend on, and to strengthen them against any other season—a fifth season of social justice. This new season subverts the conventional contract between the seasonal farmworkers and the seasons. Historically for the migrant workers, the seasons determined their ability to work and to sustain their families. The season of social justice exists as a socially constructed ideal outside of as well as inside the realm of traditional seasons. The concept of and desire for a season of social justice creates space, agency, and initiative for the farmworkers in their struggle against unjust social and economic conditions. While the farmworkers work within the conventional seasons, this new season works for them. The season of social justice is at once atemporal and time specific. The clamor for social justice has existed through time. One wants social justice always and already. And yet the desire for social justice is often particularized and focused on a specific historic moment of injustice. Within the context of the late 1960s and the urgency of the Grape Pickers strike, Chávez and the UFWOC demanded immediate social justice. *Quinta Temporada* proclaims that social justice is, in fact, on the side of Chávez and the union and that, as a result, they will prevail.

With the creation of this new season this social protest performance moves beyond the revelation of the existing social reality to a ritualistic creation of a new future reality. According to Fabre, the performance propels the audience

> into a kind of atemporality and into a historical present, into the perpetuity of community and into a future open to change. Anchored in tradition and in the past, the performance proposes through dialogue a change however momentary or limited. This finality must be analyzed as a ritual of liberation and also as a rit-

ual of reinsertion into group origins that reconnect a common past and future.[47]

The concept of a fifth season, as Fabre suggests, symbolically liberates the farmworkers from the hegemony of ranchers, while it reconnects them to a heritage of agrarian struggle and survival. A fifth season for the people of the Fifth Sun. The declaration of a fifth season of social justice in *Quinta Temporada* is a moment of spiritual, subversive, and symbolic celebration in which the spectators are expected to participate. It functions as a symbolic mediation, linking spectators and performers with the UFWOC cause and their Indian heritage, predicting the union's future victories.

The finale of *Slave Ship*, like the ending of *Quinta Temporada*, is antistructural. It attempts to induce further audience participation and to compel its audience to act. After the onstage black masses kill the White Voice in *Slave Ship*, they invite black spectators up onto the stage to dance with the performers to the jazz music of Archie Shepp. This action reinforces the celebratory and communal bond between spectators and performers. Together actors and audience become participants in a collective ritual, a "tribal" ceremony of spiritual and social significance. Just when the party reaches some loose improvisation, Baraka calls for the head of the Uncle Tom preacher to be thrown into the center of the dance floor. This symbolic, antistructural act transformed the atmosphere of the theatrical event. The shocking introduction of the preacher's head abruptly shifts the mood of the action. In a manner similar to Antonin Artaud and his Theater of Cruelty,[48] Baraka bombards his audience with violent, cruel images. Rather than purging spectators of the propensity to act—the expected response to violent images that Artaud articulated in *Theater and Its Double*—Baraka intends for this final moment of *Slave Ship* to induce the spectators' participation and compel their activism. Baraka reminds the audience through this powerful image of the unfulfilled legacy of the civil rights movement.

Fabre argues that revolutionary black theatrical productions must attempt to:

> simultaneously plunge the spectator into terror and reassure him . . . . In terrifying the spectator, the production brings back reality which is no longer doubted, for the performance must go beyond

the domain of the "magic" to reveal an order that is not dominated by the forces of destiny but regulated by the laws of history where change is necessary.[49]

Following Fabre's formula, *Slave Ship*, in its finale, jolts the audience back into the uncertain 1960s reality, in which victory over white oppression has yet to be achieved. The horrible revelation of the preacher's head further dispels the theatrical illusion and the convention of the theater as a safe environment free of the exigencies and consequences of daily life. Instead of continuing to celebrate, the spectators must confront this bloody image. The intrusion of the preacher's head into the action is not simply a symbolic act. It actually disrupts the dancing and compels the dancers to respond. The spectators need to recognize that the preacher's betrayal of his black brethren necessitated his death. This knowledge would reassure the spectators of the validity and righteousness of their struggle. BRT performances such as *Slave Ship* created dichotomous experiences intended to confront and provoke their audiences to social action. The social protest performance conflated the symbolic and the real, heightening the social significance of the performance.

Inducing Participation, Rehearsing Revolution

The practitioners of El Teatro as well as the BRT attempted systematically to manipulate the performance space and the performance text to break down the fourth wall and involve their audiences in communal celebration with a spirit of ethnic unity and a commitment to the cause of social rebellion. Neither the performances of El Teatro nor those of the BRT required the spectators' suspension of disbelief. Instead, the social protest performance engaged sympathetic spectators and performers in ritualistic and celebratory protest. Performances often occurred in an atmosphere of both festivity and apprehension. Rather than acting antithetically and diminishing the potential for social efficacy, these dual sentiments together provoked an emotional intensity in the theater that affected spectators as well as performers.

The signs and symbols contained in the social protest performance texts in consort with the social protest performance spaces incited audience participation and communion between spectators and performers.

The performance texts of both *Quinta Temporada* and *Slave Ship* contained signs and symbols that held real-life meaning for their audiences. The volatility and viability of these signs and symbols enabled the performances to act ritualistically as symbolic mediations and signifying practices. El Teatro and the BRT expected their audiences to participate in a symbolic theatrical revolution as a "rehearsal" for the resistance efforts they hoped these audience members to undertake in real life.

5

Performers and Spectators: Spiritual Communion and Subversive Celebration

In previous chapters I have attempted to reveal the ritualistic potential of the social protest performance by examining, in succession, the urgency of the surrounding social conditions, symbolic elements within the dramatic texts, signs and symbols within the performance texts, and the transformational power of the performance space. All of these components, alone and in combination, affect the social protest performance's interaction with its audience and contribute to making the social protest performance a communal and participatory experience. I now turn to confront the fundamental theatrical exchange between the performers[1] and the spectators. My objectives here are twofold: first, I want to examine how the social protest performer functions as social signifier and affects the communion between audience and performers; second, I want to analyze the dynamics of audience participation in the social performances of El Teatro and the BRT.

Valdez declared of El Teatro, "Audience participation is not a cute production trick with us, it is a pre-established, pre-assumed privilege."[2] And yet, as previous chapters have demonstrated, both El Teatro's and the BRT's performances contained deliberate strategies for inducing participatory behavior. Herbert Blau points out, in *Audience,* that the "question of participation remains the most fertile experimental issue in performance, in or out of theater. It is of course an unavoidable issue in any concept of audience, though what we mean by participation—degree of, kind, passive or active?—is a large part of the question."[3] The question for this chapter and the social protest performances of El Teatro and the BRT is not simply one of degree but, rather, of the meaning of that participation within the context of the performance and the theaters' overall social goals. Audience participation, I believe, is critical in the social protest theater, because it functions as a measure of social efficacy and a precursor to social action.

In any performance the audience acts as interpreter of meaning, decoding the signs and symbols of the performance. As Keir Elam notes, "It is with the spectators, in brief, that theatrical communication begins and ends."[4] Susan Bennett, in *Theatre Audiences*, describes this interpretation by the spectators as an active process in which the spectators must decode the sign systems available.[5] While the traditional theatrical paradigm requires this active decoding process, it also encourages the spectators to remain physically passive during the actual performance. The audience members are not expected to respond demonstratively. The audiences' physical and verbal passivity permits the performers to perform their onstage activities without threat of interruption. Social protest performances, however, challenge the convention of passivity. By invoking and inducing audience participation, by engaging the audience in the ritualistic enactment, the social protest performances disrupt conventional theatrical practices and normative patterns of audience behavior. Bennett writes:

> When audiences are consulted and involved in the structuring of the theatrical event, and are encouraged (at least in the immediate post-production period) to translate their reading of that event into action, then their role no longer maintains the fixity that dominant cultural practice assumes. In this way the production/reception process acts bi-directionally in broader cultural perspectives.[6]

The social protest performances of El Teatro and the BRT rejected the normal "fixity" of the audience. Instead, the spectators actively interacted with the performance and engaged in a dynamic dyadic, or "bidirectional," discourse with the performers.

El Teatro's and the BRT's performers worked to incite audience participation in the theater and to define and authorize the spectators' activism outside of the theater. In these ways performing in the social protest performance itself functioned as a "symbolic mediation" and a "signifying practice." Performing in the social protest theater did not, however, constitute one monolithic style, nor did it develop from one singular "method" of training and technique. As this chapter will reveal, the performing techniques of El Teatro and the BRT were quite distinct and reflective of the groups' differing approaches to social protest performance. And yet, because of the explicit social purposes of their performances, the signifying potential of the performer and performing were paramount for both El Teatro and the BRT.

In contrast to El Teatro and the BRT, American Method acting—in which the objective is to achieve a believable, realistic portrayal of the character and the role—discourages overt and explicit "indication," or what Blau terms "the conscious formation of behavior as a sign."[7] When an actor indicates, he or she uses external movements or gestures to convey an internal emotional or psychological state—such as pacing back and forth to indicate impatience. Within the American Method tradition such indication is considered bad acting. The social protest theater, on the other hand, encourages the performer to indicate. In the final moments of the performance of *Slave Ship* indicative gestures such as raised black fists pumping in the air, stomping black feet, black power handshakes exchanged with the black audience members, powerfully conveyed the rebellious sentiments of the black masses onstage to the audience and encouraged the audience to participate. The performer who portrayed Don Coyote in *Quinta Temporada* represented this prototypical farm labor contractor through external signifiers such as a coyote-like howl as he leaped onto the stage, a pronounced walk, rapid head movements, and leering eyes. There was no need for him to explore "inner monologues" or any reason for him to attempt to uncover the character's hidden psychological desires.

Within the signifying practice of performing in the social protest theater, indication, enunciating gestures, acted as "gestus" or as "heuristic devices."[8] They represented essential elements of character type, established mood, expressed social frustrations, and directed social action. If the activist/performer were effective, his or her performance was increasingly capable of affecting the thought, emotions, and participation of the audience. When a successful performer met with sympathetic spectators, the result was often dynamic. The separation between spectators and performers was eased, and they joined in cele-bratory protest.

The Activist/Performer and the Rituals of Rehearsal

In 1965 Baraka proudly declared of his new revolutionary theater, the Spirit House Movers: "We don't use Actors' Equity Members. We don't have anything to do with that; that's another world."[9] After the demise of BARTS in Harlem, Baraka moved back to his hometown of Newark, New Jersey: "We created a theater company, the Spirit House Movers, named after a group of brothers who frequented a tavern near a loft where we had our rehearsals, who actually moved furniture. We wanted to move the black masses."[10] The most important criteria for involvement with the Spirit House Movers was a strong commitment to the principles of the Black Arts Movement and a belief in the broader Black Power movement. "To the Spirit House came many of the artists and musicians, directors and performers, writers and poets, who had developed the Black Arts in New York City and some from local envi-rons."[11] As the renown of Baraka and the Spirit House spread to urban areas throughout the country, young socially committed artisans came from all over, including the South, and even California, to join the Spirit House Movers.[12] By 1969 the company consisted of ten members, seven men and three women.[13] Baraka served as the artistic and spiritual director. Under Baraka's leadership the Spirit House Movers rehearsed and developed a core of social protest works to be performed in reper-tory. These included *Black Mass* and *Slave Ship* by Baraka and *The Prayer Meeting* by Ben Caldwell.

In 1965 Valdez created a core performing troupe of five members. All were farmworkers active in the UFWOC strike movement. The per-formers' experience in the fields, he believed, helped them to commu-nicate and to identify with their farmworker audience: "Our most important aim is to reach the farmworker. All the actors are farmwork-ers, and our single topic is the Huelga."[14] Although he frequently lost rehearsal time to the strike effort, in 1967 Valdez stated: "We shouldn't be judged as a theater. We're really part of a cause."[15] The activist/per-formers represented identifiable voices of protest. When the actual victims of and combatants in the current social crisis functioned as performers, they potentially exploited what semiotician Keir Elam referred to as "iconic identity."[16] While they denoted stage characters, they still represented themselves.

The development of the early *actos* of El Teatro incorporated the actual strike and farm labor experiences of its farmworker/performers. El Teatro created the *actos* through an improvisational structure that emphasized the collective effort of the performing troupe as a whole. According to Valdez, "Starting from scratch with a real-life incident, character or idea everybody in the Teatro contributes to the development of an *acto*."[17] Valdez would provide the performers with an outline that served as a basis for group improvisational creation.[18] Felix Alvarez, a former member of El Teatro, described El Teatro's collective creative and rehearsal process:

> We took basic themes and ideas and formulated visual concepts from them. Say the concept was liberator turning oppressor . . . we would ask for a visual concept of that, a physical representation . . . in other words, show it to me.[19]

Through focused improvisations they translated ideological concepts and social and political issues into visual actions and symbols. The process of improvisational creation in rehearsal enabled the farmworker/performers to insert themselves, their experiences, into the action of the *acto*. Valdez proclaimed that, because El Teatro's improvisational, collective playwriting foregrounded the community and the actual experiences of the farmworker/performers, "the major emphasis in the acto [was] the social vision as opposed to the individual artist or playwright's vision. . . . The reality represented in an acto [was] a social reality."[20] The collective process served to direct the performers further toward the signifying ends of El Teatro. The performers' commitment to the group and its principles was informed and reaffirmed by the collective creative process.

Not only were the *actos* created through collective improvisation, but they were also performed without a set script. This encouraged the interpolation of new improvisations at each performance. In her book *Yoruba Ritual,* Margaret Thompson Drewal discusses how improvisations in Yoruba rituals allowed for structural alterations due to the "assessments of the moment."[21] Similarly, the improvisational nature of El Teatro's performances enabled the farmworker/performers to adjust their performances to the specific social context and the occurrences of that particular day in the field. This open, improvisational performance style compelled the performers to remain alert and flexible so that they could adapt to momentary changes in the flow of the improvisation. The performer could not focus on internalizing the character and the character's motivations, but, rather, he or she needed to concentrate on the external presentation of the action and its social meanings. In order to perform spontaneous, socially relevant improvisations, the farmworker/performers had to be aware of and sensitive to the pressing political and economic concerns of their audiences.

The performance of the Spirit House Movers also required the troupe to focus on the external presentation and the social value of its art. Performances often occurred in the context of black protest rallies or events. At these gatherings Baraka would deliver a speech, after which the Spirit House Movers would stage one or more plays. During the protest rally the Spirit House Movers performed a variety of pre- and postperformance duties—introducing Baraka and the performance, lecturing, reading poetry, handing out literature, leading the spectators in revolutionary chants and cheers. Their various roles as mediating agents required that they remain cognizant of the overall revolutionary cause and the significance of the performance in its broader social context.

The importance placed on the greater social awareness of Spirit House's activist/performers and El Teatro's farmworker/performers directly correlates with the social consciousness maintained by the priest/performer or officiant in the performance of a ritual. Turner notes that, in "rituals of affliction," "ritual officiants often enact the roles of gods, cultural heroes, ancestors, or demons as described in cultural myths."[22] Fierce spiritual commitment and emotional investment mark these enactments. Yet the ritual officiants remain focused on the purposes for and consequences of their actions. They perform these rituals to exorcise afflicting spirits. By mastering and manipulating symbols through ritual action, the ritual performer wields authority and the power to transform conventional hierarchies.[23] Similarly, the activist/performer or farmworker/performer—by effectively negotiating the rhythms, symbols, and action of performance—asserted the power to transform not only the theatrical illusion but outside social interaction as well.

Fundamental to the ritual officiant's committed performance was a perception of his or her actions as critical to the collective good of the gathered community. Situated within the urgencies and the ongoing social dramas of the 1960s and 1970s, El Teatro and the BRT wanted their social protest performers to recognize the social import of their actions and encouraged them to perceive of themselves as committed social artisans. Discussing the unique position of black activist/performers in the 1960s and the 1970s, Gilbert Moses argues:

> To do something significant at the time was important. Here was an opportunity to speak to the times, to fashion our own messages and to create our own plays. Theater offered them [the performers] the possibility to be artists and to be black people. Being an activist was exercising the highest form of art.[24]

Moses suggests that, within the atmosphere of urgency, socially conscious art held an exalted status. Moses points to the fusion of arts and activism within the ideology and practices of social protest theater. By conflating art and activism, not only did the social protest performance serve social ends, but the performers' conception of themselves as activists propelled and inflated the value of their art. The performers' sense of the political, social, and cultural significance of their work kept the actors from being absorbed by the role, consumed by their identification with the characters. Moreover, the performers' awareness of the social import of the performance foregrounded its political function and prevented it from becoming aestheticized as mere diversionary entertainment.

To inculcate further the activist/performers' social awareness and to increase their collective sensibility, Baraka and the Spirit House Movers created a "Unity Prayer" that expressed their spiritual, cultural, and political unity. The Spirit House Movers recited the "Unity Prayer" before rehearsals and performances:

> The essence of Black People is unity, the essence of the Spirit House Movers will be unity. Unity of Mind, Body and Spirit. Unity of all things (God). Responsible for each other, All for One,

One for All, We will not act unless for all. We are all parts of one
another.[25]

The rhetoric of this prayer implied that, for black people, unity was an
essential, endemic racial characteristic. To more contemporary sensibilities the homogenized, organicized view of black people expressed in
this prayer is extremely romantic and unrealistic. Yet promoting an
essential cultural identity, black cultural pride and unity were significant strategies in Baraka and the BRT's performer training. The absolutism of the "Unity Prayer" reaffirmed for the Movers that their art did
not simply serve themselves but was to benefit "all" black people. The
recitation of the "Unity Prayer" was a private ritual ceremony that the
Spirit House Movers engaged in and that served a cohesive and revi-
talizing function for the performers. It acted as a symbolic mediation
uniting the Movers with an idealized black community and the cause of
black liberation. Chanting the prayer reinforced the group's solidarity.
    In addition to the prayer, classes and other activities that the
Movers participated in at Spirit House informed their understanding of
black identity and their belief in the need for black social activism.
Spirit House taught classes in black arts, African-based culture, history,
and religion. Study groups examined important revolutionary works
such as *The Wretched of the Earth* by Frantz Fanon and *Quotations from
Chairman Mao Tse-tung*, from a decidedly black nationalist perspective.
These readings connected Spirit House and the black nationalist movement in the United States to a radical chain of revolutionary struggles
against colonial oppression emerging in the Third World. The educational, spiritual, and theatrical practice at Spirit House also indoctri-
nated the repertory company in a secular/spiritual ideology of black
cultural nationalism. On a fundamental level these activities instilled
communality. They reinforced the Movers' collectivity as a community
of interest. The Movers united around a shared political ideology as
well as a shared vision of effecting change through the social protest
theater.
    For El Teatro the uniting principle and communal activity was La
Huelga. The Spirit House Movers and the Black nationalist movement
did not have such a central unifying event nor a unifying site, such as
Delano. As a result, the Spirit House Movers relied more heavily than
El Teatro did at first on such ritualistic activities as the communal

recitation of the "Unity Prayer" to generate and reinforce collective commitment and social significance. With El Teatro's farmworker/performers, on the other hand, participation on the picket lines, attendance at strike meetings and rallies, worship at the regular services held by the shrine erected in the back of César Chávez's truck, all reaffirmed the collective consciousness of El Teatro's spiritual/political mission. The farmworker/performers of El Teatro recognized that the social significance of their theatrical activities was clearly and directly connected to their participation in La Huelga.

As the troupe moved away from the immediacy of the strike, in Delano, to Del Rey in 1967 then to Fresno in 1969 and, finally, in 1971, to their current home in San Juan Bautista, Valdez instituted communal practices and a doctrine of spiritual faith rooted in the Mayan and Aztec origins of Chicano culture. In 1971 Valdez wrote his spiritual manifesto, *Pensamiento Serpentino*. The foundation of *Pensamiento Serpentino* is the Mayan affirmation "in lach'ech," or "you are my other self."[26] Through his reclamation of this Mayan dictum Valdez proclaimed the essential unity of El Teatro members and of all humanity.[27] In addition, Valdez argued in *Pensamiento Serpentino* that Chicanos needed to "Mexicanize" themselves and perceive themselves as "Neo-Mayans," because "los Mayas really had it together. . . . Their communal life was not based on intellectual agreement/it was based on a vision of/los cosmos/porque el hombre pertenecía/a las estrellas [the cosmos/because man belongs to the stars]."[28] The philosophical platform presented in this poetic essay became the basis for El Teatro's spiritual and aesthetic practice. Spiritual ceremonies, based on Mayan rituals, initiated the performers in Valdez's neo-Mayan religious ideology. Phil Esparza, the current managing director of El Teatro, admitted that, initially, he and the other performers were apprehensive when Valdez asked them to engage in these ritual practices.[29] Soon, however, through the rehearsal process and preproduction activities, the members came to understand and accept this new spiritual orientation.

Richard Schechner has theorized that "the essential ritual action of theater takes place during rehearsals."[30] Through the "rituals" of rehearsal El Teatro members, and the Spirit House Movers, increased their spiritual faith and united around common aesthetic and ethical ideals. Their theatrical exercises and sociopolitical activities helped to build the performer group into a community of shared experience. Jean

Marie Pradier, in an article entitled "Towards a Biological Theory of Body in Performance," writes:

> the strong ties which characterize interpersonal communication among groups united by a common aesthetic or ethical ideal is greatly determined by intensive emotional processes, linked by aesthetic activity as well as personal involvement.[31]

Both El Teatro and the BRT exhibited the strong interpersonal communication that Pradier describes. The intragroup unity potentially translated into cohesive, committed ensemble performances. Consequently, these "rehearsal rituals," study groups, and classes should not be perceived as tangential to, but rather as critical components of, social protest performer training. These activities placed collective commitment and social activism in the foreground. The performers were to understand the signifying intentions of the performance and to use their own cultural awareness in communicating cultural consciousness to their audience.

The rehearsal process for Moses's 1969 production of *Slave Ship* at the Chelsea Theater Center also included rehearsal rituals of cultural and sociopolitical indoctrination. And yet, unlike either the original El Teatro performers or the Spirit House Movers, the performers in *Slave Ship* were professional actors cast through an audition process.[32] The level of social commitment varied among the cast members. Given the theatrical background of his cast, Moses, himself an experienced professional, could have chosen to draw principally on the performers' professional experience and focus his rehearsal process solely on conventional performance techniques such as blocking, movement, and motivation. Yet Moses believed that, in order to communicate revolutionary fervor to their audiences effectively, the performers needed a strong foundation in black consciousness. Through the rehearsal process he encouraged the performers' commitment to and knowledge of black cultural nationalism. At the initial rehearsals Moses had the cast read and study African and African American history and Yoruba language and culture. They also studied and discussed current philosophies of Black Power. They developed a greater awareness of the social context for and political objectives of their performances.

It would be naive, however, to assume that the entire *Slave Ship* cast became politicized through the rituals of rehearsal. Still, by compelling the actors to engage in consciousness-raising activities, by emphasizing the importance of activism and of communing with the audience, the rehearsal process for *Slave Ship* reoriented the professional actors' thinking about the performance and their roles within it. Moses's focus on the signifying intention of the performance required that the professional actors employ different skills and even conceive of themselves differently. Moses's rehearsal process encouraged them to perceive of themselves as socially committed black artisans and to recognize "being an activist" as "exercising the highest form of art." Through his rehearsal process he observed that the cast became committed to "communing with the audience; to coming together and healing; to raising awareness to a new level."[33] Moses considered the ensemble bonding of the performers in rehearsal an important precursor to the desired communion of the performers with the audience.

Yet attributing the achievements of the performance of *Slave Ship* solely to the cast's development of a greater political consciousness is also overly simplistic and diminishes the aesthetic achievement of Moses and his cast. The rehearsals as well as the performances of *Slave Ship* required the creativity, improvisational skills, and adaptability of the performers. Despite their recent indoctrination into the black liberation cause, they still needed a level of artistic skill and technical proficiency in order to effect Moses's directorial concept and to engage the audience.

As part of his overall aesthetic concept, Moses employed the techniques of experimentalists Jerzy Grotowski, Richard Schechner, and Antonin Artaud in his rehearsal process. In so doing, he expanded and even subverted the original objectives of these experimental performance theories. While Grotowski imagined his theater as a therapeutic experience and Artaud expected his bombardment of violent, cruel images to purge the audience's propensity for violence, Moses intended to arouse his audience's militancy and direct them to take action in their own lives.[34] His appropriation of the theories and practices of Grotowski, Schechner, and Artaud furthered the performers' articulation of the signifying intentions of the performance. The experimental performance techniques used by Moses worked in concert with the educative training in black nationalism and social activism to support his subversive, oppositional agenda.

Valdez notes that, in the environment of urgency, of Delano, El Teatro had little time or opportunity to think in terms of actor training or stage techniques but simply in terms of "can you [the actor] do this, can you convey the message and perform the actions of the acto?"[35] Yet at that time he still was very much concerned with the artistic quality of the *actos* and the skills of his performers. With El Teatro's relocation to Del Rey in 1967 and then to Fresno in 1969, Valdez began a program of performer training. He instituted a program of "Ten Exercises" aimed at improving performing techniques.[36] Valdez and El Teatro developed and adapted their exercises from a variety of sources, including the San Francisco Mime Troupe and the Mexican *carpa* tradition.[37] In performer training El Teatro members discovered body movements, positions, and gestures to support the physical humor and social messages of the text. Unlike the work of Moses on *Slave Ship*, El Teatro's exercises focused on refining the performers' presentational skills, flexibility, and comic sensibilities. The distinctions in performer training underscore the profound difference in performance style between *Slave Ship* and BRT productions and the *actos* of El Teatro. Moses had his actors work from the inside out, concentrating on emotional commitment and psychological intensity. Valdez reversed this process. His work initially involved the physical, the gestural, the presentational, as means to reflect and represent the political and psychological conditions of Chicanos. Still, the training methodology of Valdez, like that of Moses, educated the performers in understanding and articulating performing as a signifying practice.

As El Teatro's performers became more proficient, the style of performance and performance values evolved. According to John Harrop and Jorge Huerta, "the early reliance upon signs hung around the performers' necks gave way to more use of masks and the actors' own physicality."[38] Even as the signs around the performers' necks disappeared and the performers became more technically skilled, the troupe retained its focus on the social purposes of its art. The training practices of El Teatro in the late 1960s and early 1970s still expected and encouraged performers to perceive of themselves as committed social activists.[39]

Since the art of acting depends on artifice, it would seem that social commitment or a perception of authentic activism should not be such critical factors. A talented actor should be able to portray a striking

farmworker or a militant black activist effectively without the prereq-
uisite commitment to the cause of social change. The value of a talented
performer in the theater is undeniable. Valdez attributes a great deal of
the *actos'* effective audience engagement to the comic genius and
improvisational ingenuity of Felipe Cantu as the "Everyman" Farmworker character.[40] Correspondingly, the fact that Moses auditioned
and selected the performers for *Slave Ship* suggests that he was concerned not only with political commitment but also with the talent and
performance skills of the professional actors whom he cast. Therefore,
one might ask whether the success of Moses's production of *Slave Ship*
or the early performances of El Teatro's *actos* could not simply be attributed to the acting abilities of the performers regardless of their social
commitment, their authenticity, or their perception of themselves as
activists.

Evaluating authenticity versus talent onstage is subjective at best
and highly debatable at worst. While I will discuss more about the politics of authenticity later in this chapter, I do not want to belabor this
argument here. Instead, I want to suggest that the actual authenticity or
social commitment of the social protest performer was not as crucial to
the social efficacy of the production as the audience's *perception* of the
actors' authenticity. Efficacy depends on audience reception and
response. And for *certain* audiences the perception of authenticity held
considerable commercial, emotional, and political currency.

For certain audiences the perception of authenticity worked to
strip away conventional theatrical illusion and foreground the relationship of the staged events to social conditions. Throughout the performance these spectators remained acutely aware that they were watch-
ing real farmworkers or real black activists onstage. Ralph Gleason
wrote of an El Teatro performance at the Committee Theater in San
Francisco on 4 May 1966:

> The most simplistic representation of growers and scabs and strik-
> ers has a kind of reality when the Teatro does it in the actos as they
> call their skits, that the professional theater companies cannot get.
> The reason is simple. It is all too real to the participants and the
> audience when it sees these men on stage and knows without
> thinking about it that they come from the picket line where they
> faced the violence and the terror they are talking about.[41]

For Gleason and others recognizing the authenticity of the activist/per-formers heightened their emotional empathy as well as the validity of the social protest performers' message: it was "all too real." The impact of this perceived "realness" made sympathetic audiences more willing to forgive or even ignore the lack of technical polish demonstrated by performers. For certain spectators this realness increased the signifying potential of the performer as well as the urgency and relevance of the performance's social messages.

The perception of authenticity helped sympathetic spectators to identify the performer as his own persona while, at the same time, rec-ognizing the performer as a character in the play or *acto*. Critics such as Jorge Huerta have associated the audience's recognition of the duality of El Teatro's farmworker/performer with the effect Brecht demanded from his epic style of acting.[42] In the Brechtian theater the actor func-tioned not only as the character but as a commentator on the actions of that character. Brecht intended for the intrusion of the actor-as-com-mentator to disrupt the audience's passive reception of the character and to compel the audience to engage intellectually with the socioeco-nomic issues reflected in the performance. Brecht's epic style of acting, while it encouraged the actor to judge the character, also compelled the audience to view the character as a social construct and to evaluate the social, political, and economic circumstances that created the character. In the work of El Teatro, as in the Brechtian epic theater, the audience's perception of the performer's dual identity prevented the performer from being subsumed into the role. The farmworker/performer, like the Brechtian actor, could then operate as a social commentator. The placards that Valdez hung around the necks of the El Teatro perform-ers served as Brechtian devices; they interrupted the theatrical illusion and forced the spectators to recognize the characters as socially con-structed archetypes. Valdez remarked, "In a Mexican way we have dis-covered what Brecht is all about."[43]

The audience's recognition of the duality of the farmworker/per-formers, however, often resulted in emotional empathy rather than the intellectual engagement and dialectical analysis that Brecht desired from his epic theater audience. Brecht's actors asked the spectators to undertake an intellectual synthesis by pointing out the inherent contra-dictions within the performance and the actions of the characters. The spectators' recognition of the duality of Valdez's farmworker/performers, or the BRT's black activist/performers, potentially heightened their social awareness and political consciousness by underscoring the correlation between the situation demonstrated by the performance and the performers' daily reality. Rather than Brechtian, I consider the impact of the audience's recognition of the activist/performers' duality to be ritualistic. As a result of this recognition, the symbolic meaning, the signifying intention of the performer, and the performative action could come increasingly to the foreground.

Audience Composition, *Communitas*, and the Perception of Authenticity

I have used the qualifiers *certain* and *sympathetic* because not all spectators, not even all the Chicano spectators who witnessed El Teatro nor all the black spectators who attended performances of the BRT, responded to the authenticity of the performers. El Teatro and BRT audiences based their perception of authenticity on a variety of factors, including their actual knowledge of the pre- and postproduction activities of the El Teatro and BRT troupe members. An audience's perception of authenticity as well as its participation in the social protest performance also depended upon the composition, the psychological and emotional disposition, and the cultural background of that audience. All of these elements contributed to the spectators' interpretation of the signs and symbols of the performance text. The relationship between the spectators' actual experience and the onstage action of the social protest play helped to determine how spectators read, responded to, and participated in the performance.

To illustrate this point I will examine the audiences for two social protest touring productions: the southern tour of *Slave Ship*, staged by Gilbert Moses and the Free Southern Theater in 1970, and the performances of El Teatro, during the UFWOC march from Delano to Sacramento in March and April 1966. I have selected the southern touring production of *Slave Ship* and the nightly El Teatro performances along the UFWOC march route because they both frequently evidenced the dynamic potential of audience participation at social protest performances. These tours featured "nontraditional" theater audiences that came to the social protest performances unburdened by Western theatrical codes of behavior. In fact, one could argue that they were not

theater audiences at all but were, instead, drawn to the evocative interplay of art, culture, politics, and spirituality. The performance event for
them was more than entertainment. Accordingly, they brought different cultural experiences and sociopolitical expectations to bear on their
decoding of messages in the social protest theater.

Most of the poor rural black spectators for the southern tour of
Slave Ship had little previous experience with the theater. Instead, they
came to the performances steeped in the rituals and traditions of the
black church, in which participation was not only encouraged but
expected. In fact, the cultural traditions of both blacks and Chicanos
encouraged active audience interaction with the performance. Thomas
Pawley, in a significant article on black theater audiences, details a history of black participatory response in the theater and relates this theatrical behavior to the tradition of call and response in the black
church.[44] Other scholars have traced this participatory behavior back to
African ritual practices. In either case the vocal and physical responsiveness of the black audience suggests a self-conscious willingness to
engage more fully in the performance and a responsibility on the part
of the audience to confirm what is happening. The black spectators'
involvement provided the performers or church minister with immediate feedback on the aesthetic effectiveness and the cultural, political,
social, and spiritual relevance.

Similarly, El Teatro's audiences of Chicano farmworkers shared a
cultural heritage of participatory art. Mexican comic burlesque performances, which El Teatro used as a source for the humor of its *actos*,
were bawdy and boisterous events that featured physical humor and
spontaneous responses from the audience. In addition to their familiarity with Mexican comedy, the Chicano farmworker audiences of El
Teatro most likely knew or had participated in the collective singing of
corridos. Corridos, or Mexican folk ballads, generally contain verses or
refrains in which the audience joins in with the performers. Purposefully, El Teatro began their performances with *corridos*—some written
specifically for El Teatro by troupe members Augustin Lira and Danny
Valdez—and invited their audiences to participate. El Teatro also took
popular songs with familiar tunes and changed the lyrics to ones that
supported the union and the strike. "Se Va el Caimal [There Goes the
Crocodile]" became "El Picket Sign."[45]

In Chicano culture, as in black culture, history and folklore have traditionally been transmitted orally. For Chicanos the telling of *cuentos*, folktales, has remained an oral and participatory art. The Chicano farmworker spectators brought these cultural references with them to the theater. Like the black rural audiences for *Slave Ship*, they were generally inexperienced with and little restricted by conventional, Western theatrical expectations and rules of audience behavior. As a result of their cultural experiences, these spectators transformed the conventional Western relationship between audience and stage. They made the exchange between audience and stage a more interactive process.

In addition to their cultural background the southern blacks and Chicano farmworkers who came to *Slave Ship* and the *actos* brought with them recent and firsthand knowledge of discrimination and racism, economic and political struggle. The black southern audiences for *Slave Ship* had direct, personal knowledge of black unrest, resistance, and rebellion. Certainly, not all or even the majority of the spectators for the Free Southern Theater's production of *Slave Ship* were black revolutionaries or social activists. They were, on the whole, working people, farmers and sharecroppers, with an awareness of their own subservient position within a system of economic and cultural oppression. Still, they had been affected by the urgency of the black liberation struggle going on around them. Many had witnessed the events and aftermath of the Mississippi Freedom Summer of 1966, the civil rights marches, sit-ins, boycotts, and freedom rides. Most had watched the rise of black political power and voter registration throughout the South and had seen the spread, locally and nationally, of Black Power and black nationalistic ideologies, including the radicalization of Stokely Carmichael and the Student Nonviolent Coordinating Committee (SNCC). The tumult and upheaval of the black liberation struggle influenced their lives outside of the social protest theater, their reception of the social protest performance, and even their decision to attend the performance. These were audiences already sympathetic to the messages they would hear disseminated in *Slave Ship*.

While not ethnically homogeneous, the participants in the UFWOC march did include many who could be classified as social activists. Their decision to join and willingness to participate in the twenty-five-day march from Delano to the state capital, Sacramento, testified to their commitment. In addition to a core group of union leaders and strike organizers, the marchers came to include Chicano student activists from throughout the state, liberal union sympathizers, and migrant workers from local towns, who had participated in that day's march or who inhabited that particular community. As the number of marchers increased, the marchers' vision of themselves as social agents and the march as a significant political and cultural event grew as well. The marchers were conscious of the union's goals and the unjust treatment of itinerant farmworkers. They watched the nightly performances of El Teatro already sensitized to the need for active support of La Huelga.

Even before the marchers along the UFWOC march route and the black rural southern spectators for *Slave Ship* entered into their respective theatrical spaces, they composed ideological and cultural communities of interest. They shared common bonds around notions either of culture, or ethnicity, or social and political struggle. In addition to their ideological orientation, the collective activity of marching each day in the hot sun, along with the El Teatro performers, brought the marchers together as a community. They cooperated toward a short-term goal, the completion of the march, and a long-term goal, victory for the UFWOC in its struggle with the major grape growers for a union contract. The black audiences for *Slave Ship* represented a community not simply because of their racial homogeneity but because of the geographical identification, their rural orientation and experiences, that imbued them with a particular set of values and norms of everyday life. Community, as Anthony Cohen articulates, is "largely a mental construct, whose 'objective' manifestations in locality or ethnicity give it credibility. It is highly symbolized, with the consequence that its members can invest it with their selves."[46] The symbolic construction of communities outside the theater influenced the willingness of these audiences to commune with the social protest performers and performance once inside the theater. The integrity of these ideological and cultural communities affected the spectators' responsiveness to and decoding of the performances.

Victor Turner argues that, the more a group consciously identified itself as a group or community, the more likely *communitas* would be manifested in the social interaction of that group. The term *communitas*, appropriated from the ritual theories of Turner, refers to a form of social interrelatedness and interconnectedness. The feeling of *communi-*

tas is unstructured, spontaneous, and immediate. It is ephemeral and can seldom be sustained for long. When people experience *communitas* they discover "a flash of mutual understanding," profound illumination, and "intersubjective communication." Turner writes that "individuals who interact with one another in the mode of spontaneous communitas become totally absorbed into one synchronized fluid event." He acknowledges that there is something "magical" about the power of *communitas*.[47] When *communitas* was present, the performers and spectators of El Teatro and the BRT experienced a feeling of wholeness, optimism, and possibility.[48]

The audience's perception of authenticity was affected by, and in turn affected, the development of *communitas*. For sympathetic audiences—such as those along the UFWOC march route and the southern tour of *Slave Ship*—the perception of the performers as authentic activists facilitated what Baz Kershaw refers to in *The Politics of Performance* as "the incorporation of the company [the activist/performers] into the community [the gathered spectators]."[49] By inviting the company of performers into their community, as Kershaw suggests, the spectators formed a new community of interest in the theater, and *communitas* was possible. The spectators' ideological understanding of their own oppression potentially fused with their cultural identification with the "authentic" performers. The emergence of *communitas* fueled the spiritual, ritualistic communion of spectators and performers. The union of spectators and performers around issues of ideology, culture, the perceptions of authenticity and activism, helped to legitimize and confirm the rhetoric of the performance and the goals of El Teatro and the BRT.

The Politics of Authenticity

While the advocacy of particular perceptions and positions of authenticity by both El Teatro and the BRT augmented their promotion of social activism and ethnic unity, at times it also fostered restrictive and essentialist covenants and even produced factionalism. By endorsing certain strategies and ideologies of Chicano and black authenticity, El Teatro and the BRT dismissed and disregarded others. Perceptions of authenticity necessarily exclude as they include. In fact, both El Teatro and the BRT would incur ideological opposition from other Chicano and black activist groups as a result of this inclusionary/exclusionary dialectic of authenticity.

In the urgency arising from the struggle for Black Power of the 1960s and 1970s, black groups and individuals jockeyed, postured, and positioned themselves as being more authentic or even "blacker" than others.[50] During this time the Black Panther Party engaged in a vehement battle with Baraka and Ron Karenga, the leading exponents of black cultural nationalism, over nationalist ideologies and perceptions of authenticity. The Black Panthers ridiculed and rejected the politics of Baraka and his Spirit House. They objected to Baraka's culturally based approach to black revolution and conceived of it as politically naive. As a consequence, editorials in the *Black Panther Paper* sarcastically labeled Baraka's philosophy "pork chop nationalism." The politics of Baraka and Karenga contrasted decisively on a number of fronts with those of Eldridge Cleaver and the Black Panthers. The conflict escalated in 1967, when members of Karenga's US organization killed two Black Panthers during an armed shootout near the University of California, Los Angeles campus. Immediately after the UCLA shooting Baraka and the Spirit House Movers received a letter from the Jersey City branch of the Black Panthers that threatened to "rub them out."[51] Clearly, the Black Panthers' perception of black activist authenticity explicitly excluded the practices of Baraka and the BRT. Knowledge of the differing perspectives on authenticity by Baraka and the Panthers reinforces Paul Gilroy's comment that "none of us enjoys a monopoly on black authenticity."[52] Definitions of authenticity are situational and dependent upon the perceptions of those who invoke them.

In the 1970s, as Valdez and El Teatro moved away from the political pragmatism of the *acto* to a more religious and mystical style of theater, they also encountered opposition and resistance from other Chicano activists over issues of activism and authenticity. Radical factions within El Teatro Nacional de Aztlán (TENAZ), a national network of Chicano teatros formed in 1971, objected to Valdez's decision to investigate the spiritual Mayan and Aztec roots of Chicano culture through the theater. Valdez believed that his new theatrical project was fundamental to understanding Chicano identity and authenticity. Others, including the Argentinean theater activist and author of *Theater of the Oppressed*, August Boal, disagreed. They maintained that El Teatro's new spiritualism neglected the "real" issues of employment, poverty, and discrimination confronting Chicanos. Eventually, this tension and inter-Teatro factionalism led Valdez to withdraw El Teatro's membership in TENAZ, an organization he had originally helped to found. The politics of authenticity practiced by TENAZ came to exclude El Teatro. At times the promotion of authenticity restricted rather than encouraged diverse forms of ethnic cultural expression.[53]

Despite its restrictiveness, the advocacy of authenticity remained an important element within the policies and practices of El Teatro and the BRT in the period 1965 to 1971. Moreover, it is still a powerful rhetorical tool within contemporary politics of identity and representation. Claims of authenticity structure privileged contrasts separating the authentic from the inauthentic. Such privileged contrasts can valorize the voice, presence, and subjectivity of the previously silent and disenfranchised. Consequently, new political subjects repeatedly turn to assertions of authenticity to generate consensus and even political action.

Within the contemporary theater demands for authenticity still wield power because of their continued impact on the politics of casting, staging, and audience identification. Jill Dolan, in her recent book *Presence and Desire*, challenges whether a heterosexual actress is capable of effectively performing a lesbian character before a lesbian audience.[54] Dolan's consideration of lesbian authenticity in *Presence and Desire* reasserts the need for marginalized groups to control their own representations and to see themselves accurately portrayed. Concerned with maintaining the cultural sensibilities and artistic integrity of his work, celebrated contemporary black playwright August Wilson has refused to allow the filming of his 1986 Pulitzer Prize–winning play, *Fences*, to go forward without a black director.[55] In 1992 Valdez again found himself entangled by issues of authenticity over his casting of Italian-American actress Laura San Giacomo as the famous artist Frida Kahlo, in his proposed film "Frida and Diego." Latina actresses in Los Angeles picketed Valdez and the production demanding that a Latina be auditioned and cast in the role of Kahlo.[56] Valdez countered with an alternative perspective on authenticity in casting. Kahlo, Valdez argued, was not only Latina but a product of mixed birth. While her mother was Mexican, her father was a German Jew. As a consequence, he was justified in casting a non-Latina in the role.[57] Stung by the criticism, Valdez first canceled the project indefinitely. Then in 1993 he determined to mount a reimagined—and still unproduced—version of the project entitled "The Two Fridas" and featuring San Giacomo as well as a Mexican actress, Ofelia Medina, as Kahlo. All these contemporary examples evidence the continued utility and power of authenticity within spheres of representation. Proclamations of authenticity in the 1960s and 1970s were then as they are now: dangerous but desirous strategies of privilege and self-determination implemented and manipulated within debates of culture and politics.

Audience Participation and Preaching to the Converted

Certainly, perceptions of authenticity influenced the reception of the audiences along the UFWOC march route to Sacramento as well as those for the touring production of *Slave Ship*. These audiences consisted of self-selective and largely homogeneous constituencies. The performances before these audiences could be said to represent what Marco De Marinis terms "closed performances" that required a "model spectator."[58] De Marinis's term *closed performances* specifically refers to marginalized, alternative productions that appeal to specific interest groups and particular audiences away from the more commercial mainstream. De Marinis would classify performances within the commercial mainstream or from the Western culture's classical theatrical canon as "open." And yet, while the productions of the American commercial mainstream—on and off Broadway and in regional theaters across the country—operate under the premise of accessibility to a wide audience, they still require specialized knowledge and processes of indoctrination in order for audiences to accept their premises. They are not truly open. These productions have a long history of being closed to the interests and perspectives of underrepresented groups. At the time that El Teatro and the BRT emerged in the mid-1960s, the American mainstream theater continued, overtly and covertly, culturally and economically, to exclude Chicanos and blacks from participating in its productions. The creation of theater by, for, and about Chicanos and blacks by El Teatro and the BRT was in part a response to their lack of access to closed mainstream performances.

Despite its decidedly Western bias, De Marinis's theory on closed performances and model spectators is useful to this discussion of the social protest performance audience. For, as De Marinis cautions, "If ... a closed performance is performed for a spectator far removed from its model spectator, then things will be different."[59] Accordingly, the reception and conception of the meanings of El Teatro's and the BRT's productions changed when they were performed before spectators who were outside of their respective "model" constituencies. Valdez and El Teatro mixed Spanish and English as well as *calo*, Chicano slang, in the dialogue of the *actos* to appeal particularly to Chicano audiences and to reflect the real speech patterns of their model Chicano farmworker spectators. The barriers of language, their discomfort with English, was another factor in many campesinos' feelings of exclusion from the American mainstream culture and of inclusion within the bilingual productions of El Teatro.

Although the original production of *Slave Ship* at the Chelsea Theater Center was attended by more than just black spectators, Moses and Baraka directed the production at arousing and inciting black participation. Wole Söyinka recounted the impressions of a white critic who felt isolated and rejected by the cast of *Slave Ship*, who, at the end of the play, only shook hands with the black audience members:

> It was a shock to him [the white critic] to find literally that the play, and his ordeal, was not over, that he had to experience yet another level of his unsuspected rejection. He, in spite of these feelings of identification which had been fed into him from the universality of suffering, found that his emotive identification existed only for him and was not necessarily reciprocal in itself with the essential truths of the evening.[60]

Appealing to the "universality of suffering" was not an objective of social protest theater. Social protest performances asserted self-determination and pride in one's own class or group. El Teatro's and the BRT's advocacy of closed performances and closed audiences subverted and inverted the exclusion of Chicano and blacks from the dominant culture's theatrical performances and valorized their difference. The ability of their productions to form an emotional bond with the audience depended on the audiences' own social and political consciousness. Closed audiences of model spectators often represented, therefore, "an element in the co-production of the play's meaning."[61]

By tailoring their theaters to and for specific constituencies, El Teatro and the BRT were, at times, "preaching to the converted." Certain critics have denigrated the process of preaching to the converted for being detrimental and redundant.[62] They have faulted social protest performances for not reaching those audiences most in need of conversion. Yet it must be understood that the primary goal of the social protest performance was not conversion. This is not to suggest that conversion was impossible but, rather, that El Teatro and the BRT perceived a distinct purpose and advantage in addressing an audience of those already faithful to their cause. Situated within the urgent movement for social change, the immediate intention of their performances was to rededicate the spectators to the struggle. Both El Teatro and the BRT maintained that their loyal ethnic constituency should not be only the audience for the performance event but the critics as well. Valdez wrote that Chicano *teatro* "must be popular to no other critics except the pueblo itself."[63] In a similar vein Etheridge Knight remarked of the BRT that "the Black artist, in creating his own aesthetic, must be accountable for it only to Black people."[64] For the audience of the converted, the social protest performance reaffirmed the virtues of the revolutionary cause and heightened the audience's optimism by predicting revolutionary victory. In addition, the audience of the converted, who shared a sense of community, of values and beliefs, was more predisposed to respond collectively and to commune with the activist/performers as cocelebrants in the ritualistic social protest event. The oppositional strategies of El Teatro and the BRT attempted to reinforce and reproduce collective responses in the theater.

Herbert Blau and other theater scholars, however, have argued that the possibilities for achieving collective participation and communal ritualistic reception are inherently flawed. Blau maintains that the "participation mystique" is simply that, a mystique, since the response to any performance, in the end, is not participatory or communal but, rather, solitary: "This is the last blight on the participatory illusion: the enduring gravity of the theater is not a collective one but solitary."[65] The common critical perception is that, regardless of the manner in which the performance encourages communal response, each individual audience member interprets the performance's signs for him- or herself. Every spectator's readings must be different, reflective of his or her own individuality. Because of the primacy of individual experience, collective responses and readings are difficult, if not impossible, to achieve.

Expanding this critical rejection of communal response, Michael Vanden Heuvel maintains that the composition of a theater audience is profoundly different from that for a ritual and the possibility of transforming the former into the latter is extremely problematic:

> The inherent difficulties in forming the assembly into a congregation rather than an audience of spectators removed from the ritual action (a problem encountered by Peter Brook's performers as well during their polyglot performances in Africa 1980), in making performances efficacious instead of affective or merely entertaining, and in creating a reiterative context instead of an imitative one proved impossible to circumvent for groups as diverse as Schechner's Performance Group, El Teatro Campesino and the Bread and Puppet Theater.[66]

Yet, in grouping together the social protest theater El Teatro Campesino with the experimental Performance Group and Bread and Puppet theaters, Vanden Heuvel's critical analysis fails to consider the markedly different nature of the audiences for these theaters. The dynamics of creating a congregation do not merely depend on the activities of the performance group but also rely significantly on the values, beliefs, and cultural orientation that the spectators bring with them to the theater. The constituent audiences for El Teatro and the BRT contextualized the theatrical experience based on their own social and cultural experiences. They came to the theater predisposed to function as a congregation, orientated toward communal participation in the proceedings.

While white Americans are, by and large, acculturated to think of themselves as individuals, Chicanos and black Americans are more often conditioned by internal and external sociocultural factors to think of themselves as representative of their particular group. My intention here is not to essentialize processes of Chicano and black socialization nor to promote monolithic group identities. I do want to point out, however, the potential cultural differences that encourage Chicano and black collective reception. The dominant culture has classified Chicanos and blacks collectively as other, as outside the cultural norm. It has imposed negative group stereotypes and enduring group labels upon Chicanos and blacks that have often defined and delimited their existence in this society. Terms such as *wetback* and *illegal imigrant* negatively affect any and virtually every Chicano by inference and association. Due to the external forces of racism and discrimination as well as to the internal social and cultural insecurities of being a "minority," many Chicanos and blacks have been conditioned to believe that their individual actions or the public behavior of others from their ethnic group speak for the group and reflect on the "race" as a whole. Jill Nelson, in her memoir, *Volunteer Slavery*, notes how blacks have been socialized to believe in their own collective culpability: "when you're a Negro in America, it's usually not just you who's making the mistake, its y'all, the race, black folks in toto."[67]

Because blacks and Chicanos have faced persecution and repression simply because they were black or Chicano, they have, at times, needed to identify themselves collectively, to protect themselves through solidarity with the group in order to increase their chances of survival in a racist culture. In the 1960s and 1970s Chicano and black power and cultural nationalist movements valorized collective identities and cultural communality as a means to political empowerment. Collective action was believed to be critical to black and Chicano strategies of social and cultural rebellion. Accordingly, because of their cultural and political history and socialization as well as their knowledge of and involvement with the more immediate politics of black and Chicano power, blacks and Chicano audiences in the 1960s and 1970s were predisposed to adopt a group identity and to respond communally to the social protest performances of El Teatro and the BRT.

At one performance of *Slave Ship* in Baton Rouge, Louisiana, along the 1970 Free Southern Theater tour, an aroused audience, bolstered by the militant participatory action of the production, stood at the end of the performance ready to riot. If not for the fact that the doors of the theater remained bolted until the fervor had somewhat subsided, this audience would have carried through on its resolve.[68] At another performance of *Slave Ship*, in West Point, Mississippi, the entire audience rose to its feet and joined in with the actors, waving fists and chanting, "We gonna rise up!"[69]

Correspondingly, Valdez observed and absorbed the overwhelming response of audiences in towns along the march route to Sacramento in 1966 and declared that "the response of the audience in all these towns was a small triumph in the greater triumph of the NFW March."[70] Valdez maintained that the most successful performance on the pilgrimage to Sacramento occurred in Freeport, a small town nine miles outside of the state capital. The leaders of the march expected to meet with California governor Edmund Brown along the march route; at the last minute, however, the governor changed his schedule. Nevertheless, at the El Teatro performance in Freeport that night loudspeakers and sirens announced the governor's arrival at the rally. El Teatro company member Augustin Lira, sporting a huge paunch, stepped out of a car as the "Governor." During the course of Lira's performance the Governor changed from being an ally of the ranchers to being an ardent, Spanish-speaking supporter of La Huelga. As the shocked ranchers dragged Lira from the stage, the large audience laughed and cheered vigorously. The image of a pro-Huelga governor fostered a mood of festivity, *communitas,* and subversive celebration in which both spectators and performers participated. Such energized, participatory responses challenged theatrical conventions and reaffirmed the ritualistic potential of the social protest theatrical event.

When audiences stood and chanted at performances of *Slave Ship* in Baton Rouge and at the Governor's appearance in Freeport, it clearly constituted a collective, communal response. The participants united in celebratory protest. Such collective reactions did not dissipate nor negate the individual experience in the theater; rather, they served to connect the individual reaction to the wider community's experience in the theater and to the cultural and social developments outside of the theater.[71] As Kershaw argues, the collective impact of and response to a performance intensifies the individual spectator's experience as well as the performance's possible efficacy:

> For if a whole audience, or even a whole community responds in this way to the symbolism of a "possible world," then the potential of performance efficacy is multiplied by more than the audience number. To the extent that the audience is part of a community, then the networks of the community will change, however infinitesimally, in response to changes in the audience members.[72]

When the spectators understood the meaning of the play's events within their own experience and carried this meaning with them out of the theater, theatrical participation then had the opportunity to be transformed into social action. As testament to the communal participation in and social efficacy of the southern tour of *Slave Ship*, Moses observed that the numbers of black people participating in voter registration efforts dramatically increased in certain cities immediately following the performances of *Slave Ship*.[73] After viewing an El Teatro performance in Bakersfield, two Chicano migrant workers, who had previously worked as "scab" workers in Delano, disavowed their strikebreaking activities and pledged allegiance to the union strike effort.[74]

Audience Participation and Social Efficacy

Despite accounts of increased activity at voter registration drives in southern cities subsequent to performances of *Slave Ship* and of strikebreakers joining the union after viewing a performance of El Teatro, establishing a direct correlation between social action and the social protest performance is problematic. The social efficacy of social protest theater remains extremely difficult to prove. Rarely are posttheatrical events documented. Furthermore, attributing postperformance activism solely to theatrical attendance is impossible when a myriad of other social and psychological circumstances concurrently exist. Through reviews, firsthand accounts, and other qualitative and quantitative methodologies, however, the participatory responses of the spectators at a social protest performance can be observed and documented. These records of participation can provide significant insight into the efficacy of the ritualistic social protest performance. For audience participation, I contend, not only alters conventional exchanges between audience and stage but also testifies to the meaning of the play's action for the participant community.

Active participation in the social protest performance reconfigured the relationship between the spectator and the performance apparatus, positing the spectator in the subject position. Hence, the audience of marchers, in Freeport, recognized themselves, their struggle, their march, as the subject of the performance. They participated in the symbolic transformation of the Governor into Huelgista. Similarly, black spectators in Baton Rouge actively participated in *Slave Ship*'s symbolic overthrow of the White Voice. By participating, the spectators no longer functioned as passive audience members but as cocelebrants. As subjects, the spectators understood that the performance was not only for them but also about them and involving them. Subjectivity empowered and was empowered by active participation.

Writing about audience reception and Sri Lankan rituals, Ranjini Obeyesekere differentiates "participants" from "spectators" at a ritual event.[75] While spectators are interested in the entertainment, or "liminoid," aspects of performance, participants are those principally involved with the performance's efficacy and social meaning. Margaret Thompson Drewal, in her research on Yoruba ritual, observed how improvisational participation drew people into the ritual performance.[76] Spontaneous participation in the ritual event was transformative. It constructed new relationships and generated multiple discourses "always surging between harmony/disharmony, order/disorder, integration/opposition."[77] Similarly, participation in the ritualistic social protest performance also created new relationships and new discourses between audience members and performers. When the audience members participated, the social protest performance experienced a dynamic and immediate duality—wavering between harmony and disharmony, order and disorder, insurrection and reconciliation. The emotional, vociferous participation at the performances of *Slave Ship* in Baton Rouge, Louisiana, and West Point, Mississippi, evidenced this duality. The audience response demonstrated not "spectatorship" but "participation" and active involvement with the play's message. The audience's decision to participate can be perceived as both a practical and symbolic act of rebellion and audience participation, a critical indicator of social efficacy.

Some critics, however, have argued that a vociferous response in the theater dissipated potential social action outside of the theater. Following Aristotelian theory, these critics have interpreted the participation of spectators in the social protest performance as a cathartic release and not an indication of their active commitment. After viewing a performance of *Slave Ship* at the Chelsea Theater Center, critic Charles Reichenthal commented that he did not perceive a groundswell of black outrage and white fear in the theater:

Instead one recalls the emotional catharsis brought about. And that emotional purging happens to both black and white audience members. In a very real sense, this blood letting in "Slave Ship" backfires if the play is supposed to leave the black man filled with hate and the white man filled with anxiety. I found, oddly enough, that upon leaving the theater, there had been created a bond between white and black spectators that was strong and visible . . . . The theatrical catharsis had aided both to take clearer looks at their backgrounds and beliefs.[78]

Reichenthal interpreted the emotional outpouring from spectators as a purgation and release of emotion. He did not concur with Stefan Brecht that *Slave Ship* was a revolutionary call to arms for young black Americans.[79] As evidenced by other reviews and critical commentaries on the performance of *Slave Ship*, Reichenthal's perception was clearly a minority view. His discussion of the cathartic consequences of audience participation, however, directly correlates with repeated criticisms of social protest theater.

Morgan Himelstein, in his critique of the Workers' Theater Movement of the 1920s and 1930s, concurred with Reichenthal that an emotional participatory response in the theater was a cathartic response. Himelstein maintained that this cathartic response in the theater defused the potential for agitational action outside of the theater: "The emotional catharsis induced by the drama made the theater a less satisfactory weapon than the [Communist] Party theorists had imagined. Apparently they had never read Aristotle's *Poetics*."[80] The inability to link postperformance social action directly to interperformance participation leaves audience participation and its role in social protest performance open to speculation.

Augusto Boal, in his important work on revolutionary theater, *Theater of the Oppressed*, differentiates revolutionary theater and the participatory response it engenders from Aristotelian tragedy and its cathartic response.[81] In a section entitled "Catharsis and Responses, or Knowledge and Action" Boal foregrounds Brecht's concept of theater as a social process and uses Brechtian theories to develop his own concept of a revolutionary "Theater of the Oppressed." Boal postulates that, while the orientation of the Greek tragic hero is toward the past, the revolutionary protagonist focuses on the future. In an Aristotelian tragedy the hero gains knowledge of his or her own tragic flaws and loses the propensity to act. The revolutionary hero, on the other hand, recognizes the flaws in society that must be addressed and develops the willingness to fight for remedy.

Boal maintains that the revolutionary audience becomes increasingly radicalized as it participates in the radical transformation of the revolutionary hero. The spectators are not purged of the desire to act socially but are empowered with the will to struggle in their own lives. Rather than cathartic release, therefore, the fervent participation of spectators is a sign of conscious empowerment. According to Boal, demonstrative action inside the theater did not preclude or dissipate social action outside of the theater. Instead, it fueled the revolutionary fires. Applying Boal's theories to the social protest performances of El Teatro and the BRT, the active, emotional responses of audiences to the *actos* in Bakersfield or to *Slave Ship* in Baton Rouge represent signs of conscious empowerment. As these spectators watched the Farmworker character in the *actos* or the black masses in *Slave Ship*, they become more empowered to act in their own lives. Their participation intensified the interplay of material and symbolic forces within the social protest performance. Audience participation attested to the effectiveness of the social protest performances as symbolic mediations and signifying practices and demonstrated that the audience felt connected to and invested in the ritualistic performance events.

Urgency and the Uncommitted

At times along the UFWOC march to Sacramento and the Free Southern Theater tour of *Slave Ship*, as well as other moments during the period 1965–71, El Teatro and BRT performances were attended by those outside the "closed" cultural group. In addition, not all blacks or Chicanos who attended were sympathetic to the liberation cause. What happened when the audience was not totally closed? Could the social protest performance convert the nonconverted?

The effect of the production on the converted as well as the nonconverted depended significantly on external social conditions. Because of the surrounding atmosphere of social upheaval, the performance event increasingly became an affective and effective arena for representing and negotiating change. The urgencies present in the Chicano and black communities of the 1960s and 1970s affected the non-converted Chicanos and blacks, along with members of the dominant culture, as they entered into the theater. Moreover, the divisions between outsider and insider, cultural and political status, are not fixed or subject to strict "black and white" binarisms. As demonstrated by the responses of white critics such as Stan Machlin to Slave Ship[82] or Ralph Gleason to the actos, these social protest performances possessed the potential to reach across difference to those "outside" spectators who could identify and empathize with the performers. The appeal of ritualistic social protest theater is potentially infectious.

Still, for those who remained adamantly outside of the matrix of cultural or antistructural communitas, whose individual identity distanced them from the collectivity encouraged by the performance event, who came to the theater with traditional cultural preconceptions, conversion was not impossible, but it was unrealistic. In contrast to the committed and participatory audience members, these spectators perceived their attendance of the performance as a liminiod, or leisure, activity, not as a liminal, sociocultural necessity.[83] Such audiences may have not been sympathetic to the technical simplicity of the productions nor engaged in the perception of authenticity. The potential efficacy was diminished, as these spectators refrained from active participation and remained within conventional patterns of audience-stage exchange.

The surrounding social conditions affected audience reception and, as a result, the potential efficacy of social protest theater. As Johannes Birringer, in Theater, Theory, Postmodernism, argues: "And those who might ask whether political revolutions can be rehearsed in the theater, I would answer that it depends on the conditions under which one works toward changing the perceptions of conditions."[84] The performance and reception of social protest theater depended on the existence of an urgent, dynamic social environment. When the audience participated with activist/performers in the social protest performance, they responded not only to the signs, symbols, and messages within the performance text but also to the immediate call for social action in the outside social environment and in the social dramas within their own daily lives.

6

The Rituals of Social Protest Theater: Reconsiderations and Conclusions

The social protest performances of El Teatro Campesino and the Black Revolutionary Theater movement linked the political, the cultural, the aesthetic, and the spiritual. Through the presentation of social protest dramas these two groups agitated for the dismantling of the dominant power structure and a reordering of cultural, social, and theatrical practices in the United States. Conceived during the Delano Grape Pickers strike of 1965 and the Black Power rebellions of the mid-1960s, El Teatro and the BRT both professed cultural pride and group unity as critical corollaries to self-determination and revolutionary social action. When most effective, the social protest performances of El Teatro and the BRT became cultural celebrations and ritual communions, as spectators and performers participated together in subversive, celebratory protest.

While El Teatro and the Black Revolutionary Theater movement developed around very different organizing principles and attempted to design original, culturally specific forms of theater, the works they created exhibited striking commonalities, attributable to their shared purposes of merging culture and politics and affecting social change. They both discovered a theatrical paradigm that reflected the consecrative and productive, the revolutionary and conservative, potentialities of ritual. Just as tribal communities and preindustrial societies invoked rituals as means of redress in times of immediate social crisis, El Teatro and the BRT used protest performances to mediate, illuminate, and mandate change in their insistent social struggles. Ritualistically, the social protest performance not only reaffirmed the values, heritage, and solidarity of marginalized blacks and Chicanos but also presented new models for change in the U.S. social order. The cultural affirmation of the performance supported the transformative action and new revolutionary symbols within the performance text. Jean Comaroff writes that "the power of ritual may come to be used under certain circumstances, to objectify conflict in the everyday world and to attempt to transcend it."[1] Similarly, El Teatro and the BRT employed ritualistic social protest performances to dramatize their causes of social urgency and to imagine transcendent social change. The social protest performances of El Teatro and the BRT intended to generate real social action through participation by performers and spectators in symbolic reformulations. Their social protest performances acted as symbolic mediations and signifying practices, uniting participants with the social protest cause and directing them toward insurgency.

The Exchange between Stage and Audience

When most successful, the social protest performance was an interactive process. All elements of the exchange between audience and stage contributed to make the performance a participatory, collective communion. As the spectators and performers came together in a spontaneous cultural and ideological community, the performance embodied a tenuous but dynamic duality—a duality common to rituals of transformation and endemic to social protest theatrical efficacy. At this moment the performance reflected the surge between harmony and disharmony, order and disorder, which ritual scholar Margaret Thompson Drewal observes in Yoruba rituals,[2] and the consecrative and reproductive capabilities of ritual, which Robert Weimann identifies.[3] Cultural reaffirmation and celebration fused with revolutionary fervor and militancy. As Baz Kershaw argues, the efficacious social protest performance challenges the spectators' ideological community, but at the same time, dialectically, it comforts the spectators and confirms their social purpose.[4] The performance and its resultant celebration could plunge the audience "into terror, and reassure them," which Geneviève Fabre suggests was fundamental to the efficacy of black revolutionary theater.[5] When the spectators communed together with the actors in celebratory protest, they recognized not only the import of the performance but also the significance of their own presence at and participation in the event.

Audience participation was critical to social protest performance. It can be read as an act of symbolic rebellion; when an individual spontaneously participated, it testified to the meaning and the import of the performance for that individual. This is not to suggest that participation in the social protest performance implied total social commitment or immediately translated into social action. As this book has shown, many factors contribute to audience participation. Research in advertising and persuasion theory has shown that a key step in persuading an individual to take action outside, after an advertising appeal, is to convince that individual to perform a simple action, during the persuasive appeal, such as signing his or her name on a piece of paper. This technique, known as the "foot-in-the door-technique for inducing compliance," was first identified by J. L. Freedman and S. C. Fraser in 1966.[6] Freedman's and Fraser's work, as well as subsequent experiments in persuasion, have shown that there is a direct correlation between the initial act of complicity and the long-term efficacy of the persuasive appeal.[7] The participatory involvement of the audience in the social protest performance parallels this basic persuasive principle. The audience's decision to participate actively was, in effect, like signing one's name in the foot-in-the-door technique. It affected the spectators' self-image and signified agreement with the overall strategy of the social protest performance.

When performer Augustin Lira, as a Spanish-speaking governor, shouted "Viva La Huelga!" to the audience gathered along the UFWOC march route in Freeport, California, in 1966, the spectators responded vociferously with fists clenched in defiance, "Viva La Huelga!" They participated in the subversive theatrical event and laughed and cheered as shocked "ranchers" dragged the pro-Huelga governor from the stage. This participation bolstered the marcher's political conviction and belief in the strike cause. Despite the nonappearance of the real California governor, Edmund Brown Sr., who was expected to meet with the union leadership, the marchers were not discouraged. The marchers' involvement in the Freeport performance signified and even demonstrated their resolve to continue their march to Sacramento. Audience participation in the social protest performances of El Teatro and the BRT significantly testified to the effectiveness of the social protest performance's agitational messages.

In the Absence of Urgency: Urgency and Efficacy

As demonstrated in the work of El Teatro and the BRT, the social context was also integral to the efficacy of the social protest performance. The social protest performance worked not in a vacuum but in synergistic communion with the urgent social activities occurring in society. Dramatic social events poignantly demonstrated the current state of turmoil, upheaval, and dissatisfaction. These real-life dramas were then interpreted and refracted through the radical lens of the social protest performance. The palpable presence of urgency created an atmosphere conducive to the performance of social theater. Urgency situated and contextualized every aspect of the social protest performance. Both spectators and performers came to the performance conditioned by the dramatic social events transpiring around them. Their involvement with these events affected their readings of, responses to, and participation in the social protest event. Urgent social and cultural times propelled the repositioning of the theater by blacks and Chicanos. In the 1960s and early 1970s black and Chicano social protest theaters became significant institutions for the promulgation of alternative cultural representations.

Yet urgency, by definition, is ephemeral; the demand for immediate change does not last forever. On 29 January 1970 the twenty-six major growers signed a union contract with the UFWOC effectively ending the Grape Pickers strike and thereby altering the original urgency and direction of El Teatro Campesino. By the mid-1970s black America no longer reverberated with urgent cries for change: the Black Power movement had dissolved; the Spirit House in Newark had virtually stopped operating as a social protest theater in 1971, as Baraka moved away from active involvement with theatrical performance and would soon change his political ideology. The pressures of Watergate and the approaching end to the war in Vietnam foregrounded a new set of issues in the national agenda, and race was again marginalized. Without the necessary environmental conditions, social protest theaters could not produce efficacious performances. Performing a social protest piece away from its constituent audience and outside of an atmosphere of urgency diluted its potential efficacy and altered the participatory, ritualistic nature of the performance event.

What happens to social protest theater, then, after the urgency dies? Each of El Teatro's and the BRT's activists/performers had to determine for themselves, individually, whether their greater commitment was to the theater or to the social cause. Some members of the Spirit House Movers embarked on professional acting careers, while others devoted themselves full-time to grassroots activism. In addition, social protest theaters and their leaders had to reevaluate their processes and consider future directions. Ideologically, both Valdez and Baraka moved away from the essentialist dogma that characterized their work in the 1960s and early 1970s to embrace the "universality of suffering" and to explore the commonalities of culture. Baraka rejected the separatism of black cultural nationalism and adopted Marxist socialism. Even as he endorsed a more inclusive class analysis of American racism, Baraka's adoption of socialism moved him further into the radical fringe of black political thought. Valdez relinquished the agitational voice of the *acto* and experimented with a new form, the *mito*. With the *mito* he undertook a search to unearth the mythical, spiritual, primordial, roots of Chicano experience. This search led Valdez to advocate spiritual harmony and a collective unity of all people. The ideological shifts of these theater artists exemplified the cultural permutations, political schisms, and paradigmatic changes evolving within black and Chicano communities—the search for new strategies and solutions after the immediacy of liminal, revolutionary times had passed. Urgent, insistent times create an atmosphere for social protest theater, and the effect of those times cannot be overstated.

With the dissolution of the conditions of urgency in the 1970s, another significant difference between El Teatro and the BRT surfaced. The BRT ceased to be a viable, productive theatrical or social force. El Teatro, on the other hand, moved to San Juan Bautista, California, in 1971, where—although no longer the signal performance organization in contemporary Chicano theater—it continues to operate. Clearly, the politics and aesthetics of El Teatro have changed considerably since its inception with the Delano Grape Pickers strike. In 1967 Valdez proclaimed: "We shouldn't be judged as a theater. We're really part of a cause."[8] Then, during a 1983 interview he stated:

We're still cultural, still political but first and foremost theater is what we do for a living and who we are. We're not afraid to sell tickets; this may seem at variance with our radical theatrical origins but it's a reality. We've got to pay rent, pay taxes, provide a decent living for our actors and staff.[9]

The differences between Valdez's two statements testifies to the social and artistic evolution of El Teatro. Most recently, Valdez has become more and more involved with film and television productions, and he is now the new chair of the theater program at California State University, Monterey. In the absence of urgency, new decisions have to be made and priorities established.

The contemporary discourses of blacks, Chicanos, and other underrepresented groups have evolved away from the naive, absolutist arguments of earlier urgent times and have moved toward promoting linkages, acknowledging the commonalities of oppression and struggle. Current feminist reconsiderations of both the Chicano and Black Power movements have probed the positioning of women and women's issues within the two movements and recognized their inherent male-centrism. The essentialist views of social liberation espoused by these movements failed to include gender issues and the cultural stratification of women in their platforms for change. Baraka, in his 1984 autobiography, admits:

Ron Karenga's doctrine [of cultural nationalism] made male chauvinism a revolutionary legitimacy. The doctrine said there was no such thing as equality between men and women, "they were complementary." . . . When brothers went by, the women were supposed to "salimu" or "submit," crossing their arms on their breast and bowing slightly.[10]

Correspondingly, Valdez suggests that the social climate of the times and the cultural orientation of El Teatro's farmworker audiences did not allow for the promotion and representation of women.[11] Both the BRT and El Teatro subjugated women to subordinate roles within their respective theater companies and limited representations of women. They exhibited an uneven distribution of power and reflected the social development and gender stratifications of that time.

And yet by speaking directly and only to a specific disenfranchised group, the social protest performance of El Teatro and the BRT reinforced group identity, consciousness, and self-worth. As El Teatro and the BRT protested the oppression of Chicanos and blacks within the dominant culture, they asserted their difference as a strength and as a site of resistance and empowerment. Their cultural identity, their otherness and marginality, became loci of pride, communal consciousness, and social awareness. In the process they deconstructed and decentered social and theatrical norms. The strategy of decentering is a preliminary step toward what many contemporary critics have identified as a postmodern "politics of difference."[12] Within this postmodern paradigm the normative center is destabilized and contested by the margins, and marginality is reimagined as a position of power and agency. A politics of difference foregrounds and acknowledges differences while recognizing positions of negotiated consensus and commonality. A politics of difference builds coalitions as a strategy of resistance and reform. Stuart Hall theorizes in "New Ethnicities" that

> a politics can be constructed which works with and through difference, which is able to build those forms of solidarity and identification which make common struggle and resistance possible but without suppressing the heterogeneity of interests and identities, and which can effectively draw the political boundary lines without which political contestation is impossible, without fixing those boundaries for eternity.[13]

As expressed by Hall, the politics of difference are tactical, differential, situational, and ephemeral. New ethnicities and political coalitions are constructed according to temporal, conditional social needs. The practices of El Teatro and the BRT exhibit the beginnings of a politics of difference as they worked "with and through difference" to build group solidarity and identity around issues of commonality, struggle, and resistance.

The work of El Teatro and the BRT has helped to change scholarly and aesthetic conceptions of American theater and drama. Since the 1960s American drama, affected by the concurrent social, political, cultural, and demographic developments, has moved away from previous normative and normalizing conventions and perceptions—to become more inclusive. Definitions of the American dramatic "canon" have been broadened to embrace the works of underrepresented peoples. Certainly, the insistent efforts of El Teatro and the BRT to create an alternative, oppositional theatrical practice have aided in this decentering. El Teatro and the BRT rejected the dominant culture's representations of Chicanos and blacks and created their own. They demanded that their previously silenced voices be recognized on the American stage. The social protest performances of El Teatro and the BRT of the period 1965 to 1971 still have an impact on cultural production today. The aesthetic practices of contemporary playwrights—such as Cherríe Moraga and August Wilson—are indebted to the social protest performances and cultural agitation of El Teatro and the BRT.[14] While the groups did not effect the demise of the Western aesthetic that they originally imagined, they have claimed space within the new American dramatic canon.

As with much of contemporary Chicano and black cultural practices, the performance works of El Teatro and the BRT were concerned fundamentally with questions of identity. Yet, while contemporary Chicano and black discourses often valorize the multiplicity of Chicano and black identities, the work of El Teatro and the BRT celebrated more homogenized identities for the two groups and the notion of a collective racial or cultural memory. More recent theories on race and ethnicity as well as current Chicano and black cultural productions have refuted and rejected the identity politics and the organicized perspectives on race offered by Chicano and black cultural nationalism of the 1960s and 1970s. And yet there remains a desire expressed recently by some Chicano and black theater practitioners, cultural critics, and scholars to recuperate elements of cultural nationalism and identity politics. Despite the fragmentation of contemporary postmodern circumstances and the pessimism of contemporary critical theories that problematize any invocation of community, the concept of community—of collective ethnic identity—remains an appealing one to those interested in empowering the underrepresented and promoting social change.

Black cultural critic Wahneema Lubiano perceives black nationalism as a "contestatory ground" whose operations and implications need to be rethought.[15] She points out that black nationalism in the 1960s and 1970s "valorized community" and "temporarily elided the material differences among different stratifications of black Americans in order to make politics possible."[16] Often effectively, black nationalism conceived of black people as a political class, a "community," in order to foment its agenda of revolutionary social change. Through his current work playwright August Wilson attempts to reinvigorate a black nationalistic consciousness while recognizing the multiplicity of black experiences. In fact, Wilson still considers himself a black nationalist. He writes: "My youth was fired in the kiln of black cultural nationalism as exemplified by Amiri Baraka in the sixties. . . . The ideas of self-determination, self-respect, and self-defense which it espoused are still very much a part of my life as I sit down to write."[17] He asks that African Americans recognize and reclaim their "African-ness."[18] This is a challenging and perhaps, at times, even contradictory project that has the potential, like the cultural nationalism of the 1960s and 1970s, to romanticize Africa, to dissolve black difference, and to homogenize and essentialize black identity.

Similarly, Cherríe Moraga, in her latest book, *The Last Generation*, revises and reasserts the concept of Chicano nationalism:

> I mourn the dissolution of an active Chicano Movement. . . . What was right about Chicano Nationalism was its commitment to preserving the integrity of the Chicano people. . . . Chicanos are an occupied nation within a nation, and women and women's sexuality are occupied within the Chicano nation. . . . I cling to the word "nation" because without the specific naming of a nation, the nation will be lost.[19]

Moraga imagines a different Chicano nationalism from that of the 1960s and 1970s—a Chicano nationalism that includes the previously excluded. Even as she calls for a recognition of diversity, however, Moraga's invocation of the term *nation* structures borders of authenticity and exclusivity. Yvonne Yarbro-Bejarano notes: "No matter how opposed we may be to essentializing constructions of racial identity, no one wants to give up the romance of being Chicano. . . . It is the possibility of collective struggle as a people that gives meaning to and sustains the notion of 'Chicano.'"[20] As Yarbro-Bejarano observes, the notion of Chicano nationalism is both seductive and problematic; it presumes essential boundaries of identification and restricts diversity. Still, this underlying essentialism does not negate the attraction of cultural nationalism. As evidenced by Moraga and Wilson, many contemporary black and Chicano artists and scholars find themselves faced with a complex and perplexing dialectic as they attempt to uncover a discursive practice that allows for the recuperation of nationalistic strategies of community and identity politics while foregrounding the constructed nature of race and ethnic categories.

The performance practices of El Teatro and the BRT can provide insight into this contemporary conundrum. In the social climate of the 1960s and early 1970s collectivity and community were not just illusory and romanticized concepts but were tangible and identifiable in the performance practices of El Teatro and the BRT. The audiences who attended the productions of El Teatro and the BRT generally represented self-selective "closed" communities. Yet it would be a mistake to assume that these were ontological or essential communities that were formed along the exclusionary lines of Chicano and/or black ethnic and cultural identity. Rather, they represented "communities of interest," constructed as a direct result of the social, cultural, economic, and political needs of their constituents.[21] The exigent demands of Chicano and black social, cultural, and political life in the 1960s and 1970s necessitated the formation and militant advocacy of these communities of interest. The needs of these communities produced tactical declarations of collective identity, *Chicanismo* and Black Power, in the social protest theater. The ritualistic theatrical practices of El Teatro and the BRT manipulated and reinforced these notions of community and collective consciousness in order to achieve their social and political ends. In and through their work El Teatro and the BRT linked cultural technologies to the realm of the political. The complex and even contradictory cultural politics of El Teatro and the BRT, during those earlier times of urgency, provide new contemporary political subjects and artists of color with examples of strategic uses of essentialism and demonstrate the power of social protest theater to generate and support collective social agency.

The Universality of Social Need

The practice of ritualistic social protest performance is not limited to El Teatro and the BRT. Rather, it has been a model employed, in various degrees, to mediate other oppressed peoples' struggles. As Norma

Alarcón has pointed out, in times of political and social insurrection the marginalized and disenfranchised have turned to "communal modes of empowerment."[22] Concurrently, the protest theaters of these oppressed peoples emerge and invoke ritualistic social protest performances to encourage community empowerment and to inculcate a spirit of collective faith and revolutionary optimism. Similar strategies can emerge from movements that have variant social ends. El Teatro and the BRT developed around decidedly different organizing principles, and yet they both discovered ritualistic social protest performance practices.

When the feminist theater movement in the United States originated in the mid-1970s, it too used aspects of ritualistic social protest theater. In direct contrast to the plays of the BRT and El Teatro, feminist theater performances challenged the oppression of women, championed women's rights, and celebrated the personal and political nature of women's experiences. And yet, in marked similarity to the social protest performances of the BRT and El Teatro, the feminist performances of the 1970s were ritualistic and celebratory. Performances were directed specifically at closed, constituent audiences of women. And female spectators and performers joined together in a bond of determination and communion.

As seen with the feminist theater of the 1970s, with the gay theater movement of the 1970s and 1980s, with the theater around the AIDS epidemic of the 1980s and 1990s, invariably in times of crisis, previously oppressed communities turn to social protest performance. Social protest theater directly responds to the social and political needs of the disenfranchised and disempowered. For those without power in the society, theater offers a means of empowerment and, as a result, has repeatedly been used as a social weapon.

Each historic moment and cultural constituency has its own specific demands and defines its own particular social protest theater. With each new cause of urgent social need, new social protest theaters have emerged, each believing in the singularity of its purpose and the individuality of its efforts. And yet the performances of these various groups bear striking similarities. Implicitly and explicitly, they reflect the transformative, generative, and regenerative power of ritual. The ritualistic social protest performance remains a potentially dynamic and powerful theatrical event.

Notes

Chapter 1

1. By "social protest performances" I mean those performances that have an explicit social purpose, that direct their audiences to social action. My definition presupposes that social protest performances emerge solely from marginalized peoples and oppositional positions. Social protest performances function as counterhegemonic strategies through which underrepresented groups challenge the dominant social order and agitate for change. The representational apparatus of the social protest performance serves to reinforce, reimagine, and rearticulate the objectives of social and political resistance. I use the term *social protest performance*, rather than *radical theater*, to indicate that these performances actively protest against a very specific and urgent cause of social need. Social protest performance is an ever-evolving genre appearing wherever oppressed people assert their subjectivity and contest the status quo.

2. I have chosen to begin my analysis with 1965 because this is the year in which both of these theater movements originated. The year 1971 marks an ideological and geographical shift for El Teatro Campesino, as the group moved from Fresno to its current home in San Juan Bautista, both in California. They also turned from their improvisational-agitational theatrical form known as the "acto" to the more mystically oriented "mito." By 1971 the activism of Spirit House in Newark had declined, as Baraka became less involved in the day-to-day operations of the theater and increasingly active in local and national electoral politics. He had campaigned successfully for the election of Newark's first black mayor, Kenneth Gibson, in 1970. Thus, after 1971 both El Teatro and the BRT moved away from an agenda of activist protest.

3. I will focus exclusively on those social protest performances initiated by Amiri Baraka (LeRoi Jones) in the two manifestations of his Black Revolutionary Theater, the Black Arts Repertory Theater School (BARTS) in Harlem (1965) and the Spirit House in Newark, New Jersey (1966–74). Baraka's theaters, BARTS and Spirit House, represent two of the more significant black social protest theaters of the 1960s and 1970s. Concentrating solely on the plays and performances of BARTS and Spirit House will make for intriguing parallels with the work of El Teatro and will help to balance this comparative study of social protest theater. Because I am limiting my examination of black social protest performance to the theaters of Baraka, I will use the term *Black Revolutionary Theater (BRT)* rather than the more inclusive and established delineations of black theater of the period, such as *Black Arts Movement* or *Black Theater Movement*.

4. See Jorge Huerta, *Chicano Theater: Themes and Forms* (Tempe, AZ: Bilingual Press, 1982).

5. See Yolanda Broyles-González, "El Teatro and the Mexican Popular Performance Tradition," *El Teatro Campesino: Theater in the Chicano Movement* (Austin: University of Texas Press, 1994), 3–78.

6. Mbongi Ngema, the South African playwright and creator of the musical theater pieces *Sarafina* and *Asinimali*, has reported that his knowledge of the performance practices of El Teatro greatly influenced his own performance methods and ideas of social protest performance.

7. Yolanda Broyles-González discusses the problems with using "the great-man/text-centered/chronological-linear approach" to assess the work of Valdez and El Teatro Campesino. She argues that focusing on the great man obscures the work of the community and denigrates from the participatory achievement of the women involved with the group. See Yolanda Broyles-González, "Introduction," *El Teatro Campesino: Theater in the Chicano Movement* (Austin: University of Texas Press, 1994), xiii.

8. I must acknowledge that through my decision to focus on the early performances of El Teatro and those of the BRT, I am limiting this study to the works of male playwrights and male-centered theaters. Certainly, women were involved in the Chicano theater movement and in the later practices of El Teatro. Nelda Perez was one of the founding members of Teatro de la Esperanza at the University of California at Santa Barbara in 1968. Olivia Chumacero, Yolanda Para, Dolores Rodriguez, and Socorro Valdez all became members of El Teatro Campesino's performance troupe in the 1970s. (See Yolanda Broyles-González, "Toward a Re-Vision of Chicano Theater History: The Women of El Teatro Campesino," in *Making Spectacle*, ed. Lynda Hart [Ann Arbor: University of Michigan Press, 1989], 209–38; "Toward a Re-Vision of Chicano Theater History: The Role of Women in El Teatro Campesino," *El Teatro Campesino: Theater in the Chicano Movement* [Austin: University of Texas Press, 1994], 129–64; and Jorge Huerta, *Chicano Theater: Themes and Forms* [Ypsilanti, MI: Bilingual Press, 1982], 68–81.) Women playwrights and theater practitioners were also involved with the

Black Arts Movement. Sonia Sanchez was one of the more significant play-wrights. Barbara Ann Teer created the National Black Theater in Harlem, in 1968, where she designed performances that she termed "black rituals" with performers whom she called "liberators." (See Jessica B. Harris, "The National Black Theater: The Sun People of 125th Street," in *The Theater of Black Americans*, vol. 2: *The Presenters/The Participators*, ed. Errol Hill [Engle-wood Cliffs, NJ: Prentice-Hall, 1980], 85–94.) My purpose is not to diminish the accomplishments of these and other women through exclusion but, rather, to heighten our understanding of two male-dominated theaters, El Teatro and the BRT, within their particular sociohistorical context.

9. See Geneviève Fabre, *Drumbeats, Masks and Metaphor* (Cambridge, MA: Harvard University Press, 1983); and Mance Williams, *Black Theater in the 1960s and 1970s* (Westport, CN: Greenwood Press, 1985), for examinations of black revolutionary theater. See Huerta, *Chicano Theater*, for a discussion of the evolution of El Teatro Campesino. See Broyles-González, *El Teatro Campesino*, for a discussion of El Teatro's methodology and the roots of its collective practice. Richard Scharine, in *From Class to Caste in American Drama* (Westport, CN: Greenwood Press, 1991), discusses both black and Chicano social protest theater; however, he treats them separately rather than comparatively.

10. One difference between El Teatro and the BRT that potentially problema-tizes any comparisons is their respective longevity. Unlike Spirit House, El Teatro is still an existing, practicing theater company. From its inception in 1965 until the present El Teatro has undergone a significant geographical, theatrical, and ideological pilgrimage. In 1967 El Teatro moved from its original base in Delano to the small city of Del Rey, California. From Del Rey the troupe migrated to the much more urban Fresno in 1969. This move was followed, in 1971, by a return to the group's rural roots as El Teatro relocated to its current theatrical home, the peaceful and pastoral San Juan Bautista. For the purposes of limiting and balancing this comparative analysis of social protest performance, I will restrict my consideration of El Teatro to its early years and its rural beginnings in Delano, when its social protest performances were most specifically connected to "La Huelga," the Grape Pickers strike. When I discuss El Teatro in this book, unless other-wise indicated, I will be referring, with historical perspective, to the earliest configurations and practices of this theater troupe. By considering only the early performances of El Teatro in conjunction with the concurrent black social protest performances of BARTS and Spirit House, I will be able to isolate, identify, and examine what I will argue are comparable social protest performances before particular constituencies and at specific histor-ical moments.

One might also question why I propose to do a comparative study of El Teatro and the BRT when their "differences" appear to be so marked. From the outset the terms of the comparison might seem too skewed or unbal-anced. Why compare a theatrical "troupe," El Teatro, with a theater "movement," the BRT? For, although El Teatro inspired the birth of the "Chicano theater movement," it is only one theater group, whose practices have mainly been localized in California. The BRT, on the other hand, suggests a conglomerate of groups and a movement that—during the 1960s and 1970s—was national in scope. My definition of the BRT in this study is purposefully not so inclusive.

11. Homi Bhabha, "Interrogating Identity: The Post Colonial Prerogative," in *The Anatomy of Racism,* ed. David Theo Goldberg (Minneapolis: University of Minnesota Press, 1990), 188.

12. Fabre, "The Militant Theater," *Drumbeats, Masks and Metaphor,* 103.

13. See Harry J. Elam Jr., "Revolution and Ritual: Luis Valdez' *Quinta Temporada* and LeRoi Jones' *Slave Ship,*" *Theatre Journal* 38.4 (1986): 463–72, in which I examine black revolutionary theater and the Chicano *teatro* in the 1960s and 1970s.

14. See bell hooks, "Is Paris Burning?" *Black Looks* (Boston: South End Press, 1992), 145–56; also see Stuart Hall, "New Ethnicities," *Black Film/British Cinema,* ICA Documents no. 7 (London: ICA, 1988), 27–31.

15. hooks, "Is Paris Burning?" 152–53.

16. Despite the avowed social purposes of El Teatro, white mainstream newspaper critics and theater scholars who observed the troupe's early performance work critiqued the performances using conventional modes of aesthetic and theatrical analysis. Not surprisingly, their commentaries neglected or even ignored the social power of the performances. Instead, these critics cited what they perceived as El Teatro's theatrical naïveté and aesthetic "primitivism." They devalued El Teatro's performances, calling the works "raw," "crude," and "technically unskilled." See John Brokaw, "Teatro Chicano: Some Reflections," *Educational Theater Journal* 29 (December 1977): 33–44. Also see Sylvia Drake, *Los Angeles Times,* 4 October 1969, sec. 2, 7. Oblivious to the negative judgments of these white critics, the Chicano farmworkers, who formed the bulk of the audience for these early performances, appreciatively embraced El Teatro's conjunction of politics and aesthetics within the performance space. Distracted from their grape picking chores, drawn in by the immediacy and political significance of the performances, the Chicano farmworkers often became active participants in the theatrical event. They laughed, cheered, and personally identified with El Teatro's farmworker/performers.

During the same period the response of black audiences to the performances of the Black Revolutionary Theater movement (BRT) also contrasted sharply with the published opinions of white theater critics. The BRT emerged in the mid-1960s determined to create theater by, for, and about black people. In accord with the concurrent Black Power movement, the BRT advocated violent racial revolution. The theater became a weapon in the struggle to achieve these racialized revolutionary ends. In a 22 November 1969 review white critic Clive Barnes of the *New York Times* called *Slave Ship*—by the principal playwright of the BRT, Amiri Baraka

(LeRoi Jones)—a "black militant racist play" that was "artistically as ragged as burlap." Fellow *New York Times* critic Walter Kerr concluded that the play was "underdeveloped, repetitive, monotonous, unmoving." See Clive Barnes, "The Theater: New LeRoi Jones Play," *New York Times,* 22 November 1969, 46. See Walter Kerr, "Is This Their Dream?" *New York Times,* 23 November 1969, sec. 2, 3. Black spectators, however, like their Chicano contemporaries, were unaffected by such criticism. They attended the production in significant numbers and fervently participated in the supposedly "unmoving" theatrical event.

17. For examples of black and Chicano theatrical criticism of the 1960s and 1970s, see: Jorge Huerta, "Chicano Theater: A Background," *Aztlán* (Fall 1971): 63–78; Nicolás Kanellos, "Folklore in Chicano Theater: Chicano Theater as Folklore," in *Popular Theater for Social Change,* ed. Gerado Luizunaga (Los Angeles: UCLA Latin American Studies Center Publications, 1978), 158–77; Larry Neal, "The Black Arts Movement," *Drama Review* 12.4 (Summer 1968): 36–46; and Addison Gayle Jr., *The Black Aesthetic* (New York: Vintage Books, 1970). My point here is not to denigrate the works of criticism from the 1960s and 1970s but, rather, to suggest that they did not possess the historical distance and critical methodologies now available. Consequently, there is a need to reexamine the drama of El Teatro and the BRT with contemporary critical tools and historical perspective.

18. See Yolanda Broyles-Gonzáles, "Toward a Re-Vision of Chicana/o Theater History: The Roles of Women in El Teatro Campesino," *Teatro Campesino* (Austin: University of Texas Press, 1994), 129–64. See Yvonne Yarbro-Bejarano, "The Female Subject in Chicano Theatre: Sexuality, 'Race,' and Class," *Theatre Journal* 38.4: 389–407. See David Lionel Smith, "The Black Arts Movement and Its Critics," *American Literary History* 3.1 (Spring 1991): 93–110.

19. See Paul Gilroy, "Cultural Studies and Ethnic Absolutism," in *Cultural Studies,* ed. Lawrence Grossberg, Cary Nelson, and Paula Treichler (New York: Routledge, 1992), 187–99; also see Henry Giroux, "Living Dangerously: Identity Politics and the New Cultural Racism," in *Between Boarders: Pedagogy and the Politics of Cultural Studies,* ed. Henry Giroux and Peter McLaren (New York: Routledge, 1994), 29–55; and Angie Chabram-Dernersian, "I Throw Punches for My Race, but I Don't Want to Be a Man: Writing Us—Chica-nos(Girl, Us)/Chicanas—into the Movement Script," in *Cultural Studies,* ed. Lawrence Grossberg, Cary Nelson, and Paula Treichler (New York: Routledge, 1992), 81–95. See bell hooks, "An Aesthetic of Blackness," *Yearning: Race, Gender, and Cultural Politics* (Boston: South End Press, 1990), 103–14. See Norma Alarcón, "Traddutora, Traditora: A Paradigmatic Figure of Chicano Feminism," *Cultural Critique* 13 (1989): 57–87.

20. Kobena Mercer, "'1968': Periodizing Politics and Identity," *Welcome to the Jungle* (London: Routledge, 1994), 287.

21. In her book *Essentially Speaking* Diana Fuss argues that the contemporary poststructuralist African American literary theories of Houston A. Baker

and Henry Louis Gates are implicitly essentialist in their appeals to an African American vernacular criticism. Both Baker and Gates reference African American criticism of the 1960s and 1970s in their work (Fuss, *Essentially Speaking* [New York: Routledge, 1989]). Also see Houston A. Baker, *Blues, Ideology, and Afro-American Literature* (Chicago: University of Chicago Press, 1984); Henry Louis Gates, *The Signifying Monkey* (New York: Oxford University Press, 1988); and Cherríe Moraga, *The Last Generation* (Boston: South End Press, 1993).

22. Kobena Mercer, "'1968': Periodizing Politics and Identity," 287.

23. See Hall, "New Ethnicities," 27–31; Cornel West, *Keeping Faith* (New York: Routledge, 1993); hooks, *Yearning*; Gloria Anzaldúa, *Borderlands/La Frontera: The New Mestiza* (San Francisco: Spinsters/Aunt Lute, 1987); and Henry Giroux, *Disturbing Pleasures* (New York: Routledge, 1994).

24. See Wolfgang Iser, *The Act of Reading: A Theory of Aesthetic Response* (Baltimore: Johns Hopkins University Press, 1978); Herbert Blau, *Audience* (Baltimore: Johns Hopkins University Press, 1990); and Susan Bennett, *Theater Audiences* (London: Routledge, 1990).

25. See John Dollimore and Alan Sinfield, *Political Shakespeare: New Essays in Cultural Materialism* (Manchester: Manchester University Press, 1985); Stephen Greenblatt, *Renaissance Self-Fashioning: From More to Shakespeare* (Chicago: University of Chicago Press, 1980); and Richard Wilson and Richard Dutton, *New Historicism and Renaissance Drama* (London: Longman Press, 1992).

26. Catherine Bell, "The Dynamics of Ritual Power," *Journal of Ritual Studies* 4.2 (Summer 1990): 300.

27. See hooks, *Yearning*; Donna Haraway *Primate Visions* (New York: Routledge, 1989); and Jill Dolan, *The Feminist Spectator as Critic* (Ann Arbor: University of Michigan Press, 1988).

28. See Jean and John Comaroff, *Modernity and Its Malcontents* (Chicago: University of Chicago Press, 1993); Victor Turner, *From Ritual to Theater* (New York: PAJ Publications, 1982); and Richard Schechner, *Between Theater and Anthropology* (Philadelphia: University of Pennsylvania Press, 1985).

29. Victor Turner, *The Forest of Symbols: Aspects of Ndembu Ritual* (Ithaca, NY: Cornell University Press, 1967), 19.

30. Comaroff and Comaroff, "Introduction," *Modernity and Its Malcontents*, xiv.

31. Comaroff and Comaroff, "Introduction," xvi.

32. Comaroff and Comaroff, "Introduction," xxx.

33. Jean Comaroff, *Body of Power, Spirit of Resistance* (Chicago: University of Chicago Press, 1985), 119.

34. Comaroff and Comaroff, "Introduction," xxix.

35. Victor Turner, *The Drama of Affliction* (Oxford: Clarendon Press, 1963), 6–7.

36. Mary Douglas, *Purity and Danger* (London: Routledge and Kegan Paul, 1966), 62.

37. Margaret Thompson Drewal, *Yoruba Ritual: Performers, Play Agency* (Bloomington: Indiana University Press, 1992), 13.

38. Drewal, *Yoruba Ritual,* 19.
39. Comaroff, *Body of Power,* 194.
40. Erving Goffman, "Performances," in *Ritual, Play and Performance,* ed. Richard Schechner and Mary Shuman (New York: Seabury Press, 1976), 95.
41. See Michael Vanden Heuvel, *Performing Drama/Dramatizing Performance* (Ann Arbor: University of Michigan Press, 1991), 40–41; Hilary Ursala Cohen, "Ritual and Theater: An Examination of Performance Forms in the Contemporary American Theater" (Ph.D. diss., University of Michigan, 1980). Cohen argues that the structure of ritual and theater are too inherently different for either to encompass the other. She concludes that few theatrical groups have ever performed a ritual. Cohen maintains that the features of ritual that are most difficult to achieve are "forming the assembly into a congregation rather than an audience, making efficacious rather than affective performances, and creating a reiterative rather than imitative context" (*Dissertation Abstracts International* 41.2 [August 1980], 461-A).
42. More recent ritual theorists such as Ranjini Obeyeskere do not agree with Turner that those gathered at ritual ceremonies uniformly act as a congregation. Obeyeskere differentiates between audience members who act as *spectators* and those who act as *participants* in the ritual enactment. See "The Significance of Performance for Its Audience: An Analysis of Three Sri Lankan Rituals," in *By Means of Performance,* ed. Richard Schechner (Cambridge: Cambridge University Press, 1990), 118–30.
43. Turner, *From Ritual to Theater,* 20–60.
44. Turner, *From Ritual to Theater,* 34.
45. Turner, *From Ritual to Theater,* 32, 33, 55.
46. Mieke Bal, "Experiencing Murder: Ritualistic Interpretations of Ancient Texts," in *Victor Turner and Cultural Criticism,* ed. Kathleen M. Ashley (Bloomington: Indiana University Press, 1990), 6.
47. Eric MacDonald, *Theater at the Margins* (Ann Arbor: University of Michigan Press, 1993), 25.

Chapter 2

1. Luis Valdez, quoted in "New Grapes," *Newsweek,* 31 July 1967, 79.
2. Larry Neal, "The Black Arts Movement," *Drama Review* 12.4 (Summer 1968): 29.
3. John Dollimore and Alan Sinfield, "Foreword," in *Political Shakespeare,* ed. John Dollimore and Alan Sinfield (Ithaca, NY: Cornell University Press, 1985), viii.
4. See Jorge Huerta, *Chicano Theater: Themes and Forms* (Ypsilanti, MI: Bilingual Press, 1982), 16–23, for a more detailed explanation of the *acto.*
5. Chantal Mouffe, "Hegemony and New Political Subjects: Toward a New Concept of Democracy," in *Marxism and the Interpretation of Culture,* ed. Lawrence Grossberg and Cary Nelson (Urbana: University of Illinois Press, 1988), 95.

6. Mouffe, "Hegemony and New Political Subjects," 100, 95.
7. Angela Davis does point out in her article "Black Nationalism: The Sixties and the Nineties," *Black Popular Culture* (Seattle: Bay Press, 1992), that Huey Newton wrote an article in the Black Panther paper in the spring of 1970 "urging an end to verbal gay bashing, urging an examination of Black male sexuality, and calling for an alliance with the developing gay liberation movement. This article was written in the aftermath of Jean Genet's sojourn with the Black Panther Party, and Genet's *Un Captif Amoureux* reveals suppressed moments of the history of sixties nationalism" (323). Davis goes on to note that such limited actions as that by Huey Newton have almost been "eradicated" by contemporary perceptions of black nationalism during the 1960s and early 1970s.
8. Kobena Mercer, "'1968': Periodizing Politics and Identity," *Welcome to the Jungle* (London: Routledge, 1994), 296.
9. Mouffe, "Hegemony and New Political Subjects," 89.
10. Mouffe, "Hegemony and New Political Subjects," 89.
11. Mercer, "'1968': Periodizing Politics and Identity," 296.
12. David Goodwin, *Cesar Chavez: Hope for the People* (New York: Fawcett Columbine, 1991), 129.
13. Rodolfo Acuña, *Occupied America: A History of Chicanos*, 3d ed. (New York: HarperCollins, 1988), 311.
14. Mercer, "'1968': Periodizing Politics and Identity," 303.
15. See Acuña, *Occupied America*, for a detailed history of Chicano resistance efforts.
16. During the 1960s the sense of urgency among Chicanos grew in direct proportion to the increase in the numbers of Mexican immigrants coming to the United States. With the rise in population, Chicanos and recent Mexican immigrants became increasingly aware of the economic and social discrimination they faced and the dearth of legal and social services available to them. Feelings of hopelessness and frustration multiplied as a result. Soon these feelings were directed into social action. Because of its large concentration of Chicanos—and their encounters with problems of poverty, unemployment, and cultural oppression—California became a center of Chicano activism in the 1960s and the site of visible conditions of urgency. In Los Angeles alone the Mexican immigrant population mushroomed by 113 percent in the 1960s. At the same time, unemployment remained extremely high for this population. Confrontations between the Los Angeles Police Department and Chicanos occurred frequently. Education for Chicanos in California was also a significant problem. Chicanos found themselves repeatedly discriminated against in the California school system, segregated in substandard schools without quality teachers and without any educational focus on the Spanish language or Chicano culture. In 1968 close to ten thousand Chicano students walked out of five Los Angeles high schools demanding change. The Chicano community of East Los Angeles formed the Educational Issues Coordinating Committee (EICC) to

facilitate and manage this walkout. Organized protests were also mounted by Chicano college students. By the fall of 1967 Chicano college student organizations had emerged on college campuses throughout the state of California. They engaged in a variety of protest activities, demanding political access for Chicanos and calling for changes in their educational life on campus, including the establishment of Chicano studies programs.

17. Patricia Gurin, Arthur A. Miller, and Gerald Gurin, "Stratum Identification and Consciousness," *Social Psychology Quarterly* 43.1 (1980): 33.

18. Mouffe, "Hegemony and New Political Subjects," 91.

19. John O'Neal, quoted by Bernard Weiner in "New Focus for Peoples' Festival," *San Francisco Chronicle*, 16 April 1983, 36.

20. Victor Turner, "Are There Universals of Performance in Myth, Ritual, and Drama?" in *By Means of Performance*, ed. Richard Schechner (Cambridge: Cambridge University Press, 1990), 17.

21. Avant-Garde practitioners—such as Richard Schechner and Peter Brook—looked to the Third World for theatrical inspiration and also appropriated ideas from the social protest theaters of El Teatro and the BRT. The *Drama Review*'s publication of articles on El Teatro, in the summer of 1967, and its "Black Theater" issue, in the summer of 1968, demonstrated the interest of alternative theater practitioners and theorists in the methodologies and practices of El Teatro and the BRT. As I will discuss in chapter 5, black director Gilbert Moses appropriated the techniques of white experimentalists Jerzy Grotowski, Richard Schechner, and Antonin Artaud during his rehearsals for the 1969 production of *Slave Ship* by Amiri Baraka at the Chelsea Theater Center in Brooklyn, New York. Interestingly, Peter Brook came to San Juan Bautista in 1973 to work with El Teatro Campesino. Brook and El Teatro exchanged ideas about ritual in the theater. Their collective work informed the philosophy and practice of both groups. See "A Return to Aztec and Mayan Roots," *Drama Review* 18.4 (December 1974): 56–71.

22. In Oakland, California, the Black Panther Party was founded in 1966. The following year in Detroit, Michigan, the Republic of New Africa (RNA) was established. Both preached black nationalism and self-determination. While the Black Panthers "espoused black control of the inner cities," the RNA proposed a separate black state in the South. See August Meier and Elliot Rudwick, "Introduction," in *Black Protest in the Sixties*, ed. August Meier, Elliot Rudwick, and John Bracey Jr. (New York: Mark Wiener Publishing, 1991), 19–20.

23. Cleveland Sellers, *The River of No Return: The Autobiography of a Black Militant and the Life and Death of SNCC* (New York: William Morrow, 1973), 166–67.

24. The national Chicano Moratorium on the War in Vietnam, organized by the Brown Berets and other militant Chicano organizations, erupted in violence as over twenty thousand Chicanos gathered in Los Angeles on 29 August 1970. Overzealous police clashed with demonstrators, resulting in a riotous confrontation and mass arrests. One casualty of this event was Rubén

Salazar, a reporter for the Los Angeles Spanish-language television station, KMEX-TV. Prior to the moratorium Salazar had been active in publicizing issues of police abuse. Ironically, his death at the hands of deputies from the Los Angeles County Sheriff's office became a highly politicized incident of police brutality, around which the Chicano community rallied together.

25. William L. Van Deburg, *New Day in Babylon: The Black Power Movement and American Culture, 1965–1975* (Chicago: University of Chicago Press, 1992), 171.

26. Stuart Hall, "New Ethnicities," *Black Film/British Cinema*, ICA Documents no. 7 (London: ICA, 1988), 30.

27. Meier and Rudwick, "Introduction," 19–20.

28. Paul Gilroy, *"There Ain't No Black in the Union Jack"* (Chicago: University of Chicago Press, 1987), 234–35.

29. Amiri Baraka, quoted by Saul Gottlieb, "They Think You're an Airplane and You're Really a Bird," *Evergreen Review* (December 1967): 51.

30. Gilroy, *"There Ain't No Black in the Union Jack,"* 36.

31. Ibid., 235.

32. See Acuña, *Oppressed America*, 307–11.

33. bell hooks, "An Aesthetic of Blackness," *Yearning: Race, Gender, and Cultural Politics* (Boston: South End Press, 1990), 107.

34. Norma Alarcón, "Chicana Feminism: In the Tracks of 'The' Native Woman," *Cultural Studies* 4.3 (October 1990): 254.

35. Yolanda Broyles-González, "Toward a Re-Vision of Chicano Theater History: The Women of El Teatro Campesino," in *Making A Spectacle,* ed. Lynda Hart (Ann Arbor: University of Michigan Press, 1989), 216.

36. Antonio Gramsci, "Americanism and Fordism," in *Selections from the Prison Notebooks,* ed. and trans. Quintin Hoare and Geoffrey Nowell Smith (New York: International Publishers, 1971), 279–89.

37. Present in protest strategies of the later gay rights and women's movements as well as the more contemporary antiabortion, animal rights, and even the far right-wing conservative militia movements is the continued significance of race as a metaphor for social antagonism and the replication of strategies of civil disobedience inherited from the civil rights and Black Power movements. The declarations of gay rights or gay power drew directly from the cries for civil rights and Black Power. Within the women's movement the practices of consciousness-raising and collective women's empowerment reflected on the strategies of black cultural nationalism and black consciousness-raising. Inequalities and new political subjects continue to emerge, oppression continues to be redefined, and the goals of democracy repositioned. Appropriating leftist strategies, the militia movement, an overwhelmingly white male right-wing configuration, staged a march on Washington in the spring of 1995, reminiscent of the 1963 march orchestrated by Dr. Martin Luther King. At the Washington Monument the militiamen, now reconstructed as oppressed peoples, listened to the warning from former Watergate burglar–turned–talk show host G. Gordon

Liddy that their rights were "now under attack by the government." New developments in social antagonisms reinforce Mouffe's argument that "there is no one paradigmatic form in which democratic antagonisms can be articulated." Rather, the articulation of new social antagonisms "depends on the discourses and relations of forces in the present struggle for hegemony."

38. Telephone interview with Luis Valdez, 27 February 1996.

39. Telephone interview with Valdez.

40. Angela Y. Davis, "Black Nationalism: The Sixties and the Nineties," in *Black Popular Culture*, ed. Gina Dent (Seattle: Bay Press, 1992), 322.

41. Davis, "Black Nationalism," 323.

42. For example, the now famous May 1969 battle to designate a "People's Park" in Berkeley, on the trash-strewn residue of a demolished block of houses, on many levels incorporated ritual practices—practices instituted by factions on both the Left and the Right. The coalition of leftists who worked to establish People's Park saw their actions and the park they would create as having a privileged status within the social practices and politics of Berkeley as well as within the movement for oppressed people's rights. Building the park was a symbolic act, a ritual practice. For, as the leftist groups engaged in construction of the park, their actions functioned as a symbolic mediation connecting them, they believed, to the higher cause of "social freedom" and linked their activities to other historic struggles against oppression. The response of the University of California, Berkeley, administration can be construed as equally ritualistic. As a "signifying practice" to reinforce its values and its hegemony over its land, the university administration erected a fence around the park and attempted to bulldoze the property. The highly politicized mood of the times and the actions of the university administration, of Governor Ronald Reagan in calling the National Guard to Berkeley, as well as of the students, Vietnam activists, and leftist groups in protecting People's Park all served to intensify the meanings of the park. "On May 30, 1969, upwards of twenty-five thousand marched peacefully through Berkeley to the park, while bayoneted Guardsmen lined the fence and police sharpshooters manned the rooftops" (Todd Gitlin, "The Spring of Hope, the Winter of Despair," *The Sixties: Years of Hope, Days of Rage* [New York: Bantam Books, 1993], 358). In its particular historic moment and as a result of the ritual practices around its existence, this small indistinct piece of land became more than a park. It reached an elevated, symbolic, and even spiritual status. For, as Catherine Bell contends: "The social or cultural context of ritual does not exist separately from the act; the context is created in the acts. In other words, ritualization is *historical* practice" (Catherine Bell, "The Dynamics of Ritual Power," *Journal of Ritual Studies* 4.2 [Summer 1990]: 310).

43. Davis, "Black Nationalism," 324.

44. Yolanda Broyles-González, "El Teatro and the Mexican Popular Perfor-

mance Tradition," *El Teatro Campesino: Theater and the Chicano Movement* (Austin: University of Texas Press, 1994), 59.

45. Broyles-González, "El Teatro Campesino," 63.

46. Broyles-González, "El Teatro Campesino," 62.

47. In the 1970s Valdez and El Teatro would turn more specifically toward these religious pageant plays as well as to an exploration of the spiritual roots of Chicano experience. His new theatrical experimentation alienated some more radical Chicanos as it moved away from the explicitly social purposes of the *actos* toward a more spiritually oriented theater.

48. Turner, *From Ritual to Theater*, 70; Ranjini Obeyeskere, "The Significance of Performance for Its Audience: An Analysis of Three Sri Lankan Rituals," in *By Means of Performance*, ed. Richard Schechner (Cambridge: Cambridge University Press, 1990), 124.

49. Turner, *From Ritual to Theater*, 70.

50. Turner, *From Ritual to Theater*, 71.

51. Amiri Baraka, *The Autobiography of LeRoi Jones/Amiri Baraka* (New York: Freundlich Books, 1984), 212.

52. Bell, "Dynamics of Ritual Power," 310.

53. Charles Patterson, *Black Ice*, in *Black Fire*, ed. Amiri Baraka and Larry Neal (New York: William Morrow, 1968), 561. All subsequent quotations from this play will be cited parenthetically in the text.

54. Eric MacDonald, *Theater at the Margins: Text and the Post-Structured Stage* (Ann Arbor: University of Michigan Press, 1993), 25.

55. Luis Valdez and El Teatro Campesino, *Las Dos Caras del Patroncito* (San Juan Bautista, CA: Menyah Press, 1971), 16. All subsequent quotations from this play will be cited parenthetically in the text. The line "Patron, you look like me!" was also somewhat ironic because the parts of the Patroncito and the Farmworker were played by the brothers Luis and Danny Valdez, respectively, who do not bear a heavy family resemblance.

56. The staging of this undressing parallels the moment in *Galileo*, by Bertolt Brecht, when the pope dresses before the audience for a council meeting to decide Galileo's fate. Standing onstage in his undergarments, the pope is simply another man, but, when he dons the vestments of the pope, he becomes God's earthly ambassador and assumes all the powers of this position. Brecht's staging separates the man, the body, from the symbols of spiritual power. This mise-en-scène reinforces for the audience the idea that the pope's power is not essential, nor internal, within the body. Rather, the pope's authority is constructed, layer by layer, as he dons his religious attire.

57. Andrea G. Labinger, "The Cruciform Farce in Latin America: Two Plays," in *Themes in Drama: Farce*, ed. James Redmond (Cambridge: Cambridge University Press, 1988), 220.

58. Lawrence B. Glick, "The Right to Equal Opportunity," in *La Raza: Forgotten Americans*, ed. Julian Samora (South Bend, IN: University of Notre Dame Press, 1966), 100.

59. Vernon M. Briggs Jr., *Chicanos and Rural Poverty* (Baltimore: Johns Hopkins University Press, 1973), 21.
60. Guillermo E. Hernández, *Chicano Satire* (Austin: University of Texas Press, 1991), 36.
61. Acuña, *Oppressed America*, 324.
62. "Shriver Prodded by Fino on Black Arts School Funding," *New York Times*, 29 December 1965, 15.
63. Sargent Shriver, quoted by John Loftus, "Election of the Poor May Be Ended, Shriver Tells House Committee," *New York Times*, 9 March 1966, 24.
64. Stephen Greenblatt, quoted by Dollimore, "Foreword," *Political Shakespeare*, 13.
65. John Weisman, "El Teatro Campesino," *Guerrilla Theater* (Garden City, NJ: Anchor Books, 1973), 19.

Chapter 3

1. Victor Turner, *The Forest of Symbols: Aspects of Ndembu Ritual* (Ithaca, NY: Cornell University Press, 1967), 28.
2. Jean and John Comaroff, "Introduction," *Modernity and Its Malcontents* (Chicago: University of Chicago Press, 1993), xx–xxi.
3. Comaroff and Comaroff, "Introduction," xx.
4. Terry Eagleton, *Marxism and Literature* (Berkeley: University of California Press, 1976), 23.
5. Fredric Jameson, *Marxism and Form: Twentieth-Century Dialectical Theories of Literature* (Princeton, NJ: Princeton University Press, 1972), 403.
6. Comaroff and Comaroff, "Introduction," xx.
7. Victor Turner, *From Ritual to Theater* (New York: PAJ Publications, 1982), 45.
8. Kimberly Benston, "The Aesthetic of Modern Black Drama: From Mimesis to Methexis," in *The Theater of Black Americans*, ed. Errol Hill (Englewood Cliffs, NJ: Prentice-Hall, 1980), 1:62.
9. Comaroff and Comaroff, "Introduction," xxii.
10. Donna Haraway, "Situated Knowledges," *Feminist Studies* 14.3 (1988): 575–600.
11. Haraway, "Situated Knowledges," 590.
12. Larry Neal, "The Black Arts Movement," *Tulane Drama Review* 12.4 (Summer 1968): 38.
13. Robert Weimann, "Ritual and Mimesis," *Shakespeare and the Popular Tradition in the Theater* (Baltimore: Johns Hopkins University Press, 1978), 1.
14. Amiri Baraka, *In Our Terribleness* (New York: Bobbs-Merrill, 1970), 89.
15. Baraka, *In Our Terribleness*, 89.
16. Amiri Baraka, *"A Black Mass," Four Black Revolutionary Plays* (New York: Bobbs-Merrill, 1969), 22. All subsequent quotations from this play will be cited parenthetically in the text.
17. Luis Valdez and El Teatro Campesino, *"La Conquista de Mexico," Actos* (San

Juan Bautista, CA: Menyah Press, 1971), 50. All subsequent quotations from this play will be cited parenthetically in the text.

18. I am indebted here to the argument put forth by Tracy Schinn-Schroeder in her undergraduate honors thesis entitled, "Amiri Baraka, Cultural Nationalism, and the Postmodern Situation" (Stanford University, May 1993).

19. Minh-Ha Trinh, "Difference: 'A Special Third World Women Issue,'" *Woman, Native, Other* (Bloomington: Indiana University Press, 1989), 96.

20. Trinh, "Difference," 80–81.

21. Yvonne Yarbro-Bejarano, "The Female Subject in Chicano Theater: Sexuality, 'Race,' and Class," *Theater Journal* (December 1986): 393.

22. Yarbro-Bejarano, "Female Subject in Chicano Theater," 392.

23. Amiri Baraka, *The Autobiography of LeRoi Jones/Amiri Baraka* (New York: Freundlich Books, 1984), 253.

24. See Angela McRobbie, "Strategies of Vigilance: An Interview with Gayatri Chakravorti Spivak," *Block* 10 (1985): 5–9.

25. McRobbie, "Strategies of Vigilance," 7.

26. Somewhat similarly to Spivak, Chela Sandoval writes that oppositional agency for any contemporary liberation movement depends on "a *tactical subjectivity* with the capacity to recenter depending upon the kinds of oppression confronted." I believe that the inherent fluidity of the theater— that when you engage in the processes of theater you are engaging in a process of strategic construction—makes it an ideal location for the practice of such "*tactical*" weaponry." See Chela Sandoval, "U.S. Third World Feminism: The Theory and Method of Oppositional Consciousness in the Postmodern World," *Genders* 10 (Spring 1991): 1–24.

27. Spivak, quoted by McRobbie, "Strategies of Vigilance," 7.

28. Amiri Baraka, "The Revolutionary Theater," *Black World* 15.5 (April 1966): 21.

29. Yolanda Broyles-González, "El Teatro Campesino and the Mexican Popular Tradition," *El Teatro Campesino: Theater and the Chicano Movement* (Austin: University of Texas Press, 1994), 6.

30. Hayden White, *The Content of the Form* (Baltimore: Johns Hopkins University Press, 1987), ix.

31. Harold Coy, *The Mexicans* (Boston: Little, Brown, 1970), 103.

32. Coy, *Mexicans*, 15.

33. Henry Louis Gates Jr., *The Signifying Monkey* (London: Oxford University Press, 1988), 92.

34. Luis Valdez, "Los Vendidos," *Actos* (San Juan Bautista, CA: Menyah Press, 1971), 36. All subsequent quotations from this play are cited parenthetically in the text.

35. Ben Caldwell, "*The Prayer Meeting or the First Militant Black Minister,*" *A Black Quartet* (New York: New American Library, 1970), 30. All subsequent quotations from this play are cited parenthetically in the text.

36. Interestingly, the Minister's words and the incidents of Brother Jackson's murder that proceed the play have an ironic and prescient quality. The jury

in Simi Valley, California, considering the 1991 videotaped beating of Rodney King in Los Angeles, similarly decided that it was Rodney King's fault for "provokin' that officer." The subsequent uprisings in Los Angeles, 29 April 1992, decried that verdict. The protest march that the Minister intends to lead at the end of the play stands to be as incendiary as the events in Los Angeles. I do not mean to suggest that the urgency in 1992 Los Angeles is synonymous with that present in 1969 at the time of the performances of *The Prayer Meeting*. Clearly, there are marked differences. I do want to point out their connection in terms of incidents of police brutality. From the earliest race riots in this country, through those of the 1960s and up to the conflagration in Los Angeles, the instigating moment of racial explosion has invariably been an unwarranted racial altercation with the police. Consequently, Caldwell's invocation of such an incident in *A Prayer Meeting* holds significant historical as well as contemporary meanings.

37. Geneviève Fabre, "The Militant Theater," *Drumbeats, Masks, and Metaphor* (Cambridge, MA: Harvard University Press, 1983), 96.
38. Victor Turner, *From Ritual to Theater* (New York: PAJ Publications, 1982), 82.
39. Barbara and Carlton Molette, *Black Theater: Premise and Presentation* (Bristol, IN: Wyndham Hall Press, 1986), 83.
40. Molette and Molette, *Black Theater*, 84.
41. Jean and John Comaroff, "Introduction," xxii.
42. Carlos Ynostraza, quoted by John Weisman, *Guerrilla Theater* (Garden City, NJ: Anchor Books, 1973), 19.
43. Richard G. Scharine, *From Class to Caste in American Drama* (Westport, CN: Greenwood Press, 1991), 188.
44. Benston, "Aesthetic of Modern Black Drama," 62.
45. Betty Ann Diamond, "Brown Eyed Children of the Sun: The Cultural Politics of El Teatro Campesino" (Ph.D. diss., University of Wisconsin, Madison, 1977), 95.
46. Jorge Huerta, *Chicano Theater: Themes and Forms* (Ypsilanti, MI: Bilingual Press, 1982), 67.
47. Huerta, *Chicano Theater*, 67.
48. Gates, *Signifying Monkey*, 3–88.
49. Broyles-González, "El Teatro Campesino and the Mexican Popular Performance Tradition," 37–38.
50. Fabre, "Militant Theater," 94.
51. Victor Turner, *Dramas, Fields and Metaphors; Symbolic Action in Human Society* (Ithaca, NY: Cornell University Press, 1974), 56.

Chapter 4

1. Jean Comaroff and John Comaroff, "Introduction," *Modernity and Its Malcontents* (Chicago: University of Chicago Press, 1993), xxi.
2. See Margaret Thompson Drewal, *Yoruba Ritual: Performance Play Agency* (Bloomington: Indiana University Press, 1992), 12–29; also see Jean

Comaroff, *Body of Power, Spirit of Resistance* (Chicago: University of Chicago Press, 1985), 8–9.

3. Jorge Huerta, *Chicano Theater: Themes and Forms* (Ypsilanti, MI: Bilingual Press, 1982), 27.

4. Clayton Riley, "Art Is What Moves You," *New York Times*, 23 November 1969, sec. 2, 3.

5. Luis Valdez, quoted by Boniface Saludes, "Viva La Huelga Heard at Cotati," *Press Democrat*, 6 May 1966, 6.

6. See Jorge Huerta, "From Temple to Arena: Teatro Chicano Today," in *The Identification and Analysis of Chicano Literature*, ed. Francisco Jiménez (New York: Bilingual Press, 1979), 100–101.

7. Beth Bagby, "El Teatro Campesino: An Interview with Luis Valdez," *Drama Review* 11 (Summer 1967): 74.

8. Telephone interview with Gilbert Moses, 23 August 1990.

9. Amiri Baraka, quoted by Theodore Hudson, *From LeRoi Jones to Amiri Baraka: The Literary Works* (Durham, NC: Duke University Press, 1973), 172.

10. Kimberly Benston, "Vision and Form in Slave Ship," in *Imanu Amiri Baraka (LeRoi Jones): A Collection of Essays*, ed. Kimberly Benston (Englewood Cliffs, NJ: Prentice-Hall, 1978), 174.

11. Telephone interview with Moses, 23 August 1990.

12. Walter Kerr, "Is This Their Dream?" *New York Times*, 23 November 1969, sec. 2, 3.

13. Don Isaacs, "The Death of the Proscenium Stage," *Antioch Review* 31.2 (Summer 1971): 250.

14. Jerry Tallmer, "Across the Footlights," *New York Post*, 21 November 1969, 64.

15. Telephone interview with Moses, 23 August 1990.

16. Telephone interview with Moses, 23 August 1990.

17. Telephone interview with Moses, 23 August 1990.

18. Baz Kershaw, *The Politics of Performance: Radical Theater as Cultural Intervention* (London: Routledge, 1992), 72–73.

19. See Homi Bhabha on performative excess in his article "Of Mimicry and Man: The Ambivalence of Colonial Discourse," *October* 28 (Spring 1984): 126.

20. See Yolanda Broyles-González, "Toward a Re-Vision of Chicano Theater History: The Women of El Teatro Campesino," in *Making Spectacle*, ed. Lynda Hart (Ann Arbor: University of Michigan Press, 1989), 210.

21. Yolanda Broyles-González, "El Teatro Campesino and the Mexican Popular Performance Tradition," *El Teatro Campesino: Theater and the Chicano Movement* (Austin: University of Texas Press, 1994), 7.

22. Broyles-González, "El Teatro Campesino and the Mexican Popular Performance Tradition," 7.

23. Nicolás Kanellos, *A History of Hispanic Theater in the United States: Origins to 1940* (Austin: University of Texas Press, 1990), 97.

24. Luis Valdez and El Teatro Campesino, "*Quinta Temporada*," *Actos* (San Juan

Bautista, CA: Menyah Press, 1971), 22. All subsequent quotes from this play will be cited parenthetically in the text.

25. Juan Bruce-Novoa, *Retrospace: Collected Essays on Chicano Literature* (Houston: Arte Publico Press, 1990), 149.

26. Maria Shevtsova, "The Sociology of Theater, Part Three: Performance," *New Theater Quarterly* 19 (August 1989): 293.

27. Luis Valdez, quoted by Beth Bagby, "El Teatro Campesino: An Interview with Luis Valdez," *Drama Review* 11 (Summer 1967): 78.

28. Bagby, "El Teatro Campesino," 74.

29. Huerta, *Chicano Theater*, 24.

30. Huerta, *Chicano Theater*, 26.

31. Geneviève Fabre, "Dialectics of Masks in El Teatro Campesino: From Images to Ritualized Events," in *Missions in Conflict: Essays on U.S.-Mexican Relations and Chicano Culture*, ed. Renate von Bardeleben, Dietrich Briesemeister, and Juan Bruce-Novoa (Tübingen: Gunter Narr Verlag, 1986), 95.

32. El Teatro used a yellow pig mask to represent the Patroncito in *Las Dos Caras*. The pig mask, created by the company stage manager and mask maker, Errol Franklin, held particularly negative connotations for the farmworker audience. The pig was a derogative symbol associated with the police, the ranch owner, and other figures of authority. When Luis Valdez jumped onto stage as the Patroncito in *Las Dos Caras*, wearing the pig mask and chomping a cigar, the audience instantly booed and jeered him in recognition.

33. Fabre, "Dialectics of Masks in El Teatro Campesino," 95.

34. Armando B. Rendon, *Chicano Manifesto* (New York: Macmillan, 1971), 8.

35. Note within Rendon's words the invocation of the male pronoun and the erasure of the Chicana within his declaration of *Chicanismo*. Angie Chabram-Dernersesian discusses this in her article "I Throw Punches for My Race, but I Don't Want to Be a Man: Writing US—Chican-nos (Girl, Us/Chican*as*—into the Movement Script," in *Cultural Studies*, ed. Lawrence Grossberg, Cary Nelson, and Paula Treichler (London: Routledge, 1992), 81–95.

36. Rendon, *Chicano Manifesto*, 12.

37. Benston, "Vision and Form in Slave Ship," 178.

38. John Lahr, "On-Stage," *Village Voice* 4, December 1969, 51.

39. Benston, "Vision and Form in Slave Ship," 183.

40. Paul Carter Harrison, *The Drama of Nommo* (New York: Grove Press, 1972), 197.

41. Victor Turner, *Dramas, Fields and Metaphors: Symbolic Action in Human Society* (Ithaca, NY: Cornell University Press, 1974), 153.

42. Amiri Baraka, *"Slave Ship," The Motion of History and Other Plays* (New York: William Morrow, 1978), 141. All subsequent quotes will be cited parenthetically in the text.

43. Comaroff and Comaroff, "Introduction," xxi.

44. Stan Machlin, "*Slave Ship* Succeeds as Theater," Collected Papers of Amiri Baraka, Moorland-Spingarn Library, Howard University, Washington, DC.
45. See chapter 1.
46. Stefan Brecht, "LeRoi Jones' *Slave Ship*," *Drama Review* 14 (Winter 1970): 215, 218.
47. Fabre, "Militant Theater," 102.
48. For a discussion of the relationship between Amiri Baraka's practice and theory to the theater of Antonin Artaud, see Mance Williams, *Black Theater in the 1960s and 1970s* (Westport, CT: Greenwood Press, 1985), 21–23; and Leslie Sanders, *The Development of Black Theater in America* (Baton Rouge: Louisiana State University Press, 1988), 126–30.
49. Fabre, "Militant Theater," 103.

Chapter 5

1. I have chosen to use the terms *performing* and *performer*, rather than *acting* and *actor*, to emphasize the distinctions between performing in the social protest theater and more conventional examples of realistic method acting. The presentational style, the explicit social messages, the ritualistic communion with the audience, I believe necessitated a style of performing as well as a type of performer that were unique to the social protest performance.
2. Luis Valdez, "Notes on Chicano Theater," *Actos* (San Juan Bautista, CA: Menyah Press, 1971), 1.
3. Herbert Blau, *Audience* (Baltimore: Johns Hopkins University Press, 1990), 148.
4. Keir Elam, *The Semiotics of Theatre and Drama* (London: Methuen, 1980), 97.
5. Susan Bennett, *Theatre Audiences* (London: Routledge, 1990), 179.
6. Bennett, *Theatre Audiences*, 180.
7. Herbert Blau, *To All Appearances* (New York: Routledge, 1992), 128.
8. Blau, *To All Appearances*, 128.
9. Amiri Baraka, "The Task of the Negro Writer," *Negro Digest* (April 1965): 65.
10. Amiri Baraka, "Black Theater in the 1960s" (MS, 1986), 16.
11. Baraka, "Black Theater in the 1960s," 16.
12. Paulla Ebron, currently an assistant professor in the Anthropology Department at Stanford University, upon seeing a lecture/performance of Baraka and the Spirit House Movers in 1968, decided to leave college and join the Spirit House Movers. Other equally motivated and socially conscious young black people from around the country did so as well.
13. Larry Miller, "Spirit House," *Black Theater* 2 (1969): 34.
14. Luis Valdez, "El Teatro Campesino, Its Beginnings," in *The Chicanos: Mexican American Voices*, ed. Ed Ludwig and James Santibáñez (Baltimore: Penguin Books, 1971), 115.
15. Luis Valdez, quoted in "New Grapes," *Newsweek*, 31 July 1967, 79.

16. Elam, *Semiotics of Theater and Drama*, 22.

17. Valdez, "El Teatro, Its Beginnings," 115.

18. Telephone interview with Luis Valdez, 27 February 1996.

19. Felix Alvarez, quoted by Carlos Morton, "Felix Alvarez—A Mito Come True: An Interview," *Tenaz II* (1971): 11.

20. Luis Valdez, "The Actos," *Actos* (San Juan Bautista, CA: Menyah Press, 1971), 6.

21. Margaret Thompson Drewal, *Yoruba Ritual: Performers, Play, Agency* (Bloomington: Indiana University Press, 1992), 22.

22. Victor Turner, *From Ritual to Theater* (New York: PAJ Publications, 1982), 110.

23. Drewal, *Yoruba Ritual*, 10.

24. Telephone interview with Gilbert Moses, 23 August 1990.

25. Spirit House Movers, "Unity Prayer Creed of the Spirit House Movers and Players" (1966), Amiri Baraka Papers, Moorland-Spingarn Library, Howard University, Washington, DC.

26. Luis Valdez, *"Pensamiento Serpentino," Early Works* (Houston, TX: Arte Publico Press, 1990), 173.

27. Interestingly, during the mid-1970s in San Juan Bautista, El Teatro—in a manner similar to avant-garde groups of the period, such as the Living Theater—lived and worked communally. The group of now thirty members lived on and collectively farmed the land around El Centro Campesino Cultural. In addition, Valdez, like Baraka and the Spirit House Movers, instituted a "Unity Creed" in order to reinforce the spiritual and communal philosophy of the troupe. "We are a family composed of families of married and single people, children and adults, compadres and comadres, uncles and aunts, brothers and sisters, who live communally. We are all brothers and sisters because we have a Common Father. . . . He who created us, He who uplifted us, Our Father of the Astros, GOD THE FATHER." See Carlos Morton, "El Teatro Campesino," *Drama Review* 18.4 (December 1974): 71–76.

28. Valdez, *Pensamiento Serpentino*, 172–73.

29. Telephone interview with Phil Esparza, 29 September 1993.

30. Richard Schechner, *Performance Theory* (New York: Routledge, 1988), 180.

31. Jean Marie-Pradier, "Towards a Biological Theory of the Body in Performance," *New Theatre Quarterly* 6.21 (February 1990): 95.

32. Both Valdez and Baraka eventually became involved in processes of auditions. Yolanda Broyles-González discusses the disruptive effect of auditions on the El Teatro ensemble in 1978. See her essay "El Teatro Campesino: From Alternative Movement to Mainstream," *El Teatro Campesino: Theater and the Chicano Movement* (Austin: University of Texas Press, 1994), 218.

33. Telephone interview with Moses, 23 August 1990.

34. Telephone interview with Moses, 23 August 1990.

35. Conversation with Luis Valdez, 22 February 1993.

36. Christiane Rahner, "The Background of the Chicano Theater and the Artistic and Political Development of Teatro Campesino" (Master's thesis, University of California, San Diego, 1980), 46.

37. See Broyles-González, "El Teatro Campesino and the Mexican Popular Tradition," 1–77.

38. John Harrop and Jorge Huerta, "The Agricultural Pilgrimage of Luis Valdez," *Theater Quarterly* 5.17 (March–May 1973): 32.

39. As El Teatro evolved in the 1970s, the troupe's acting philosophy and training regime became more and more a synthesis of Mayan spiritualism and practical theater exercises. In San Juan Bautista in the early 1970s Valdez developed an actor warm-up and workshop entitled "The Theater of the Sphere." The name related to the perfect sphere of the sun (the sun was a significant source of energy to El Teatro and its Indian ancestors) and the circular Mayan calendar. The workshop involved a process of "centering." The purpose of this centering was to gain physical, mental, and emotional control over oneself and one's environment. Valdez maintained that humans needed to be in harmony with other human beings and nature itself. In addition, the warm-up sought to "engender the actors in a complete state of belief so that . . . they will be literally recreating life according to their ancestors. There will be no physical, emotional or intellectual resistance"(Carlos Morton, "La Serpiente Sheds Its Skin: El Teatro Campesino," *Drama Review* 18.4 [December 1974]: 76). Through the warm-up, in effect, Valdez attempted to "retribalize" the actors and structure, foster, and maintain spontaneous *communitas*. The actors lived, worked, and worshiped communally at El Centro Campesino Cultural. Valdez remarked, "We'll be getting deeper and deeper into ourselves, because the Sixties was a time of outward explosion, while the Seventies is a time of inward explosion" (quoted by Morton, "La Serpiente Sheds Its Skin," 75). Victor Turner warned that "the inherent contradictions between spontaneous communitas and a markedly structured system are so great, however, that any venture which attempts to combine these modalities will constantly be threatened by structural cleavage or by the suffocation of communitas" (*From Ritual to Theater*, 49–50). Eventually, by the end of the 1970s El Teatro disbanded its plan of communal living. Still, the principles of the acting warmup, workshops, and the acting work of El Teatro at that time were based on the interaction of spiritual, emotional, mental, and physical elements and related to what Valdez termed the "Six Footsteps of God."

The Six Footsteps of God

Zero represents meditation or the pre-beginning step of our exercise, and the post-ending of all our actions. It precedes and follows our improvisations. It is no-thing, no-being. It means being as still as you can.

One or "I am" means unity. It is consciousness of one's existence, how everybody is in my life, my dream, my movie. It is also being conscious of one's heartbeat; sense your heart vibrating and beating throughout every part of your body. You are a pulsating heartbeat.

Two is duality, in which the seeker explores the dual nature of respiration (inhalation and exhalation), in and out, back and forth, up and down, left and right. It refers to the entire dualistic nature of the body and helps the seeker realize his God and Devil, Man and Woman duality.

Three is the triangle, the clash of two opposing forces ending up in a new thrust, in a new direction. It is the Marxist Trinity: thesis, antithesis, and synthesis. It is also the trinity of The Father, The Son, and the Holy Ghost. Furthermore, your cosmic or third eye is a synthesis of your two eyes. Neither left nor right views, just vision.

Four or "Kan" means serpent in Mayan. It is also the illusion of the material, where things seem to be stable but actually everything is in motion. "Kan" means balance; try to balance on your hands, feet, or head.

Five signifies the living pyramid. It is presence. You fill up a room with presence, your spirit, your being. It is also a conscious, deliberate, creative, free flowing exercise, followed by a free free exercise and then a free free free exercise.

Six or "Cimi" means death: The Death of the ego of the old self, in preparation for the rebirth of the new. It is a point at which the actor goes beyond mere consciousness of himself and becomes aware of himself as actor and audience simultaneously. (Taken from Morton, "La Serpiente Sheds Its Skin," 76)

Julio Gonzales, a member of the company in the 1970s, who later assisted Valdez in the instruction of the workshop, detailed how "The Six Footsteps of God" workshop was expanded to "twenty footsteps each representing dates on the Mayan calendar. A series of exercises were assigned to each date" (telephone interview with Julio Gonzales, 15 September 1993). During the 1980s and 1990s the acting workshops and training principles of Valdez and El Teatro have continued to evolve. Unfortunately, the exercises have never been formally recorded. Currently, Valdez and El Teatro are in the process of writing down the various exercises and constructing a workbook. Valdez also teaches a workshop, now entitled "The Vibrant Being." The basis of this workshop is still his early philosophical, spiritual, neo-Mayan theories from *Pensamiento Serpentino*. For a more recent discussion of the Theater of the Sphere, see Yolanda Broyles-González, "Theater of the Sphere: Toward the Formulation of a Native Performance Theory and Practice," *El Teatro Campesino: Theater in the Chicano Movement* (Austin: University of Texas Press, 1994), 79–128.

40. Conversation with Luis Valdez, 22 February 1993.
41. Ralph J. Gleason, "Vital, Earthy and Alive," *San Francisco Chronicle,* 4 May 1966, 41.

42. See Jorge Huerta, *Chicano Theater: Themes and Forms* (Ypsilanti, MI: Bilingual Press, 1982), 16.

43. Luis Valdez, "El Teatro Campesino," *Ramparts* (July 1966): 55.

44. Thomas Pawley, "Black Theatre Audiences," in *The Theatre of Black Americans*, ed. Errol Hill (Englewood Cliffs, NJ: Prentice-Hall, 1980), 2:109–19.

45. Nicolás Kanellos, "Folklore in Chicano Theater and Chicano Theater as Folklore," in *The Chicano Experience*, ed. Stanley A. West and June Macklin (Boulder, CO: Westview Press, 1979), 167.

46. Anthony Cohen, quoted by Paul Gilroy, *"There Ain't No Black in the Union Jack"* (Chicago: University of Chicago Press, 1987), 235.

47. Victor Turner, *The Anthropology of Performance* (New York: PAJ Publications, 1986), 133, 47, 48.

48. Victor Turner, *Drama, Fields and Metaphors* (Ithaca, NY: Cornell University Press, 1975), 114.

49. Baz Kershaw, *The Politics of Performance: Radical Theater as Cultural Intervention* (London: Routledge, 1992), 247.

50. For blacks in the 1960s and 1970s being perceived as "down with the cause" or as a "righteous black brother or sister" held significant cultural currency. Journalist Jill Nelson subtitles *Volunteer Slavery*, her autobiographic exposé on her experience as a reporter for the *Washington Post*, "An Authentic Negro Experience." In *Volunteer Slavery* Nelson relates how, growing up as a child of the black bourgeoisie in the 1960s and 1970s, she longed for what she then considered an authentic "Negro experience." *Authentic* connoted urban, activist, and proletariat, connected to the lives of the black masses. Her middle-class experience was perceived as outside of the traditional contexts of black existence and therefore suspect and, consequently, excluded from definitions of black authenticity. Implicitly and explicitly, her memoir assails such monolithic thinking.

51. Amiri Baraka, *The Autobiography of LeRoi Jones/Amiri Baraka* (New York: Freundlich Books, 1984), 279.

52. Paul Gilroy, "Nothing but Sweat Inside My Hands: Diaspora Aesthetics and Black Arts in Britain," *Black Film/British Cinema*, ICA Documents no. 7 (London: ICA, 1988), 44.

53. For further discussion of the inclusionary/exclusionary dialectic of authenticity in cultural expression, see Paul Gilroy, *The Black Atlantic* (Cambridge, MA: Harvard University Press, 1993), 96.

54. Dolan's discussion of authenticity and lesbianism in *Presence and Desire* was prompted by her own initial inclination to use heterosexual women in the performance of scenes from a lesbian play, *Dos Lebos*, at the Women and Theater Program preconference to the American Theater in Higher Education Conference in August 1987. The audience would have known prior to the performance of the sexuality of the performers. Consequently, just as in the social protest performances of El Teatro and the BRT, theatrical mediation before and after the performances would have influenced the audience's perception of authenticity and reception of the performance. After

the ideological objections of feminist theater critic and scholar Sue-Ellen Case, however, Dolan reconsidered the ramifications of casting heterosexuals. With revised insight Dolan maintains:

> For a lesbian spectator a heterosexual woman would not be believable as a lesbian. As much as she might empathize with or do visualization exercises to project herself into a lesbian role, a heterosexual woman will never know, in her body, what it feels like to be queer in a homophobic culture. She has never developed the survival instincts to break the code, to signify and to read what dominant representations suppress. (See *Presence and Desire* [Ann Arbor: University of Michigan Press, 1994], 145)

55. See August Wilson, "Why I Want a Black Director," in *May All Your Fences Have Gates,* ed. Alan Nadel (Des Moines: University of Iowa Press, 1994), 200–204.
56. See "Culture Watch: Miscast Protest," *Los Angeles Times,* 19 August 1992, "Metro" sec., pt. B, 6; "Luis Valdez Speaks Out on Frida Controversy," *Daily Variety,* 21 August 1992; Judith Green, "Tables Turned in Hispanic Casting Dispute, Writer Director Valdez Finds He's in an Ironic Situation," *San Diego Union Tribune,* 8 September 1992, "Lifestyle" sec., sec. E, 4.
57. Conversation with Luis Valdez, 22 February 1993.
58. Marco De Marinis, "The Dramaturgy of the Spectator," *Drama Review* 31.2 (Summer 1987): 103.
59. De Marinis, "Dramaturgy of the Spectator," 103.
60. Wole Söyinka, "Drama and the Revolutionary Ideal," in *In Person: Achebe, Awoonor, and Soyinka,* ed. Karen L. Morell (Seattle: Institute for Comparative and Foreign Area Studies, University of Washington, 1975), 80.
61. Sue-Ellen Case, *Feminism and Theatre* (New York: Methuen, 1988), 116.
62. See Morgan Himelstein, *Drama Was a Weapon* (New Brunswick, NJ: Rutgers University Press, 1963).
63. Luis Valdez, "Notes on Chicano Theater," *Actos* (San Juan Bautista, CA: Menyah Press, 1971), 2.
64. Etheridge Knight, quoted by Larry Neal, "The Black Arts Movement," *Drama Review* 12.4 (Summer 1968): 80.
65. Blau, *Audience,* 190.
66. Michael Vanden Heuvel, *Performing Drama/Dramatizing Performance* (Ann Arbor: University of Michigan Press, 1991), 40–41.
67. Jill Nelson, *Volunteer Slavery* (New York: Noble Press, 1993), 149.
68. Val Ferdinand, "A Report on Black Theatre: New Orleans," *Negro Digest* (April 1970): 28–29.
69. Ferdinand, "Report on Black Theatre in America: New Orleans," 28–29.
70. Luis Valdez, "El Teatro Campesino—Its Beginnings," in *The Chicanos: Mexican American Voices,* ed. Ed Ludwig and James Santibáñez (Baltimore: Penguin Books, 1971), 117.
71. Kershaw, *Politics of Performance,* 35.

72. Kershaw, *Politics of Performance*, 28.
73. Telephone interview with Gilbert Moses, 23 August 1990.
74. "New Grapes," *Newsweek*, 31 July 1967, 79.
75. Ranjini Obeyesekere, "The Significance of Performance: An Analysis of Three Sri Lankan Rituals." In *By Means of Performance*, ed. Richard Schechner (Cambridge: Cambridge University Press, 1990), 130.
76. Margaret Thompson Drewal, *Yoruba Ritual: Performers, Play Agency* (Bloomington: Indiana University Press, 1992), 7.
77. Drewal, *Yoruba Ritual*, 7.
78. Charles Reichenthal, "Underlites," *Flatbush Life*, 6 December 1969, 20.
79. Stefan Brecht, "LeRoi Jones' *Slave Ship*," *Drama Review* 14 (Winter 1970): 218.
80. Himelstein, *Drama Was a Weapon*, 228.
81. Augusto Boal, *Theatre of the Oppressed* (New York: Urizen Books, 1979), 1–50, 100–106.
82. See chapter 4.
83. See my discussion of the liminal and liminoid in chapter 1.
84. Johannes Birringer, *Theatre, Theory, Postmodernism* (Bloomington: Indiana University Press, 1991), 166.

Chapter 6

1. Jean Comaroff, *Body of Power, Spirit of Resistance* (Chicago: University of Chicago Press, 1985), 119.
2. Margaret Thompson Drewal, *Yoruba Ritual: Performers, Play, Agency* (Bloomington: Indiana University Press, 1992), 7. See chapter 5.
3. Robert Weimann, "Ritual and Mimesis," *Shakespeare and the Popular Tradition in the Theater* (Baltimore: Johns Hopkins University Press, 1978), 5.
4. Baz Kershaw, *The Politics of Performance: Radical Theater as Cultural Intervention* (London: Routledge, 1992), 33, 246–48.
5. Geneviève Fabre, "The Militant Theater," *Drumbeats, Masks and Metaphor* (Cambridge, MA: Harvard University Press, 1983), 103. See chapter 4.
6. See J. L. Freedman and S. C. Fraser, "Compliance without Pressure: The Foot-in-the-Door Technique," *Journal of Personality and Social Psychology* 4 (1966): 195–202.
7. See Richard E. Petty and John T. Cacioppo, *Attitudes and Persuasion: Classic and Contemporary Approaches* (Dubuque, IA: William C. Brown and Company, 1981), 167–69.
8. Luis Valdez, quoted in "New Grapes," *Newsweek*, 31 July 1967, 79.
9. Luis Valdez, quoted by Bernard Weiner, in "Corridos: Mexican Ballads of Love, Lust and Death," *San Francisco Chronicle Datebook*, 17 April 1983, 40.
10. Amiri Baraka, *The Autobiography of LeRoi Jones/Amiri Baraka* (New York: Freundlich Books, 1984), 275.
11. Telephone interview with Luis Valdez, 27 February 1996.
12. See Anna Yeatman, *Postmodern Revisions of the Political* (London: Routledge,

1994); Stuart Hall, "New Ethnicities," *Black Film/British Cinema*, ICA Documents no. 7 (London: ICA, 1988), 27–31; Chela Sandoval, "U.S. Third World Feminism: The Theory and Method of Oppositional Consciousness in the Postmodern World," *Genders* 10 (Spring 1991): 1–24; Cornel West, "The New Cultural Politics of Difference," *Keeping Faith* (New York: Routledge, 1993), 3–32.

13. Hall, "New Ethnicities," 28.

14. August Wilson cofounded a black nationalist theater in Pittsburgh in the late 1960s. He believes that his current work is building on that earlier black nationalist tradition. Interestingly, his play *Ma Rainey's Black Bottom*, even as it is set in the 1920s, features the character Toledo, who preaches the tenets of 1960s black nationalism and discusses African retentions. Wilson through his plays continues to assert that African Americans must rediscover their "African-ness." Cherríe Moraga's play *Heroes and Saints* (1990) appropriates and revises the concept of a disembodied head from Luis Valdez's cultural nationalistic drama *The Shrunken Head of Pancho Villa* (1970). While Valdez uses a bodiless male character, Bellarmino, Moraga creates a bodiless Chicana, Cerezita. Moraga's play confronts issues of social protest and Chicana empowerment. George Wolfe's play *The Colored Museum* satirizes and critiques issues from the African-American theater of the 1960s and 1970s. Wolfe discusses "the madness of race" in a manner similar to Amiri Baraka in his controversial 1964 drama, *Dutchman*. See Harry J. Elam Jr., "Signifyin(g) on African-American Theater: *The Colored Museum* by George Wolfe," *Theater Journal* 44 (1992): 291–303.

15. Wahneema Lubiano, "Black Nationalism" (MS, 1994), 8.

16. Lubiano, "Black Nationalism," 13.

17. August Wilson, "Preface," *Three Plays by August Wilson* (Pittsburgh: University of Pittsburgh Press, 1991), ix.

18. David Savran, "An Interview with August Wilson," *In Their Own Words* (New York: Theater Communications Group, 1988), 296.

19. Cherríe Moraga, "Queer Aztlán: The Re-formation of Chicano Tribe," *The Last Generation* (South End Press, 1993), 148, 150.

20. Yvonne Yarbro-Bejarano, "'The Miracle People': Cherríe Moraga's 'Heroes and Saints' and Contemporary Chicano Theater" (MS, 1994), 28.

21. Yeatman, *Postmodern Revisions of the Political*, 92–105.

22. Norma Alarcón, "Chicana Feminism: In the Tracks of the 'Native' Woman," *Cultural Studies* 4.3 (October 1990): 254.

Bibliography

Books

Acuña, Rodolfo. *Occupied America: A History of Chicanos*. 3d ed. New York: HarperCollins, 1988.

Althusser, Louis. *For Marx*. London: Verso NLB, 1969.

Anzaldúa, Gloria. *Borderlands/La Frontera: The New Mestiza*. San Francisco: Spinsters/Aunt Lute, 1987.

Ashley, Kathleen M. *Victor Turner and Cultural Criticism*. Bloomington: Indiana University Press, 1990.

Aston, Elaine, and George Savona. *Theatre as Sign System: A Semiotics of Text and Performance*. New York: Routledge, 1991.

Baker, Houston A. *Blues, Ideology, and Afro-American Literature: A Vernacular Theory*. Chicago: University of Chicago Press, 1984.

Bakhtin, Mikhail. *Rabelais and His World*. Translated by Helene Iswolsky. Bloomington: Indiana University Press, 1984.

Baraka, Amiri. *Blues People: Negro Music in America*. New York: William Morrow, 1963.

———. *Home: Social Essays*. New York: William Morrow, 1966.

———. *Four Black Revolutionary Plays*. New York: Bobbs-Merrill, 1969.

———. *In Our Terribleness: Some Elements and Meaning in Black Style*. New York: Bobbs-Merrill, 1970.

———. *Raise Race Rays Raze: Essays since 1965*. New York: Random House, 1971.

———. *The New Nationalism*. Chicago: Third World Press, 1972.

———. *Black Fire*. New York: William Morrow, 1972.

———. *The Motion of History and Other Plays*. New York: William Morrow, 1978.

———. *The Autobiography of LeRoi Jones/Amiri Baraka*. New York: Freundlich Books, 1984.

Bennett, Susan. *Theater Audiences*. London: Routledge, 1990.

Benston, Kimberly. *Baraka: The Renegade and the Mask*. New Haven: Yale University Press, 1976.

———. *Imamu Amiri Baraka (LeRoi Jones): A Collection of Essays*. Englewood Cliffs, N.J.: Prentice-Hall, 1978.

Bigsby, C. W. E. *Confrontation and Commitment: A Study of Contemporary American Drama, 1959–1966*. Columbia: University of Missouri Press, 1986.

Birringer, Johannes. *Theatre, Theory, Postmodernism*. Bloomington: Indiana University Press, 1991.

Blau, Herbert. *Audience*. Baltimore: Johns Hopkins University Press, 1990.

———. *To All Appearances*. New York: Routledge, 1992.

Boal, Augusto. *Theater of the Oppressed*. New York: Urizen Books, 1979.

Bradby, David, and John McCormick. *People's Theatre*. London: Croom Helm, 1978.

Brecht, Bertolt. *Brecht on Theatre*. Ed. John Willett. New York: Hill and Wang, 1964.

Briggs, Vernon M., Jr. *Chicanos and Rural Poverty*. Baltimore: Johns Hopkins University Press, 1973.

Brown, Lloyd W. *Amiri Baraka*. Boston: Twayne, 1980.

Broyles-González, Yolanda. *El Teatro Campesino: Theater in the Chicano Movement*. Austin: University of Texas Press, 1994.

Bruce-Novoa, Juan. *Retrospace: Collected Essays on Chicano Literature*. Houston: Arte Publico Press, 1990.

Case, Sue-Ellen. *Feminism and Theatre*. New York: Methuen, 1988.

Comaroff, Jean. *Body of Power, Spirit of Resistance: The Culture and History of a South African People*. Chicago: University of Chicago Press, 1985.

Comaroff, Jean, and John. *Modernity and Its Malcontents: Ritual and Power in Postcolonial Africa*. Chicago: University of Chicago Press, 1993.

Coy, Harold. *The Mexicans*. Boston: Little, Brown, 1970.

Cruse, Harold. *The Crisis of the Negro Intellectual*. New York: William Morrow, 1967.

Dent, Gina. *Black Popular Culture*. Seattle: Bay Press, 1992.

Dolan, Jill. *The Feminist Spectator as Critic*. Ann Arbor: University of Michigan Press, 1988.

———. *Presence and Desire: Essays on Gender, Sexuality and Performance*. Ann Arbor: University of Michigan Press, 1994.

Dollimore, John, and Alan Sinfield. *Political Shakespeare: New Essays in Cultural Materialism*. Manchester: Manchester University Press, 1985.

Douglas, Mary. *Purity and Danger: An Analysis of Concepts of Pollution and Taboo*. London: Routledge and Kegan Paul, 1966.

Drewal, Margaret Thompson. *Yoruba Ritual: Performers, Play, Agency*. Bloomington: Indiana University Press, 1992.

Eagleton, Terry. *Marxism and Literature*. Berkeley: University of California Press, 1976.

Elam, Keir. *The Semiotics of Theater and Drama*. London: Methuen, 1980.

Fabre, Geneviève. *Drumbeats, Masks and Metaphor: Contemporary Afro-American Theatre.* Cambridge: Harvard University Press, 1983.

Fanon, Frantz. *Black Skin, White Masks.* Translated by Charles Markmann. New York: Grove Press, 1967.

Fuegi, John. *Bertolt Brecht: Chaos, According to Plan.* Cambridge: Cambridge University Press, 1987.

Fuss, Diana. *Essentially Speaking: Feminism, Nature and Difference.* New York: Routledge, 1989.

Gates, Henry Louis, Jr. *The Signifying Monkey: A Theory of Afro-American Literary Criticism.* New York: Oxford University Press, 1988.

Gayle, Addison, Jr. *The Black Aesthetic.* New York: Vintage Books, 1970.

Gilroy, Paul. *"There Ain't No Black in the Union Jack: The Cultural Politics of Race and Nation."* Chicago: University of Chicago Press, 1987.

———. *The Black Atlantic: Modernity and Double Consciousness.* Cambridge: Harvard University Press, 1993.

Giroux, Henry. *Disturbing Pleasures: Learning Popular Culture.* New York: Routledge, 1994.

Giroux, Henry, and Peter McLaren. *Between Boarders: Pedagogy and the Politics of Cultural Studies.* New York: Routledge, 1994.

Goldberg, David Theo. *The Anatomy of Racism.* Minneapolis: University of Minnesota Press, 1990.

Goodwin, David. *Cesar Chavez: Hope for the People.* New York: Fawcett Columbine, 1991.

Gramsci, Antonio. *"Americanism and Fordism."* In *Selections from the Prison Notebooks,* ed. and trans. Quintin Hoare and Geoffrey Nowell Smith. New York: International Publishers, 1971.

Greenblatt, Stephen. *Renaissance Self-Fashioning: From More to Shakespeare.* Chicago: University of Chicago Press, 1980.

Grossberg, Lawrence, and Cary Nelson. *Marxism and the Interpretation of Culture.* Urbana: University of Illinois Press, 1988.

Grossberg, Lawrence, Cary Nelson, and Paula Treichler. *Cultural Studies.* New York: Routledge, 1992.

Haraway, Donna. *Primate Visions: Gender, Race, and Nature in the World of Modern Science.* New York: Routledge, 1989.

Harrison, Paul Carter. *The Drama of Nommo.* New York: Grove Press, 1972.

Hay, Samuel. *African American Theatre: An Historical and Critical Analysis.* Cambridge: Cambridge University Press, 1994.

Hernández, Guillermo E. *Chicano Satire: A Study in Literary Culture.* Austin: University of Texas, 1991.

Hill, Errol. *The Theater of Black Americans: A Collection of Critical Essays.* Englewood Cliffs, NJ: Prentice-Hall, 1980.

Himelstein, Morgan. *Drama Was a Weapon: The Left-Wing Theatre in New York, 1929–41.* New Brunswick, NJ: Rutgers University Press, 1963.

hooks, bell. *Black Looks: Race and Representation.* Boston: South End Press, 1992.

——. *Yearning: Race, Gender, and Cultural Politics.* Boston: South End Press, 1990.

Hudson, Theodore. *From LeRoi Jones to Amiri Baraka: The Literary Works.* Durham, NC: Duke University Press, 1973.

Huerta, Jorge. *Chicano Theater: Themes and Forms.* Ypsilanti, MI: Bilingual Press, 1982.

Iser, Wolfgang. *The Act of Reading: A Theory of Aesthetic Response.* Baltimore: Johns Hopkins University Press, 1978.

Jameson, Fredric. *Marxism and Form: Twentieth Century Dialectical.* Princeton, NJ: Princeton University Press, 1972.

Kanellos, Nicolas. *A History of Hispanic Theater in the United States: Origins to 1940.* Austin: University of Texas Press, 1990.

Kershaw, Baz. *The Politics of Performance: Radical Theater as Cultural Intervention.* London: Routledge, 1992.

Laclau, Ernesto, and Chantal Mouffe. *Hegemony & Socialist Strategy: Towards a Radical Democratic Politics,* London: Verso, 1985.

Ludwig, Ed, and James Santibáñez. *The Chicanos: Mexican American Voices.* Baltimore: Penguin Books, 1971.

Lyons, Charles R. *Bertolt Brecht: The Despair and the Polemic.* Carbondale: Southern Illinois University Press, 1968.

MacDonald, Eric. *Theater at the Margins: Text and the Post-Structured Stage.* Ann Arbor: University of Michigan Press, 1993.

Meier, August, and Elliot Rudwick. *Black Protest in the Sixties.* New York: Mark Wiener Publishing, 1991.

Mercer, Kobena. *Welcome to the Jungle: New Positions in Black Cultural Studies.* London: Routledge, 1994.

Molette, Barbara, and Carlton Molette. *Black Theater: Premise and Presentation.* Bristol, IN: Wyndham Hall Press, 1986.

Moraga, Cherríe. *The Last Generation: Prose and Poetry.* Boston: South End Press, 1993.

Nadel, Alan. *May All Your Fences Have Gates: Essays on the Drama of August Wilson.* Des Moines: University of Iowa Press, 1994.

Nelson, Jill. *Volunteer Slavery: My Authentic Negro Experience.* New York: Noble Press, 1993.

Petty, Richard E., and John T. Cacioppo. *Attitudes and Persuasion: Classic and Contemporary Approaches.* Dubuque, IA: William C. Brown, 1981.

Reinelt, Janelle G., and Joseph R. Roach. *Critical Theory and Performance.* Ann Arbor: University of Michigan Press, 1992.

Rendon, Armando B. *Chicano Manifesto.* New York: Macmillan, 1971.

Sainer, Arthur. *The Radical Theatre Notebook.* New York: Avon Books, 1975.

Saldívar, Ramón. *Chicano Narrative: The Dialectics of Difference.* Madison: University of Wisconsin Press, 1990.

Samora, Julian. *La Raza: Forgotten Americans.* South Bend, IN: University of Notre Dame Press, 1966.

Sanders, Leslie. *The Development of Black Theater in America*. Baton Rouge: Louisiana State University Press, 1988.

Savran, David. *In Their Own Words: Contemporary American Playwrights*. New York: Theater Communications Group, 1988.

Scharine, Richard. *From Class to Caste in American Drama: Political and Social Themes Since the 1930s*. Westport, CT: Greenwood Press, 1991.

Schechner, Richard. *Between Theater and Anthropology*. Philadelphia: University of Pennsylvania Press, 1985.

———. *By Means of Performance: Intercultural Studies of Theatre and Ritual*. Cambridge: Cambridge University Press, 1990.

———. *The Future of Ritual: Writings on Culture and Performance*. New York: Routledge, 1993.

———. *Performance Theory*. New York: Routledge, 1988.

Schechner, Richard, and Mary Shuman. *Ritual, Play and Performance: Readings in the Social Sciences/Theatre*. New York: Seabury Press, 1976.

Sellers, Cleveland. *The River of No Return: The Autobiography of a Black Militant and the Life and Death of SNCC*. New York: William Morrow, 1973.

States, Bert O. *Great Reckonings in Little Rooms: On the Phenomenology of Theater*. Berkeley: University of California Press, 1985.

Trinh, Minh-Ha. *Woman, Native, Other: Writing Postcoloniality and Feminism*. Bloomington: Indiana University Press, 1989.

Turner, Victor. *The Anthropology of Performance*. New York: PAJ Productions, 1986.

———. *The Drums of Affliction: A Study of Religious Processes Among the Ndembu of Zambia*. Oxford: Clarendon Press, 1968.

———. *Dramas, Fields and Metaphors: Symbolic Action in Human Society*. Ithaca: Cornell University Press, 1974.

———. *The Forest of Symbols: Aspects of Ndembu Ritual*. Ithaca: Cornell University Press, 1967.

———. *From Ritual to Theater: The Human Seriousness of Play*. New York: PAJ Publications, 1982.

Valdez, Luis. *Actos*. San Juan Bautista: Menyah Press, 1971.

———. *Early Works*. Houston: Arte Publico Press, 1990.

———. *Zoot Suit and Other Plays*. Houston: Arte Publico Press, 1992.

Van Deburg, William L. *New Day in Babylon: The Black Power Movement and American Culture, 1965–1975*. Chicago: University of Chicago Press, 1992.

Vanden Heuvel, Michael. *Performing Drama/Dramatizing Performance: Alternative Theatre and the Dramatic Text*. Ann Arbor: University of Michigan Press, 1991.

Weimann, Robert. *Shakespeare and the Popular Tradition in the Theater: Studies in the Social Dimension of Dramatic Form and Function*. Baltimore: Johns Hopkins University Press, 1978.

Weisman, John. *Guerrilla Theater: Scenarios for Revolution*. Garden City, NJ: Anchor Books, 1973.

West, Cornel. *Keeping Faith: Philosophy and Race in America*. New York: Routledge, 1993.

West, Stanley A., and June Macklin. *The Chicano Experience*. Boulder, CO: Westview Press, 1979.

White, Hayden. *The Content of the Form: Narrative Discourse and Historical Representation*. Baltimore: Johns Hopkins University Press, 1987.

Williams, Mance. *Black Theater in the 1960s and 1970s: A Historical-Critical Analysis of the Movement*. Westport, CT: Greenwood Press, 1985.

Wilson, August. *Three Plays by August Wilson*. Pittsburgh: University of Pittsburgh Press, 1991.

Wilson, Richard, and Richard Dutton. *New Historicism and Renaissance Drama*. London: Longman Press 1992.

Yeatman, Anna. *Postmodern Revisions of the Political*. London: Routledge, 1994.

Journal Articles

Alarcón, Norma. "Chicana Feminism: In the Tracks of 'The' Native Woman." *Cultural Studies* 4.3 (October 1990): 248–56.

———. "Traddutora, Traditora: A Paradigmatic Figure of Chicano Feminism." *Cultural Critique* 13 (1989): 57–87.

Bagby, Beth. "El Teatro Campesino: An Interview with Luis Valdez." *Drama Review* 11 (Summer 1967): 70–80.

Baraka, Amiri. "In Search of the Revolutionary Theater." *Black World* 15.5 (April 1966): 20–25.

———. "The Task of the Negro Writer." *Negro Digest* (April 1965): 65, 75–76.

Brecht, Stefan. "LeRoi Jones' *Slave Ship*." *Drama Review* 14 (Winter 1970): 212–19.

Brokaw, John. "Teatro Chicano: Some Reflections." *Educational Theater Journal* 29 (December 1977): 33–44.

Broyles-González, Yolanda. "Toward a Re-Vision of Chicano Theater History: The Women of El Teatro Campesino." In *Making Spectacle*, ed. Lynda Hart (Ann Arbor: University of Michigan Press, 1989), 209–38.

———. "What price 'mainstream'? Luis Valdez' *Corridos* on stage and film." *Cultural Studies* 43 (October 1990): 281–93.

Chabram, Angie C., and Rosa Linda Fregoso. "Chicana/o Cultural Representations: Reframing Alternative Discourses." *Cultural Studies* 4.3 (October 1990): 203–16.

Chabram-Dernersian, Angie. "I Throw Punches for My Race, but I Don't Want to Be a Man: Writing Us—Chica-nos(Girl, Us)/Chicanas—into the Movement Script." In *Cultural Studies*, ed. Lawrence Grossberg, Cary Nelson, and Paula Treichler, 81–95. New York: Routledge, 1992.

De Marinis, Marco. "The Dramaturgy of the Spectator." *Drama Review* 31.2 (Summer 1987): 100–114.

Elam, Harry J., Jr. "Revolution and Ritual: Luis Valdez' *Quinta Temporada* and LeRoi Jones' *Slave Ship*." *Theatre Journal* 38.4 (1986): 463–72.

———. "Signifyin(g) on African-American Theater: *The Colored Museum* by George Wolfe." *Theater Journal* 44 (1992): 291–303.

———. "Of Angels and Transcendence: An Analysis of *Fences* by August Wilson and *Roosters* by Milcha Sanchez-Scott." In *Staging Difference: Cultural Pluralism in American Theatre and Drama*, ed. Marc Maufort, 287–300. New York: Peter Lang, 1995.

———. "Social Urgency and the Performance of *Slave Ship* by Amiri Baraka," In *The Crucible of Crisis: Performing Social Change*, ed. Janelle Reinelt, Ann Arbor: University of Michigan Press, 1996, 13–33.

Fabre, Geneviève. "Dialectics of Masks in El Teatro Campesino: From Images to Ritualized Events." In *Missions in Conflict: Essays on U.S.-Mexican Relations and Chicano Culture*, ed. Renate von Bardeleben, Dietrich Briesemeister, and Juan Bruce-Novoa, 93–100. Tübingen: Gunter Narr Verlag, 1986.

Ferdinand, Val. "A Report on Black Theatre: New Orleans." *Negro Digest* (April 1970): 28–29.

Freedman, J. L., and S. C. Fraser. "Compliance without Pressure: The Foot-in-the-Door Technique." *Journal of Personality and Social Psychology* 4 (1966): 195–202.

Gurin, Patricia, Arthur A. Miller, and Gerald Gurin. "Stratum Identification and Consciousness." *Social Psychology Quarterly* 43.1 (1980): 30–47.

Hall, Stuart. "New Ethnicities." *Black Film/British Cinema*. ICA Documents 7 (1988): 27–31.

Haraway, Donna. "Situated Knowledges." *Feminist Studies* 14.3 (1988): 575–600.

Harris, Jessica B. "The National Black Theater: The Sun People of 125th Street." In *The Theater of Black Americans*, vol. 2: *The Presenters/The Participators*, ed. Errol Hill, 85–94. Englewood Cliffs, NJ: Prentice-Hall Press, 1980.

Harrop, John, and Jorge Huerta. "The Agricultural Pilgrimage of Luis Valdez." *Theater Quarterly* 5.17 (March–May 1973): 30–39.

Huerta, Jorge. "Chicano Theater: A Background." *Aztlán* (Fall 1971): 63–78.

———. "From Temple to Arena: Teatro Chicano Today." In *The Identification and Analysis of Chicano Literature*, ed. Francisco Jiménez, 100–101. New York: Bilingual Press, 1979.

———. "From Stereotypes to Archetypes: Chicano Theater's Reflection of the Mexicano in the United States," In *Missions in Conflict: Essays on U.S.-Mexican Relations and Chicano Culture*, ed. Renate von Bardeleben, Dietrich Brusemeister, and Juan Bruce Novoa, 75–84. Tübingen: Gunter Narr Verlag, 1986.

Kanellos, Nicolás. "Folklore in Chicano Theater: Chicano Theater as Folklore." In *Popular Theater for Social Change*, ed. Gerado Luizunaga, 158–77. Los Angeles: UCLA Latin American Studies Center Publications, 1978.

Labinger, Andrea G., "The Cruciform Farce in Latin America: Two Plays in *Themes in Drama: Farce*," ed. James Redmond, 219–26. Cambridge: Cambridge University Press, 1988.

McRobbie, Angela. "Strategies of Vigilance: An Interview with Gayatri Chakravorti Spivak." *Block* 10 (1985): 5–9.

Morton, Carlos. "El Teatro Campesino." *Drama Review* 18.4 (December 1974): 71–76.

Mouffe, Chantal, "Hegemony and New Political Subjects: Towards a New Concept of Democracy, in *Marxism and the Interpretation of Culture*, ed. Lawrence Grossberg and Cary Nelson, 89–104. Urbana: University of Illinois Press, 1988.

Neal, Larry. "The Black Arts Movement." *Drama Review* 12.4 (Summer 1968): 36–46.

———. "New Grapes." *Newsweek*, 31 July 1967, 79.

Sandoval, Chela. "U.S. Third World Feminism: The Theory and Method of Oppositional Consciousness in the Postmodern World." *Genders* 10 (Spring 1991): 1–24.

Shank, Theodore. "A Return to Aztec and Mayan Roots." *Drama Review* 18.4 (December 1974): 56–71.

Smith, David Lionel. "The Black Arts Movement and Its Critics." *American Literary History* 3.1 (Spring 1991): 93–110.

Söyinka, Wole. "Drama and the Revolutionary Ideal." In *In Person: Achebe, Awoonor, and Soyinka*, ed. Karen L. Morell, 61–88. Seattle: Institute for Comparative and Foreign Area Studies, University of Washington, 1975.

Yarbro-Bejarano, Yvonne. "The Female Subject in Chicano Theatre: Sexuality, 'Race,' and Class." *Theatre Journal* 38.4: 389–407.

Newspaper Articles

Barnes, Clive. "The Theater: New LeRoi Jones Play." *New York Times*, 22 November 1969, 46.

———. "Culture Watch: Miscast Protest," *Los Angeles Times*, 19 August 1992, "Metro" sec., B6.

Drake, Sylvia. *Los Angeles Times*, 4 October 1969, sec. 2, 7.

Gleason, Ralph J. "Vital, Earthy and Alive." *San Francisco Chronicle*, 4 May 1966, 41.

Green, Judith. "Tables Turned in Hispanic Casting Dispute, Writer Director Valdez Finds He's in an Ironic Situation." *San Diego Union Tribune*, 8 September 1992, "Lifestyle" sec., E4.

Kerr, Walter. "Is This Their Dream?" *New York Times*, 23 November 1969, sec. 2, 3.

Lahr, John. "On-Stage." *Village Voice*, 4 December 1969, 51.

Loftus, John. "Election of the Poor May Be Ended, Shriver Tells House Committee." *New York Times*, 9 March 1966, 24.

———. "Luis Valdez Speaks Out on Frida Controversy." *Daily Variety*, 21 August 1992.

Reichenthal, Charles. "Underlites." *Flatbush Life*, 6 December 1969, 20.

Riley, Clayton. "Art Is What Moves You." *New York Times*, 23 November 1969, sec. 2, 3.

Saludes, Boniface. "Viva La Huelga Heard at Cotati." *Press Democrat,* 6 May 1966, 6.

———. "Shriver Prodded by Fino on Black Arts School Funding." *New York Times,* 29 December 1965, 15.

Tallmer, Jerry. "Across the Footlights." *New York Post,* 21 November 1969, 64.

Weiner, Bernard. "Corridos: Mexican Ballads of Love, Lust and Death." *San Francisco Chronicle Datebook,* 17 April 1983, 40.

———. "New Focus for Peoples' Festival." *San Francisco Chronicle,* 16 April 1983, 36.

Plays

Baraka, Amiri. *"A Black Mass." Four Black Revolutionary Plays.* New York: Bobbs-Merrill, 1969.

———. *"Slave Ship." The Motion of History and Other Plays.* New York: William Morrow, 1978.

Caldwell, Ben. *"The Prayer Meeting or the First Militant Black Minister." A Black Quartet.* New York: New American Library, 1970.

Patterson, Charles. *"Black Ice."* In *Black Fire,* ed. Amiri Baraka and Larry Neal. New York: William Morrow, 1968.

Valdez, Luis. *"Los Vendidos." Actos.* San Juan Bautista, CA: Menyah Press, 1971.

Valdez, Luis, and El Teatro Campesino. *"La Conquista de Mexico." Actos.* San Juan Bautista, CA: Menyah Press, 1971.

———.*"Las Dos Caras del Patroncito." Actos.* San Juan Bautista, CA: Menyah Press, 1971.

———. *"Quinta Temporada." Actos.* San Juan Bautista, CA: Menyah Press, 1971.

Index